The Hemphills: Partners in Emotion

The *Hemphills:*
PARTNERS IN
Emotion

The Story of Joel and LaBreeska Hemphill

LaBreeska Rogers Hemphill

Trumpet Call Books
P.O. Box 656
Joelton, TN 37080

Trumpet Call Books
P.O. Box 656
Joelton, TN 37080

www.thehemphills.com

The Hemphills: Partners in Emotion
ISBN: 0-9671756-1-5

Cover Photo by George Bloodworth
Cameo Photo by Ken Kim, compliments of Benson Company

Unless otherwise indicated, Scripture taken from
the Holy Bible: King James Version.

Scripture quotation marked "NIV" are taken from
the Holy Bible: New International Version ®. © 1973,
1978, 1984 by the International Bible Society.
Used by permission of Zondervan Bible Publishers.

To my grandchildren:

Jasmine, Taylor, Madeleine, Nicholas,
Sarah Kate, William and any that should come after.

My hope is that by better knowing your
grandfather and me, you may better know
yourselves; to understand that to honor commitments
to God and man are worth all that we might endure.

"But the mercy of the LORD is from everlasting
to everlasting upon them that fear him, and his
righteousness unto *children's children.*"
(Psalm 103:17, emphasis added)

Table of Contents

Acknowledgements

My greatest debt while writing this book is to my husband, Joel W. Hemphill. He has carefully read the manuscript at various stages and helped guide me, in sequence, through the rough terrain of his illness, supplying dates, medicines, etc. Without his support and willingness to be totally transparent for the glory of God, I would not have attempted such private disclosure.

Thanks to Brenda McClain for encouraging me to write and to my dear friend Doris Barnette for her labor of love with my first autobiographical writings entitled *LaBreeska* in 1972. Those writings were extremely valuable and portions were used to make this book complete.

I am indebted to the late Bob Benson for the forward that he penned for those writings. The things he said were special and timeless, so I decided to add them to this book as well.

Gratitude to Kim Driver for her tireless efforts and enthusiasm to see the finished product; and to Brenda Deason, Lou Crowder and Ken Beck.

A big thank you to Chris Kline and George McPeek. Also to The Benson Company, who shared pictures from their archives and to photographers Bobby Bentz, Ralph Barrett, George Bloodworth and Victor Bruce. Also to my editor, Janet Dixon, for her assistance, faith and patience.

Many thanks to the late Bob McKenzie who from his sick-bed caused me to reach further and deeper with his probing questions.

Foreword

What makes a person smile? Why are some faces radiant? I was reading the other day about a man who said there were only a few people in life who smiled when they saw him coming. They were just glad to see him coming. They didn't have any improvement plans for him—they just accepted him as he was and met him with a smile. Furthermore, he didn't leave it to chance to meet these people; he made sure he met some of them every day because they sure were good for him.

Why do some people smile and why do some people frown? Why do some folk always seem to cheer you up? Is it because of their own sunny dispositions? And why does LaBreeska Hemphill always look so glad to see you? Somebody said, "Smile and the world will wonder what you have been up to." What does she know that we don't?

Anyone's first observation is probably that the smilers of the world have just had such an easy time so far that there is nothing to do but grin. But we secretly suspect the day is coming when life will wipe that happy look away. So I read her book looking for stories of a perfect childhood surrounded by happy memories and "living happily ever after."

But the story is not like that. There was more than the usual amount of tragedy, separation and loneliness. As a tenderhearted girl she made her way from parent to parent in a broken home. Maybe LaBreeska does know something that has eluded the rest of us. Maybe true happiness and outgoing warmth are better developed by the blows of life than by its accolades and joys.

Whatever she knows, it is worth reading the book to try to find out what makes LaBreeska smile. It is a warm, tender story that will move you to tears and maybe send you out to smile.

— the late Bob Benson
The Benson Publishing Company

Introduction

I guess we have all been guilty of thinking a day was a bad one because of some minor problem, but when we have been through some truly bad days, the joy of having a good day is intensified.

What constitutes a "bad day"? Is it getting a parking ticket, or is it when the doctor says, "We've found colon cancer and you are set for surgery Tuesday morning. And there is an even chance you will wear a colostomy for the rest of your life"?

What makes a "bad hair day"? Is it when it rains and it won't comb right, or is it when you just slick it down with water in a psychiatric hospital because you are more concerned with holding on to your mind—and anyway, they don't allow hair dryers in your unit?

The latter part of this book tells a story of some bad days: cancer, surgery, complications, diapers, sleepless nights, emotional breakdowns, depression and despair. It tells how I went from being a successful, driven and decisive person to someone who could not go alone to get my hair cut. It tells how after many years of faithful Christian ministry I lay on the sofa for almost two years, at times literally holding on, because I "felt" lost. In short, my physical problem became an emotional problem, and my emotional problem became a spiritual problem. Thoughts of suicide were my constant companion.

This is also a story of divine intervention and restoration, how God, through a miracle or miracles, brought joy out of our pain, hope out of our despair and turned our test into a testimony. Since my healing, I have shared this testimony before multiplied thousands in concerts and church services all across the United States and Canada as well as England, Scotland, Ireland and South Africa.

I have been privileged to tell it to millions on TBN, CBN, The Crook & Chase Show and the televised portion of the Grand Ole Opry. I, of course, am not proud of two stays in mental hospitals, but I tell it because there are a reported 19 million Americans who battle depression and spend $3 billion per year on antidepressant medications. (The number-two-selling drug in this country is Prozac at nearly $3 billion annually.)[1] They need to see someone who has been there and gotten back. This is a story of hope in God, our kind and loving Heavenly Father, whose Son Jesus was "wounded for our transgressions, he was bruised for our iniquities: the chastisement of our peace was upon him; and with his stripes we are healed" (Isaiah 53:5).

It's been a long time since I've had a bad day. I am overwhelmed with appreciation to those who stood by us with love and prayers. I am delighted not to be hurting physically or emotionally, but I have compassion for hurting people that I never could have had without our pain. I am the happiest man I know. I woke up from depression head over heels in love with our Jesus and LaBreeska, in that order.

LaBreeska is a great writer. Thank you, darling, for telling our story in this book.

—Joel Hemphill

Chapter 1

The Ryman

The floor director held up his hand for the countdown to airtime. We were ready to go on the backstage portion of the Grand Ole Opry to be interviewed by famed country singer and songwriter Bill Anderson. The show was beamed live internationally by the TNN satellite.

Joel looked dashing even under the scrutiny of the probing TV lights. The ivory suit he was wearing punctuated the healthy glow of a slight tan. I sat beside him in a royal blue, floor-length, two-piece suit.

It was hard to believe that we were here. Of all the exciting places our music has taken our family, including London, England to appear at the famous Wembly Country Music Festival, and even an invitation to the White House by President and Mrs. Carter, the Opry was a door that had never opened to us.

Now here sat Joel and I as guests on this legendary program. For the two of us to receive such an honor after all we had been through was comparable to the sudden appearing of a beautiful rainbow after a storm, or like standing on a mountain peak after a long trek through a dark valley.

The director was now signaling silently: Five . . . four . . . three . . . two . . . and pointing to Bill. Bill greeted the audience, and after a brief introduction and a few friendly exchanges, he directed his first question to me.

"LaBreeska, I understand that you sang in the old Ryman Auditorium when you were a child."

"That's right," I replied, "the Ryman was the first stage I ever sang on, at the tender age of nine. I was with my mother and her brothers and sisters in a gospel singing group known as The Happy Goodman Family. Back then there was a monthly Friday night gospel singing held at the Ryman, and my family participated. That was my first introduction to the stage."

Then Bill turned to Joel.

"Joel, I hear that your faith was severely tested not long ago. Would you like to tell us about it?" The question came as a pleasant surprise, and Joel eagerly responded.

"Well, Bill, in October of 1990 I was operated on for colon cancer," Joel began, "and shortly afterward complications set in that caused me to lose a great amount of weight. I lost weight until I was to skin and bones, thought I was dying and sank into a deep depression. The depression lasted almost two years and included two stays in mental hospitals. But the truth is, on a Sunday morning, November 8, 1992, I was prayed for by my pastor and church, and the Lord instantly healed me! That was the last day of depression I have ever had."

Within minutes the interview was completed, and as we were being ushered to the main auditorium, Bill whispered to Joel, "Thanks for sharing that with us," and Joel replied with a smile, "Thanks for asking."

When we reached the right wing of the stage, the televised portion of the Grand Ole Opry was already in progress and was being hosted by Little Jimmy Dickens. After a few minutes he graciously brought us on with that ever-familiar Southern drawl.

"And now, ladies and gentlemen, would you please make welcome this beautiful Christian couple from Nashville, Tennessee—Joel and LaBreeska Hemphill!"

There was thunderous applause as we stepped onto the stage and into the spotlight. Our son Trent was seated at the piano, and Bruce Andrews held ready his Martin acoustic guitar. They, along with Eddy Bell, James Freeze and the Opry staff band, played the introduction, then hand-in-hand Joel and I began to sing "Partners in Emotion," the love song that he had recently written for me.

We share a precious family
Our addresses are the same

We share mornings over coffee
And we even share a name
We've shared many joys and sorrows
Precious friends that we have known.
Tho' we're two very different people
We are one in flesh and bone

And we are partners in emotion
As the years go by
And whatever makes you sad
Brings tears to my eyes
I can't always make you happy
But I'm happy when I try
'Cause we are partners in emotion
You and I

We love flowers in the springtime
Love the colors in the fall
We love walking by the ocean
Or holding hands in the mall
We love church on Sunday morning
Amazing Grace, Never Alone
We love to bow our heads together
And we still love an old love song.[2]

The title of this song speaks volumes to those who know us best. It is a declaration that we have come through the storm and nothing has been lost. Our marriage is still intact and growing stronger with each new day.

Surely it was evident to the viewers who were watching the program that night that our song was delivered by two loving hearts knit together as one. When we came off the stage, we were wrapped up by family and friends who had come to share the victory. Mom Hemphill; Joel's sister, Anna Gayle; her husband, Jerry Hicks; Joel's brother, David, and his wife, Leah; and their daughter, LaTasha, all greeted us excitedly. These precious family members had taken many steps with us through our dark days of despair.

During that time we would never have guessed that Joel's healing and restoration would include a moment such as this. Even Bob

Whitaker, manager of the Opry, enthusiastically embraced us for a job well done.

More importantly, it felt like the Lord was giving us a big hug by allowing us the privilege of just being there: this place where all those happy sounds of music and laughter had originated when I was a child. That was a time when there was no television, and radio was our main source of entertainment and connection to faraway places such as Nashville, Tennessee. Actually, that was quite a long time ago, that Friday night when I first stepped onto the stage of the Ryman Auditorium, but one that I will never forget. . . . .

Trembling, I followed Mother from the dimly lit right wing of the auditorium into the glaring footlights of the stage. Being just a child of nine, I was just short enough that the blinding lights caught me at eye level. I couldn't see beyond them but I knew what was there: hundreds of gospel music fans, and they were watching *me.*

Suddenly I felt a wild impulse to run. . . .

It was the summer of 1949. Outside dusk had fallen. Nashville city lights twinkled and the All-Nite Gospel Singing was under way.

For days, our big rambling Kentucky house had bustled with preparation for this grand event. New and glamourous frocks had to be sewn for the entire family. Mama and Papa Goodman, and even the children, had to be dressed just right for the occasion. Finally the day arrived for the exciting journey to Music City, USA.

Resplendent in my shiny black patent leather shoes and white voile dress, I climbed the curving, concrete steps that led backstage, with Bobby eagerly leading the way.

Bobby, mother's youngest brother, just two years my senior, had been here before. Though looking rather strange with his hair carefully oiled and combed into place, he proceeded to give me a thorough rundown.

"These are the very steps that Minnie Pearl, Little Jimmy Dickens and Ernest Tubb climb every Saturday night to sing on the Grand Ole Opry," he said proudly. "This is the famous Ryman Auditorium."

I supposed everyone in the world knew who those folks were. Minnie Pearl's famous greeting "How-dee, I'm just so proud to be here!" And Ernest Tubb's singing "Walking the Floor Over You" could be heard just about every Saturday night by way of WSM Radio.

As we entered the backstage door, I was all eyes but found nothing more than a dingy, dilapidated old building with peeling paint and props and signs leaning haphazardly against the walls. This was hardly what I had expected.

Urged on by Bobby, we pushed forward and together made our way through the milling crowd of entertainers and their friends and relatives who were congregated in the wings. Then suddenly and without warning, directly before us stretched the stage. There were no curtains or walls to restrain us, and if it hadn't been for Bobby, I could have easily stumbled onto it. From the stage came the bouncy rhythm of a gospel style piano and the singing of enthusiastic performers who basked in the dazzling footlights and the roar of the crowd. Never had I witnessed anything so exciting. Then I heard the Master of Ceremonies announce: "And from Wingo, Kentucky, The Happy Goodman Family!" That was *my* family!

They went on like gangbusters—Howard, Gussie (my mother), Eloise, Stella, Junior, Ruth and Rusty. Howard was at the piano, his hands flying in the air. You could hear the music, but it didn't look as though his hands were touching the keyboard long enough to make the sounds. *He* was bouncing, his curly *hair* was bouncing and the *piano* was bouncing.

Besides my mother, I had six aunts and uncles on that stage. There were eight brothers and sisters altogether, and all were out there except Bobby. He sat backstage with me, watching proudly. There were so many in the family that their performance had a variety of arrangements. After two or three songs, some left the stage, leaving just a quartet to sing. Eloise, mother's younger sister, was singing bass. Whoever heard of a woman bass singer? Well, the Goodman Family had one! Eloise was a petite and very feminine brunette, with a voice that reached G below Low C.

I watched with my mouth open as they started to sing, "Way Down Deep in My Soul." Eloise took the lead, singing, "wa-a-a-ay . . . do-w-w-wn . . . wa-a-a-ay . . . do-w-w-wn . . . ," going lower and lower. The audience was spellbound and so was I.

I was so relieved when the song was over. I had been afraid she wouldn't make it! Then to my horror, Eloise stepped up to the microphone, looked at Howard and said, "Howard, if you can lower that just a teeny weeny bit, I think I can hit it."

I held my breath as Howard, looking worried all the time, put the song in a lower key, and away they went again. I thought the song was finished three times, but they kept dropping the key, until Eloise hit her lowest note. Needless to say, that was the highlight of the evening. The crowd went wild.

Meanwhile Bobby and I sat at the edge of the stage, looking on. Suddenly he made a statement that caught me completely off guard. "I'm going to sing on the last song," he said, "and Jimmy is too." Jimmy was Aunt Stella's little boy, three years younger than I was. Then as if a light had just come on in his head, Bobby blurted out, *"and you can too!"* About that time Mother walked up to us.

"Gussie, can't Breeska sing 'Looking for a City' with us?" asked Bobby.

Mother looked at me in surprise and said, "Why sure, if she wants to." Things were happening too fast. I couldn't absorb it all.

After Mother and Daddy's divorce, I had spent the biggest part of my time with Daddy and his parents while Mother worked. Now she was back home with her family, traveling with them and singing gospel music. This was a whole new and exciting world, and now they were saying I could be a part of it!

Before I had time to protest that I didn't even know the song, Bobby was singing it to me. "Now all you have to say is this,

Looking for a city,
Where we'll never die.
There the sainted millions
Never say good-bye.
There we'll meet the Savior,
And our loved ones too!
Come, O Holy Spirit,
All our hopes renew![3]

The trio that was left on stage had already started to sing the final number. Sure enough, it was "Looking for a City." The singers on stage would sing a verse and a chorus of the song; then another brother or sister would step from backstage into the spotlight and take the leading part. Each time when it looked as though they were about to end the song, another Goodman would step onto the stage.

Then it was time for Mother to go on. "Honey, since this is your first appearance, you come with me," she said. Somehow my legs obeyed the command, but my knees felt like jelly. *If only I could run and hide . . .*

What were the words Bobby had told me to sing? Beside me Mother began to take her lead, and gently nudged me. *Oh, yes, I remember!* And when I opened my mouth, I was surprised to hear my own voice. I hadn't even known I could do this! For the first time, I was exercising a natural heritage from my parents—the gift of music. Again Mother and I took the lead in unison as the crowd cheered.

In a matter of seconds it was over. All except for that wonderful applause. . . . I stumbled backstage, my head in a whirl. They loved me! All those strangers out there had loved me! This heady experience was too much for an unseasoned nine-year-old and left me wondering if and when I would ever get to do it again.

To start at the very beginning of my story, we need to go back to the time and place of my birth. It took place in the wee hours of the morning on February 4, 1940 in the little coal mining town of Flat Creek, Alabama.

Flat Creek, with its population of roughly 800, wasn't much different from the scores of mining towns that dotted north-central Alabama at that time. Since mining accounted for six percent of the goods produced in Alabama, it had become a way of life for many people, especially those without a proper education.

In those days it was a common sight to watch the men come home from a hard day's work, grimy from head to toe with coal dust. One could only make out the whites of their eyes or their teeth when they spoke. Wearily they returned, one by one, wearing mining helmets with carbide lamps on top and carrying their big combination water bucket-lunch box. These men all looked alike as they disappeared into the little shotgun camp houses that appeared to have never known the luxury of a coat of paint, and were all built from the same pattern. Along the sides of the narrow dirt streets, these humble little shanties were neatly planted in rows.

Coal mining was not the most desirable way to make a living. The days were long, and the work was backbreaking. But it was a source of income in a country not yet fully recovered from the Great Depression; consequently, the jobs were readily accepted. Most every boy in a mining camp had his future mapped out for him. As soon as he was big enough to work, he left school behind and entered the mines to help supplement the family income. Then his meager earnings were taken to the community commissary, where anything from eggs to mining boots could be bought. Here he exchanged his salary for enough goods to eke out a bare existence. My father was among that number.

That night the camp doctor was relieved when he stepped from the biting winter cold into the warm little house. He had been in almost every mining house in this community at one time or another, tending cases varying from child delivery to whooping cough. The anxious young man who had summoned him tonight was nineteen-year-old Erskine Rogers, my dad.

Also there to welcome him were my two "about to be" grandmothers, Mama Goodman and Mama Rogers, who quickly ushered him through the living room and into the only bedroom, where I was about to be born to a seventeen-year-old girl, not much more than a child herself.

At 1:30 a.m., I made my first appearance on the stage of life and, without reserve, demanded the role of leading lady in the hearts and lives of young Erskine and Gussie Rogers and both sets of proud grandparents.

Chapter 2

A Soft and
Gentle Breeze

LaBreeska was the name Mother had chosen for me.

When Mother was a little girl, her father had told her the story of a dark-skinned girl from the Philippine Islands with the same name. She was a Spanish girl whose lineage no doubt went as far back as the 1500s when the Spaniards began settling the tropical islands, searching for gold and silver. The Spanish ruled the islands until 1898, when the United States stepped in and declared war on Spain to help free the Filipinos.

Among the American troops sent over to fight in the Spanish-American War was my grandfather, Drew Sam Goodman. He was a square-jawed man of medium stature with a head full of unruly, dark brown curly hair that continually spilled over onto his forehead. Directly over his deep blue eyes, which spoke with a twinkle, was a forest of bushy brows that had to be trimmed with each haircut. In describing my maternal grandfather, I must not leave out his dimples. These were strong traits handed down to each child born to him, and even to his grandchildren. One writer said, "A fair face is half a fortune," and I suppose that blue eyes, naturally curly hair and dimples, along with a great deal of pride, was as close to a fortune as Papa had to give to his offspring.

The warm, tropical islands, with heavenly temperatures that barely reached 100 degrees or dropped below 70 degrees, had a way of growing on the American soldier. The soft, gentle breeze and the pulsating of the ocean was as steady as the rhythm of one's own heartbeat. The ability to know the difference between person and nature was almost impossible. All this was reason enough for young Drew Sam to decide to stay in the islands, even after his duty to his country was over. However, there was an even greater reason for his remaining: LaBreeska.[4] This dark-eyed beauty's name came from a Spanish word which meant a soft, gentle breeze.

Following the war, LaBreeska and Drew Sam were married and lived contentedly in their island paradise. Only a few short years passed, however, when one morning Drew Sam awoke to find the lovely LaBreeska dead beside him. Grief-stricken, he began to make plans to leave the isle which, with her untimely death, had lost its enchantment. For the first time in years, he longed for home.

Their only child, Little Joe, was six years old. The thought of an ocean voyage filled him with excitement. This was his first trip to the United States. Papa called in a tailor and had him make Joe an "Uncle Sam" suit from red, white and blue satin material.

It was just like Papa to come home in grand style. Everyone aboard ship was talking about the cute little boy in the "Uncle Sam" suit.

This romantic story of her father's life from years past intrigued my mother as a child, and while she was still very young, she determined one day to have a LaBreeska of her own. By the time I was three, Daddy left the coal mines for a white-collar job as an insurance salesman in the big city of Birmingham. Like many other young families of that period, we had made our first step up the ladder of social and economic progress, and it felt good.

In those days, I vividly recall Mother's terror of thunderstorms. The least bit of thunder and lightning would cause her to dissolve into hysterics. I particularly remember one bad storm. Mother was crying and wringing her hands and Daddy was gallantly trying to soothe us both. He set us down, me on his knee, his arm around Mother, and in his most dramatic voice began a fairy tale of what caused thunderstorms. Mother and I both became so engrossed in the story that, before we knew it, the storm was over and we were all laughing again.

Daddy was outgoing and, to me, very handsome. He was six feet tall and had raven-black hair. When he was around, I wasn't afraid of anything. When we went places, it seemed as though he knew everyone and everyone knew him. As I look back, I realize that he had probably never seen the ticket lady at the theater or the salesclerk at the department store or talked to this particular operator on the telephone, but he never seemed to meet a stranger. He talked with those people in a way that made me think he had known them for years. I was such a lucky child. Two of the most beautiful people in the world were my parents.

I don't know when I first detected a dark cloud hovering over our happiness. I don't know if it crept in overnight, or if it had begun forming years before. All I know is that one day it was there, black and ominous, blocking out happier times. Small and trivial disagreements became mountains, separating a young love. Tenderness gave way to harsh words. What was happening to my beautiful parents?

It was during this time that I had a horrible nightmare. I still slept in my baby bed in the hall, just outside Mother and Daddy's bedroom. One night I dreamed I was awakened by two men. There was really nothing unusual about their appearance, but their very presence frightened me. They were trying to persuade me to leave with them. They talked to me in my mind, not audibly, but continued to press me to come with them. I knew I wasn't going, but I was afraid to tell them for fear I'd make them angry, so I said I would have to ask Mother and Daddy.

The next part of the dream found me at the bedside of my parents. I could see them lying there, sleeping peacefully. Mother was on her back with one arm thrown up on her pillow, and Daddy was lying against the wall, turned on one side. When I tried to wake them, I could tell they couldn't feel my nudging. I became frantic and began beating them in the face and pulling their hair, but still they didn't feel a thing. The most amazing part of the dream was the third part. I found myself back in my own bed, telling the two men that I could not go with them. To my astonishment, they didn't try to force me, as I had feared they would. Instead, they just backed off into the horrible darkness, still watching me.

After that experience I became terrified of the dark. Although I was good-naturedly teased about it by my family, no one understood why I was afraid. I was only four at the time, so I did not understand the significance of the dream. Now I realize that this was when I first became aware that there was another dimension, the spirit world, and I had not yet learned to trust Christ for protection from evil.

During this time my secure little world crumbled before my very eyes. The crash was heartbreaking. Mother and Daddy were both young and headstrong, and their marriage could not weather the storms of adjustment and struggle, so it ended in tragedy: divorce!

I was only a child, but how well I came to know the meaning of that word *divorce*. The three of us were torn from each other. Mother could not go back to her parents. They already had too many trying to survive on Papa Goodman's insufficient veteran's check. She went to work in a factory. This meant she could not keep me with her, so it was decided that I would stay with Daddy for the time being. He and I moved about fifteen miles out into the country to live with Mama and Papa Rogers. We took all Mother's furniture with us, including her bedroom suite. The house was small and crowded as Mama and Papa Rogers still had three school-age children at home—Joyce, Faye and Jimmy. However, we were welcomed with open arms. There was not so much as a hint that we were in the way or not wanted.

Daddy tried hard to shield me from the vast emptiness left by Mother's absence. I remember his spending a lot of time with me when he came home from work in the evening, trying to make me laugh. I'm sure his pain was great too, but there was a difference. He knew why the separation had happened, but all I knew was that my mother was gone and that I felt rejected and sad. Here we were, cramped up in someone else's home when ours had been so cozy and wonderful and so completely ours. I knew we didn't belong here, even though everyone loved us.

The only real comfort I had was remembering. I thought of every little incident, no matter how small, during the time Mother, Daddy and I had been together. Mother had always been the center of my world. She and I had been together almost every hour since the time I was born. No one could compare with her. She was so full of life. Her bubbly laughter rang in my ears. I ached for her. I longed to have her hold me and to smell her perfume, or to watch her laugh and clap her hands as I skipped around the coffee table and sang, "You Are My Sunshine."

All those memories came back to haunt me as I relived every moment of my short past.

Mama and Papa Rogers

They tell me that my grandfather, Walter Harris Rogers, as a young man migrated from Wildwood, Georgia with his parents and settled in a little mining town called Republic in northern Alabama. In this little town, he met and married sixteen-year-old Mary Gertrude Hodges on January 29, 1916.

These two wonderful people were never anyone but Mama and Papa Rogers to me, my paternal grandparents.

Papa was such a lovable character, with an unmatched talent for telling funny stories and a keen memory of things that happened long ago. It was easy for him to hold the attention of the young and old alike. One moment you were sitting there, spellbound, and the next you were splitting your sides in a fit of laughter. Consequently, you found him wound tightly around your heart and felt fortunate to know him, let alone have him for your very own personal grandfather. It was not just Papa's charm that made him a great favorite of his children and grandchildren. He also had a way of making each of us feel very special. I never left Papa Rogers' presence without just knowing that I was "the prettiest and sweetest thing in seven counties," because Papa had told me so. It didn't matter which of us he talked to, he always threw in some detail of something that had happened when we were babies that everyone had forgotten except him. Many other stories we heard him tell over and over again, but they never ceased to delight us because we knew Papa was really saying, "I have loved you from the minute you came into this world, and you are very special to me."

Mama and Papa's affection was a loving cushion for the terrible blow I had just experienced. Papa made me laugh and Mama rocked me as she sang or hummed old familiar church hymns. I can still hear her singing,

> *Jesus, Jesus, how I trust Him,*
> *How I've proved Him o'er and o'er;*
> *Jesus, Jesus, precious Jesus!*
> *Oh, for grace to trust Him more.*[5]

Mama Rogers was devoted to God, Papa and her children. As I look back, it amazes me as to how she raised such a large family of happy, healthy children with such meager means. The beautiful thing called "a mother's love," written about, sung about and feebly described for centuries, always manifested itself in Mama Rogers. When I became an adult and found motherhood sometimes trying, I thought of Mama Rogers and her unlimited capacity for self-sacrifice and giving to her children. Because material things were scarce, Mama Rogers only had herself to give, and that she gave, never asking anything in return.

These surroundings should have soothed the ache in my heart and should have made me forget the past, but they didn't. They only kept me from being totally consumed by the loneliness that I felt.

Many times I cried and begged Daddy to take me with him when he left for work. He tried to calm me by explaining that he would be home by nightfall. He really didn't have to explain, for I knew where he was going, but I was frightened. I had lost Mother. Suppose he didn't come home again? I could lose him too.

Tears flowed less often as time passed and as I began adjusting to a new life, which really was a good one. One day, while busy at play, my attention was drawn to the gravel road that passed in front of my grandparents' home. Mama Rogers was coming from the mailbox.

She was walking slowly and looking at a letter in her hand when I heard her call, "Bre-e-ska." I came running in time to hear her say . . . "from your mother." I stood there, squinting into the sun and looking up at Mama Rogers, while she read the letter to me. All those words could not find lodging in my four-year-old mind; but I heard her say something about my mother, who had by this time become more myth than reality to me.

Just as Mama Rogers was about to lose my attention entirely, she bent down and handed the letter to me. A familiar ache came vividly alive as I looked at the page. There at the bottom of the letter Mother had drawn a picture of a sad little face with tears dripping down. At that moment, what I felt stabbed my heart, because I knew this was Mother crying for me. I carried the letter for days, showing it to everyone I met. Sometimes I even laughed at the funny little face, but that picture told me everything I needed to know . . . Mother was sad without me.

A few days later I was sitting on the living room floor, playing, while Mama Rogers stood nearby at the ironing board. As she ironed, she was listening to one of her favorite programs on the radio. The program ended and one of the popular talk shows began. The people were yelling and clapping as the show came on the air. The announcer shouted, "Is everybody happy?" Mama Rogers still recounted years later how I never looked up from my play, but answered the announcer solemnly, "No, I'm not happy."

To a child, months can seem like years. Mother and I were able to visit each other, though not very often. When she came to me or when I went to her, it was by means of public conveyance. Railways and busses became an important part of my young life, taking me from one parent to the other. I spent many a holiday riding on a train, listening to the rhythm of the clacking wheels underneath and watching from my window the undistinguishable world fly by in black, grotesque figures. To be moving along gave me an odd sensation and left my emotions in a state of limbo. I could sit for hours, my head resting against the seat, lulled by the vibration of the train and the monotone of fellow passengers' voices. I was aroused only now and then by the whimper of a small child or by an abrupt stop.

One Christmas Eve I watched out the window of the train coach until dawn, hoping in vain to catch a glimpse of Old Saint Nick and his eight tiny reindeer on their yearly mission of good will. I finally fell asleep in sheer exhaustion while "visions of sugar plums danced in my head."

In those days a visit from Mother was a real treat. Once she came and took me into Birmingham for the day. We rode a trolley car that ran on tracks right down the middle of the street. Trolleys were everywhere, passing each other in a clamor and making a disturbing amount of noise. Town was crowded and bustling with activity. Men in uniform were everywhere, soldier boys coming and going, embracing loved ones in public with happy hellos and sad good-byes. The thing that most caught my attention about the giant cars on steel wheels was the fact that one could not tell the front from the back. Both ends looked the same. Sparks popped like lightening from the pole on top as it made connection with the electrical current in the lines strung overhead.

Birmingham, Alabama had to be just about the biggest city in the whole world! Mother and I stepped from the trolley and hailed a taxi. I clung to her hand, knowing I could easily get lost in such an awesome place. The taxi took us a few blocks and came to a stop in front of a big brick house on a hillside, with steep steps leading up to the front porch. This was the home of Mother's Aunt Pet and Uncle James. They had been very kind to her since her divorce and were great favorites of hers.

Mother had kept a secret from me and had a reason for bringing me here. After being greeted warmly by Aunt Pet, I was led through the house out the back door. When I stepped into the backyard, I was swamped by ten of the fattest, friskiest, whitest puppies I had ever seen. Aunt Pet had told Mother to bring me to pick the one I wanted, and as soon as they were weaned, I could have it for my very own. They were full-blooded Eskimo Spitz but looked like live balls of cotton. I could not have been more thrilled. How in the world was I ever going to pick one? There they were, covering my feet, wagging their tails as if each one were begging me to pick him.

Suddenly I noticed that all of the puppies except one had black noses. His was pink. He was the only one I could tell apart from the others. He had to be mine. I picked him up, showed him to Mother, and right then and there, I named him Pinky! Oh, how I hated to leave him. I wanted to take him home with me right then but, without a fuss, I kissed him good-bye. It would only be a couple of weeks.

Mother and I made our departure, and by the end of the day I was back with Daddy, and she was gone.

With Mama Rogers' help, I counted the days until Pinky would finally be mine. Since Daddy worked in Birmingham, all he had to do was go by and pick him up. The day finally arrived when Daddy was to bring Pinky to me. I couldn't believe it when he walked through the door that night with nothing in his hands. I was so disappointed. Daddy stood there in his familiar hat and big overcoat, empty-handed. Then before I had time to say a word, he slipped his hand into one of the pockets and brought out Pinky. He leaped into my arms and licked my face as though we were long-lost friends. Mama Rogers and I fixed him a big bowl of milk. He was so hungry! He lapped it up in no time at all and became so full he could hardly walk. This was the beginning of a long and beautiful friendship that lasted until I was fourteen.

During the next few months, something happened that bears mentioning; but it was so sudden and short that, at the time, I did not realize what was taking place. Consequently, I have very little recollection of the matter.

Mother came to visit me and she and I bathed Pinky. He was snow-white when we took him out of the towel. Mother powdered and perfumed him. (Mother and perfume went together like bread and butter.) Strutting like a peacock, Pinky seemed to be very proud of himself. He and I went out to play, and when we came back to the house later, we found Mother and Daddy talking. A few days later, the three of us were together again. This was the very thing I had dreamed of and yet, somehow, it wasn't the same anymore. It was a short-lived harmony. I have no idea when Mother and Daddy decided to give up on their second marriage, but it could not have lasted over two or three months.

The episode was not a total loss, however, because in remarrying Daddy, Mother regained the custody rights to me that she had unknowingly signed away with her first divorce. When Mother left this time, she took me with her. We went to Chattanooga, Tennessee where she found work in a factory. We then moved into a boarding house. Mother was gone most of the time, working. Instead of having Mama and Papa Rogers to love and care for me and Daddy's brothers and sisters and Pinky to play with, I had the boarding house owner. She was an elderly woman who left me to myself much of the time and didn't seem to care whether or not I had anything to eat.

One morning after Mother had left for work, I remember waking up to find the big old house empty. I went to the kitchen and found some cold oatmeal on the stove. Though I was only five years old, I was sure I could fix my own oatmeal. I had seen Mama Rogers do it lots of times. I went to the refrigerator and took out butter and cream. But the butter wouldn't melt. It kept floating on top of the oatmeal in a big glob. I believe I forgot the sugar too. I had never tasted anything so nasty and finally gave up on it.

A few days later, I was alone again. This time I had two eggs in a pan of water and was trying to boil them for my breakfast when I heard a knock at the door. I peeked through the glass and there stood two men dressed in overcoats and hats. I had no idea who they were or what they wanted and cautiously opened the door. At the sight of me, one of the men jerked off his hat and cried, "How's my Beeky!"

Papa Rogers and Daddy! I was never so happy to see anyone in my life. They didn't waste any time whisking me away from that place. They didn't even give me time to get out of my pajamas. As we hurried out to the car, I was amazed to see that the sun was actually shining. I couldn't remember having seen the sun the whole time I had been in Chattanooga. Mother went to work before I got up, and the old lady that I stayed with kept the shades down and the curtains drawn. Mother realized that I needed to be where I could be outside and play and also needed to be with someone who loved and cared for me while she worked, so she had called Daddy and he came.

My return to Daddy, after staying with Mother, set the pace for the rest of my childhood. It is amazing how resilient children are. Most human beings seem to have a mechanism built in for self-preservation, a way to survive. Somehow, my young mind came up with a solution to keep my emotions off the teeter-totter while being shuffled from one parent to another.

It was simple. When I was with Daddy and his family, I made up my mind to be there 100 percent, to quit thinking and longing for Mother. Then, when I was with Mother, I did the same thing in regard to Daddy. In fact, I learned to mention them only rarely to each other. I placed each parent, and the respective relatives—even down to my cousins—in a neat slot, completely separate from the other; in other words, I led two lives!

Being torn between parents is unsettling for a child. The whole ordeal of divorce is troubling, but I believe that a child needs to know both parents, even if only one at a time. To really know my parents, as I did, helped me realize who I was and gave me a much better chance of deciding what I wanted to do with my life.

For example, one summer evening as the sun was going down, Pinky and I were playing in the backyard of Mama and Papa Rogers' home. Suddenly, I became aware of music in the air. At first I thought there must be a radio playing somewhere, but as I followed the sounds, I noticed a big gathering on a neighbor's porch.

Inside the house, some people were playing guitars and someone was singing old Jimmy Rodgers tunes. At intervals, the singing would be interspersed with the sounds of a harmonica. The porch was so packed and jammed with onlookers that I could not get near enough to see who the musicians were, but oh, that music! It made my heart sing and made a feeling of excitement stir in my veins. What I wouldn't give just to see who was making such wonderful music. Scores of neighbors must have had the same idea. But, finally realizing how dark it had become, Pinky and I set out for home.

I rushed in the back door where Mama Rogers was working in the kitchen and began breathlessly telling her of what I had just heard. "Why, honey," she said calmly, "that was your daddy."

"My daddy?"

She explained that he had gotten together with a couple of neighbor men who played guitar to have a jam session. Daddy was a one-man-show with his guitar and harmonica. The harmonica was attached to a wire device that clasped onto his chest and back and was held in place at his mouth so that he could blow while he strummed rhythm on the guitar. This way, he could sing, yodel and accompany himself with two instruments.

Mama Rogers went on to tell how Daddy used to sing and play in church. That was how he had met my mother, she said. When they went to church, Mother and her older brother and younger sister would sing "special" songs. They were called the Goodman Family Trio. Daddy played his guitar to accompany them. I left Mama Rogers' presence feeling a little blue. All those people were out there enjoying my father's music. I had never known about his talent, nor about how music had brought him and my mother together.

That was my first awakening to the music that was destined to become a large part of my life. As with my parents, it was to be through music, many years later, that I would meet my own husband.

Hard Times

Soon after I learned of my Dad's musical abilities, Mother came and took me home with her for a few months. She had left the factory and Chattanooga and had gone to live with her family in a small Georgia town. It was here that I became more acquainted with music and the kind of life that follows the gifted ones who earn their livelihood from their natural musical resources.

Mama Rogers had told me about Mother and her brother and sister's singing in church, but I had not realized how far they had gone with it. I found that there was no longer a Goodman Family Trio, but as each of the younger children had grown old enough, they too had joined the group, and now they called themselves the Goodman Family. They were still singing their own brand of happy gospel music in churches, camp meetings, revival meetings and in any other happening that needed Christian entertainment.

The Family stayed very busy with singing engagements, but did well to "break even" financially. It was a real treat if they came home with extra money. Mama and Papa Goodman and the little ones left at home existed on the pension check, a small monthly pittance paid Papa for his involvement in the Spanish-American War.

Yes, times with the Goodmans were rough. And when I say rough, I mean sometimes not having a quarter to buy a sack of potatoes. I very well remember going down to the corner grocery and asking for a quarter's worth of potatoes and telling the owner to put it on the bill. Mama Goodman sent me because I was a child. She hoped the grocer would have pity and not turn me down because they were behind on their bill. God bless the grocer, for he didn't turn me away, and once more there was food on the table.

Many times we sat down to eat with only a pot of watered-down dried beans and not even the luxury of a piece of corn bread. During these times, we didn't just sit down and ask the blessing on the food. We all knelt around the table beside our chairs and prayed earnestly. After one such meal I went out to play. One of my little playmates, who had been watching through the window while we were praying, looked at me in bewilderment and asked what we were all doing under the table!

I believe Mother's younger brother, Rusty, hated our poverty more than all the rest of us. Rusty was a gentle boy of twelve, with hair so curly you couldn't tell which end was grown to his head. One morning we got up and discovered there was nothing in the house to eat. Rusty went out back, killed a blackbird and dressed and fried it. I was hungry, but when he tried to share it with me, I only took one small bite, because he had gone to so much trouble for so little.

The worst scene of all was at the Goodman house that Christmas. Mother's folks were proud and never wanted anyone to know what a hard time they were having. We wrapped empty boxes, brick bats and stove wood and placed them under the tree because there was no money for real presents. I was so depressed I could hardly stand it. There were all those lovely packages with nothing inside. The empty boxes weren't so bad, but crude objects wrapped in the gaily colored paper made me sick. To me this was worse than not having food. However, few things drove laughter away from the Goodman house, and this lean Christmas was certainly not one of them. I can still see Mother and Stella, sitting on the floor, wrapping everything we brought to them, laughing and having a ball. Why cry? Crying was just admitting defeat. There would be more Christmases. They had to get better, for they certainly couldn't get much worse.

The Goodmans laughed away many bleak days. If things got too quiet, someone would turn on the radio to the Grand Ole Opry. In a split second, everyone would be clapping hands and singing along. What better way to forget your troubles and your woes!

There was one more boy in the Goodman household younger than Rusty—Bobby. He was two years older than I and the only member of the family with red hair. Of course, freckles usually accompany red hair and Bobby had his share. The mental picture I have of Bobby as a boy is with pant legs rolled almost to his knees, feet bare, with hair so bleached by the sun that it resembled a disorderly pile of straw.

It seemed that Mama Goodman's main concern in those days was Bobby's dirty neck and ears. He never was able to wash them to suit her. Every time she sent him to wash up and then went to inspect him, she would invariably take over with cloth and homemade lye soap. Then she would gouge and scrub while Bobby danced around screaming bloody murder.

I stood amazed. How his neck and ears could get so dirty as to bring such grief to Mama Goodman and cause a continual disruption to the household was a mystery to me. Bobby always came from these sessions red as a beet, but one thing is for sure—his neck and ears were clean.

Having nothing but boys to play with in Georgia, I lived in a world of slingshots, BB guns and fishing poles. Since Bobby was the oldest, I soon found that he was also much stronger and smarter than I was and, lest I forget, he took it upon himself, every so often, to remind me.

I followed him everywhere, wading streams for miles, looking for hidden treasure or roaming the woods behind the house, hunting. I watched as he baited and set bird and rabbit traps. My, how grand he was, even though he never caught anything. Every time we went to check the traps we could tell that little animals had been there investigating, for they had left tracks, according to Bobby.

All good things must come to an end, and my carefree days of fun and adventure were swiftly coming to a close. A new adventure was about to begin for me: school.

Mother couldn't afford to send me. The simplest necessities such as proper clothing, school supplies and lunch money were monumental to my twenty-three-year-old mother, who had no income of her own. She was also away most of the time singing, so the best thing for me to do was to return to Mama and Papa Rogers and Daddy.

We bundled up my belongings and away I went.

School Days

On my first day of school I sat down in the funny little chair that Aunt Joyce, a knowledgeable sixth grader, was calling a desk.

Then Joyce muttered something about ". . . have to go," let go of my hand and disappeared through the doorway. Suddenly I found myself alone with a room full of strangers.

Wide-eyed, I slowly began to take inventory of my surroundings. The room was tremendously big. There were rows and rows of little chairs, exactly like mine, all facing in the same direction. Kids were everywhere, laughing, scrambling over desks and even throwing things. Their camaraderie made me feel even more alone. Surely I was the only stranger here.

Then my eyes fell on three kids, sitting quietly in the back of the room. Their eyes were red from crying and they were trembling with fright, *Like scared little rabbits*, I thought. Along the wall stood a group of women smiling and chatting. It was easy to see that they were the mothers of the happy, carefree children around me. I swallowed a lump in my throat as I thought of Mother.

While deep in thought and enjoying a good deal of self-pity, I was startled when, seemingly from nowhere, a friendly arm slipped around my shoulders. I looked up into kind eyes that were peering at me through gold-rimmed glasses. Mrs. Williams, my teacher, introduced herself, and I loved her from that moment on.

I loved and enjoyed school from the beginning and was greatly disappointed a few weeks later when the teacher sent me home with the measles. I was out of commission for two whole weeks and was so horrible looking that I couldn't stand the sight of myself in the mirror.

Daddy Remarries

My first year of school was exciting, but other changes were occurring in my life at that same time. Daddy remarried. His new wife's name was Lila. She was young and beautiful. From the first, Lila cared for me as a mother. She moved right in with the rest of us and became a welcomed part of the family. Lila brought with her a comfortable air of organization. She believed that everything had a place and that's where everything should be. Because of our setup, it would have been easy for Lila to let Mama Rogers continue to be responsible for me, but that was not Lila's way. She began to teach me to care for my belongings, and she kept my hair shampooed and neatly trimmed. My clothes became her concern. She saw to it that they were starched and ironed to perfection. When we dressed for a special occasion, I walked proudly, because Lila had gone to great pains to make me look nice.

Lila never tried to take the place of Mother, but she was a very dear and special friend, and our relationship grew into something beautiful and lasting.

About the time I entered second grade, another event occurred: the arrival of my little sister Jane. I do believe she came into the world reaching for me. Just about every mental picture I have of Jane as a tot is one of her with outstretched arms, crying brokenheartedly if I got too far away. It was a chore just to get loose from her for a few minutes to play with a school chum. But I loved having a little sister— most of the time

Church had been a big part of Mama and Papa Rogers' life before I was born and even when I was a baby; but somehow over the years, they had gotten out of the habit of attending regularly. I guess it had a lot to do with the long hours Papa worked; he often came home long after dark.

Now Papa Rogers decided that we children needed to be in Sunday school and found a church for us to attend. When we arrived that first Sunday morning, the service had already begun. The church was full. As we stepped inside, we noticed the congregation was standing and singing enthusiastically. A strange feeling swept over me. Goose pimples covered my arms as they continued to sing. The only vacant seats were on the front pew, so we followed Papa to them. By the time we reached the front of the church, hot tears were stinging my cheeks. I could not control them. When the congregation was seated, I sat with my head bowed, trying once again to hide my tears. I didn't want Papa to think something was wrong with me, but he sensed something amiss and leaned over to question me, "You OK, Beeky?"

"Yes, Papa," I whispered. "I'm just sleepy."

After that Sunday, we became regular members of that wonderful little church. That is the place where I fell in love with the Lord, His people and His house; and that love firmly remains to this day.

Chapter 3

Wingo

The sun was directly overhead, pinpointing its victims with massive heat rays and causing minimal activity in the project. I was sitting outside, seeking shelter on what could scarcely be called a porch, just whiling away the time. It was summer vacation. School was out, with three whole months before I would have to succumb to the routine of homework and early rising again. But I couldn't help feeling proud, for next fall I would be in the fourth grade.

Suddenly I was aroused from my thoughts as billows of dust rolled upward and a big tan station wagon wheeled in and pulled to a stop in our front yard. Whoever could that be? Very seldom did anyone visit us. We lived too far from all our relatives and friends. I blinked my eyes as the dust began to settle. Then the front doors swung open on either side of the car.

It was Mother! And Aunt Stella! I could hardly believe my eyes. I'd had no idea they were coming for me, but here they were. Joyfully I scrambled down the steps and ran to Mother. She was tired and road-weary but was the most beautiful sight I had ever seen. And Stella, laughing and big as life, led me around to the back of the vehicle to show me a brand new bicycle! Uncle Howard had bought Bobby, Jimmy and me a new bicycle for summer vacation, and they had brought mine so that I could see it. I forgot the heat. It was time for action, so I began to gather my possessions, everything I owned. As always, when Mother came, nothing else mattered. I was dizzy with excitement because I was about to change worlds again.

Mother and Stella had lunch with Mama and Papa Rogers and freshened up a bit. Then we said our good-byes. Daddy, Lila and Jane had been gone all day. It began to look as though I would have to leave without telling them good-bye. We were out of the yard and a few blocks down the street when we met Daddy's car. Both cars stopped.

Every silver lining has to have a cloud and mine came equipped with thunder and rain, the tears of my one-year-old sister, Jane. She spotted me in the car with Mother and Stella and knew I was leaving. The thunder started. She screamed and held out her arms to me, and in my innocence, I desperately tried to figure a way to take her with me. Stella, fast on the draw, quickly produced a big beautiful doll they had brought for me, hoping to divert Jane's attention. Stella's ruse failed. We had to leave Jane screaming at the top of her lungs. My feet left the clouds and were abruptly planted on the floorboard of a well-worn dusty station wagon, taking me away from Jane.

My melancholy soon faded, though. I was too elated to be back with Mother and Stella, to hear them talk and to feel the vibrant warmth of their nearness. I wanted to hear everything they could tell me about everyone and all about where they now lived. Wingo, Kentucky? Strange, I had never heard of that place before. As soon as we arrived, I knew why.

Wingo was a small town, nine miles south of Mayfield. It boasted only a handful of stores, including a post office and a café. The actual town was stretched out in a valley, just off the highway. To get to the residential area, the main street made a distinct climb, then wound lazily to the right, exposing first the houses of seniority. These houses were painted spotless white and were surrounded by great porches, trimmed shrubbery and carpets of freshly mown grass. As we drove down the peaceful street, shaded by big oak trees, the houses became less sophisticated and more homey. Finally, we stopped in front of a rambling white frame house. It was the very last one on the right side of the street, just before the place where the city limit sign was posted and where the pavement ended.

I hopped out of the car and ran into the yard. There sat Bobby's and Jimmy's shiny new bicycles, side by side, looking as though they had never been ridden. I felt that they were just waiting for me and my bike. They were parked under one of at least a dozen large oak trees that graced the sprawling front yard. Along the concrete walkway and leading to the front porch was evidence of Mama Goodman's labors, her flowers. What a beautiful sight. It all seemed to reach out and embrace me and shout, "Welcome home!"

By now everyone had come from the house, with much hugging and kissing and just plain old commotion, which I found I had missed more than anything in my absence from the Goodmans. Jimmy, Bobby and I just had to take a ride down the street. This was the first of hundreds of miles we pedaled together on those streamlined Schwinns.

It wasn't hard for me to see that The Family was doing better.

It was a pleasant feeling to see all the changes being made. Every few weeks something new was bought for the house and Mama Goodman kept Papa and the boys busy remodeling. The sounds of hammers and saws, and the smell of new paint and wallpaper glue were common all that summer. Everyone was busy. Mama Goodman made the loveliest bedspreads and matching curtains for the girls' rooms, with ruffles everywhere. When the girls would wax the floors, the three of us kids would get old clothes and cut them up for buffing rags. Then we'd have a ball sliding and shining them. Mama Goodman was an industrious woman. Although she stood less than five feet tall, she was a giant when it came to work.

That summer Mama Goodman had Papa build chicken coops out in the backyard so she could raise poultry. It was exciting the day the biddies were delivered. Bobby, Jimmy and I were right in the middle of it all, fondling the little yellow balls of fuzz, with hundreds of squeaky cheeps ringing in our ears. All we could think of was the fun we were having, but Mama Goodman, like the busy ant, was getting ready for winter. She visualized these biddies grown into fryers and setting hens and furnishing us with eggs and chicken and dumplings. They would fill our table this winter, along with canned vegetables from Mama's summer garden.

When winter came and Mama Goodman could no longer work outside, she then had Papa hang the quilting frames and she taught me to quilt. Mama loved bright colors, so the quilts were varying shades of pink and red and contrasting blues. I have no idea how many quilts we made that winter, but there were plenty for all. Mama Goodman also taught me to embroider. We spent hours sitting in the living room near a roaring fire putting lovely designs on pillowcases, tablecloths and doilies. On such winter evenings, Papa would read and the boys would put together model airplanes. This was one of their amusements that never caught my interest.

The random lifestyle of Mother's family had its pluses and its minuses. Since their music had them in one week and out two, or vice versa, there was absolutely no set routine around the house. If they had a good trip, we were rich, but if they had a bad trip, we were poor. We had a favorite saying which aptly described our existence, "Chicken today, and feathers tomorrow."

Since Howard was the oldest and the leader of The Family's musical aspirations, the whole clan doted on him. It was at about this time that Mama Goodman remarked after one of their trips, "Howard, you children always seem so happy. Why don't you call yourselves the *Happy* Goodman Family?" And that is how their singing name evolved and how it remains to this day.

Stella, a buxom, motherly figure, was the sister that we all looked to and loved dearly. After losing her husband in the war and being left with little Jimmy, she sought companionship from God and her family. Stella stood in the shadow of three beautiful sisters but never seemed to mind because she was gifted above any of them. She had a stirring, heavy alto voice that vibrated with depth and sincerity, making her the star of the Happy Goodman Family.

At home, the hot summer evenings would find the Goodmans lounging lazily around like a pride of lions. Some stretched out on blankets underneath the oaks, others on the porch in the swing and still others taking turns with the hand-cranked ice cream freezer.

These were times that I was much in demand, and often made a pretty good haul scratching Rusty's back or combing Junior's hair for twenty-five cents a chore.

After being on the road for many miles, cramped in cars, The Family didn't fudge on relaxation or fun. All that was needed was a suggestion and everyone was ready. If one said, "Let's go swimming," it started wheels turning, and in a few minutes each of us was searching for something to swim in. I can see Rusty now, standing at Mama Goodman's sewing machine, sewing up a rip in some old pants to be cut off at the knee for his bathing suit.

A suggestion to go fishing received the same approval; consequently, everyone set about to rig the poles. Most of our fishing in those days was done forty miles away at Kentucky Dam. When we went, we stayed all day and often into the night. Mama and Papa Goodman enjoyed these outings immensely. No one was left out.

When we came home from our fishing trips, no matter what time it happened to be, Howard and Stella would clean the fish, and Stella and Mama Goodman would fry them along with delicious hushpuppies and french fries. Sometimes we would be eating this meal at midnight or at 1 o'clock in the morning. What a treat for a nine-year-old!

I recall a time when all the laughter and excitement in that big house settled down to a hush for several days. Junior had to leave for a tour of duty in the armed services. Such a sad occasion. How were we going to live without Junior for four long years? Since none of the boys had ever been separated from the family before, it was almost more than we could bear. The day Junior was to leave I found an isolated room in the back of the house where I cried and prayed for him.

Junior had always been so dear to me. If Bobby or Jimmy were giving me a rough time such as chasing me with a granddaddy long-legs, he gallantly came to my rescue. As I lay there, weeping, I remembered other times when Junior had helped me.

I could never forget the time Mother and Eloise had decided to move away. They found jobs in Louisiana and intended to make their home there. I was left behind until they were established and Mother could come for me. For a while it was business as usual without Mother. I was quite accustomed to her being away with The Family.

Late one evening, Mama, Papa, Bobby, Jimmy and I were sitting on the porch, straining our ears for the familiar hum of a certain car. Wouldn't they ever get here? The Family had been away for three whole weeks. It was time for their return. Just when we decided they had been delayed for another day, they arrived with the car horn blowing loudly. Before it could come to a complete stop, Happy Goodmans were pouring out all four doors, loaded down with presents for all of us.

Bobby and Jimmy flew from the porch and reached the car first. I was about to run through the picket gate when I stopped. Jimmy was in his mother's arms. Then it dawned on me that Mother was not coming home this time.

A familiar ache gripped my heart. I didn't go toward the car but looked around to make sure everyone was preoccupied and then faded away from the happy scene. As everyone noisily migrated up the walk and onto the porch, I ran blindly around the side of the house. Fighting back the tears and swallowing a choking lump in my throat, I hoped I could find something to make me forget my loneliness. I headed for the washhouse where my kittens were, but the thought of them didn't comfort me. There were the chicken coops, now abandoned, because the biddies were full grown and scratching about in the yard. I was determined not to give in to the pain when I felt an arm slip around my shoulders. When I looked up into Junior's face, the rushing current was unleashed, and there in his arms, I sobbed.

In a few minutes, Junior dried my eyes and said, "Come on, honey. Let's go in the house." He never told me what he had in mind, but to my delight Mother was home within twenty-four hours.

Junior left for the armed services, and right away we began receiving letters from him signed *Sam* Goodman. We were all puzzled. Finally he wrote to explain: "When I told them my name was Junior, they let me know there was no place in Uncle Sam's Army for Juniors."

So the United States Army took our Junior away from us . . . and in return gave us Sam.

The All-day Singing

It was a lovely day, crisp and green with the smell of spring in the air. We were all dressed in our Sunday best, bouncing down a gravel road in a 1940-something Buick on our way to an all-day singing and dinner-on-the-ground. What I didn't like about these all-day singings was the all day part, for they lasted from early morning till late afternoon. The thing I did like was the dinner.

All those country churches had one thing in common: long makeshift tables outside where at noontime the ladies proudly spread the meals they had brought from home. You could always count on Southern-fried chicken and banana pudding to be among the main courses.

I enjoyed the singing too, but for my own taste, they had entirely too much congregational singing and too few specials. Of course, the special singers were always The Family, or else we would have no reason to be there. I couldn't help but giggle as I watched the song leaders come up one at a time, lead the congregation in their favorite song, make it last as long as possible, then retire to the audience to be replaced by another. I'll never forget how comical they looked. I don't know why, but it seemed as though every song leader was a grandpa who looked as though he were having his last big fling. In my mind's eye I can just see one of them now: a songbook in one hand and the other waving exuberantly, and with his knee bobbing up and down, keeping time to the music. Even a child could see the satisfaction on his face as he savored every precious moment of limelight. Between stanzas he would stop the music, urge the altos or sopranos to "sing out," then away he would go again, leading the congregation with all his might. Then before the last stanza, the leader would stop the music again and give his final command in a loud musical drawl, "Everybody on the last!"

After many songs in this fashion, The Family was called to the platform to sing a few specials. Afterward, the minister would pass the hat and hopefully glean a few coins to help buy gasoline home and perhaps take us to another such event.

On this particular Sunday morning, I was feeling lighthearted as we bounced along the dirt road, and from the car window I watched the dew studded grass sparkle beneath the morning sun, like millions of tiny diamonds. Suddenly, the car began to sputter and cough and finally came to a jerky halt. Out of gas. . . . What were we going to do? There couldn't possibly be a store within ten miles, and besides this was Sunday and everything would be closed. Just as we were about to surrender to our situation, Rusty yelled, "Look! Gas!"

Ironically, we had stopped right in front of a big barn, and there nestled under the eaves was a gas barrel kept by the farmer to run his farm implements.

Oh happy day! In a few minutes, the boys had borrowed enough gasoline to take us to our destination. We hoped the farmer whose gas we had taken would be at the singing, and sure enough, he was. He felt grand and important that his gasoline had rescued the featured entertainers and therefore refused our offers to pay for it.

The Lord had performed a miracle. He made good His promise, "Lo, I am with you alway, even unto the end of the world" (Matthew 28:20).

That wasn't the only miracle that He performed that day.

That Sunday I became hot and restless and ventured outside of the church in search of a breeze and possibly a hydrant to relieve my thirst. Once outside, I don't remember finding either, but I did find several other folk milling around on the church grounds with the same idea. As I ambled around, glad to be able to stretch my legs, I came upon a couple of seedy-looking characters blowing smoke rings into the air from their crunched-up, roll-your-own cigarettes. I was fascinated.

Looking back, I am convinced that those two young men had designs on me long before I spotted them. Like serpents charming a bird, they set out to capture my attention, and succeeded. I was wary because they were unkempt and scruffy, but, at the same time, I was bored, hot and thirsty. So I inched a little closer.

Their dusty old one-seated coupe was parked right there with the door standing open, and I could see the dirty, torn interior as one of them continued to lean against the tree, still puffing little smoke rings into the air.

The trap was set and the lure effective. All they had to do next was to entice me into the car without arousing suspicion. And what better enticement could they offer a child than ice cream? They made my mouth water with the promise of good cold ice cream if I would just ride down to the store with them. But at that same moment it was as if someone was whispering in my ears, *You know there's not a store within miles of this place, and if there were, it wouldn't be open because this is Sunday*!

When I realized that they wanted me in that car bad enough to lie to me, my eyes were immediately opened to the danger that I was confronted with, and I rushed back inside the safety of the church.

The Lord rescued an eight-year-old child that day from tragedy and because He did, sexual abuse is a trauma that I have never had to overcome. Even with all my uncle's and male cousins on both sides of the family, I can truthfully say that our relationships were nothing less than wholesome. For this I am eternally grateful to them and to my Heavenly Father.

While the Happy Goodman Family and many other such gospel singing groups were merely earning a subsistence while pursuing their dreams, other people were becoming interested in gospel music as well. In Nashville, Tennessee, a man named Wally Fowler had an idea. Why not shift the Sunday all-day singings to Friday and Saturday nights and have all-night singings? He presented his plan to the public with much fanfare, and thus the all-night singing was born.

Wally Fowler moved gospel singings from traditional churches to rented auditoriums. Instead of asking one special group to perform, he invited many. The order of the proceedings was reversed. Now there were few congregational songs and much singing by the special groups. Alas, the colorful old song leader became almost obsolete.

Soon all the Southland was astir with this unheard of innovation. A singing that lasted all night! Were they really going to sing all night? People came by the hundreds to see, purchasing their tickets at the door. Never had gospel singing experienced such revolution and never had it attracted the public on such a large scale.

How well I remember my first all-night singing, held in a high school auditorium in Atlanta, Georgia in 1949, shortly after my trip to the Ryman. I was fascinated by everything going on around me. When the groups of singers came on stage for their allotted time, there was no denying where they had received their training. There were the alto leads, bass leads, baritone leads, tenor and soprano leads. The only difference from the congregational singing was that these leads were taken by individuals.

You could easily recognize the same body language found in the church song leaders, the same foot-stomping and hand-waving.

Wally Fowler was there that night with his original Oak Ridge Quartet. I laughed till I cried at their stage performance. Little Johnny New walked up to Curly Blalock (bald as a peeled onion and towering over Johnny) and motioned for him to look down at his feet. As Curly looked down, Little Johnny took out his comb, and using Curly's head as a mirror, proceeded to groom his own locks.

In those early days, each group had to gather around one microphone. The public address system left something to be desired. Many microphones sounded as though they might be nothing more than amplified Pet milk cans. As much as I love progress, there is something to be said for the interest created by switching the mike back and forth between members of the group to whomever may be taking the lead. The groups played this up. At times one member would actually take the mike away from another, sending the audience into fits of laughter.

I remember giggling behind my hand at the precise Blackwood Brothers, shaking their heads back and forth as they sang an overemphasized vibrato. I thought their style would never work. Needless to say, I was wrong and Blackwood has become a household word to gospel music lovers for decades.

Hovie Lister and The Statesmen's Quartet had a male tenor singer whose voice was so high that the other quartet members referred to him as *Sister* Cat Freeman. This delighted the fans.

My favorite group of that period was the Harmoneers' Quartet. They had a short, chubby first tenor whose name was Happy Edwards. He would sing "Heaven's Parade" until he was so wet with perspiration that he had to pull off his coat but kept right on singing. By the end of the number, the whole group would be holding him up, and then before leaving the stage, Happy would jump up in the air and send his feet in opposite directions. All of these antics were out of place in church, so the gospel music stage became the platform for a whole new breed of family entertainment.

There was another popular group called the Rangers' Quartet from Texas. They wore heavy mustaches, which I thought appeared rather homely, but their singing was amazing. They had an Irish tenor named Denver Crumpler, who was one of the best in the business, and David Reese, their monkeyish piano player, kept the audience rolling with laughter.

But gospel singing was more than entertainment. The groups wanted their audiences to enjoy the evening; but before they finished, they moved into a more serious vein and sang songs with great meaning, describing heaven or the nail prints in the hands of the crucified

Jesus. Although you laughed and had fun, before the night was over hearts were touched by the message of the gospel. For this reason, gospel music grew fast in popularity. Its supporters would drive hundreds of miles to the next concert, never tiring of the same songs, because with those songs came a renewing of the Spirit and a liberty to express oneself. These were fundamentals missing from many churches.

Happily, I can say gospel concerts were never limited to one church organization. All faiths and denominations came and, for a few hours, laid aside the man-made fences that separate believers from one another. There, with one accord, we become united in Christian fellowship. This is one of the greatest contributions gospel music has made to the world of Christendom.

So from the womb of the church came forth gospel singings as we know them today—a happy music, full of joy, hope and promise. The church is our mother and God is our Father. We are bound together with a common goal to proclaim the good news of the risen Savior to a lost world.

Nine Cousins

Goodmans of all sizes and descriptions were crammed into our 1952 Chrysler limousine as we rolled merrily along toward Burnwell, Alabama. Sitting in one of the folding jump seats in the middle of the car, I was filled with eager anticipation. School was out and we were on our way to visit Aunt Flossie Nix, Mama Goodman's sister, and her family. I was especially happy because I was going to stay over and spend several weeks at the farm with my cousins.

Uncle Hershel had pioneered the gospel in that area and was now the pastor of a small country church. He and Aunt Flossie had nine children. Their farm offered many places to explore for city slickers such as ourselves. I was going to have a wonderful vacation!

One of the most interesting things about Aunt Flossie's boys was their nicknames. They were Mock, Snip, Doodle and Clabbert, and then there was Jimmy Donald and the youngest was simply Dan.

The girls were named Margaret, Martha (pronounced Marthy) and Melvie. Marthy and I, near the same age, were best of friends. When we arrived, my cousins were glad to see me because we had a lot of catching up to do. We laughed and talked on into the night with great expectations of the days ahead. However, I was about to learn what life on the farm was really like.

On the first day after the family left, Aunt Flossie came into the bedroom early and said, "Time for you girls to get up! Marthy, you and Breeska have a choice this morning. Had you rather wash dishes and clean the kitchen or pick tomatoes?"

Marthy was about to answer when I spoke up quickly, "Pick tomatoes!" I had never done that before and was ready for adventure and the great outdoors. What was the use of being in the country if we had to stay cooped up in the house? Marthy seemed a little reluctant but readily gave in to my enthusiasm. Before long Dan, Clabbert, Marthy and I were off to the tomato patch, leaving the kitchen to poor Margaret.

It was a beautiful day. The cool morning air was fresh and sweet as we walked along the dirt road, swinging our empty buckets and chattering happily about the many things we would do during my stay: go swimming in the blue hole and eat all the home-grown watermelon I wanted.

"Where is that tomato patch, anyway?" I asked Marthy.

"Not too much farther now, we're almost there," she said.

In a few minutes we turned off the main road and found ourselves in a wide-open field. Tomatoes were everywhere! The boys started picking right away and showed me how; but as I reached for the first big red tomato, there perched on top of it was an awful looking little varmint.

"What is that?" I shouted. After inspecting the tomato, the boys and Marthy laughed.

"Why, it's just a little ole bug," Clabbert said. "He won't bother you none. Just knock him off!"

I tried. But by that time another annoyance was becoming increasingly evident. The hot sun was beating down mercilessly on my back. What had happened to that lovely breeze that had followed us from the house? Time passed slowly. Soon I was sweaty, itchy and thirsty. My thoughts returned to the house and Margaret in that cool kitchen.

"Marthy, why didn't you tell me how bad tomato picking was?"

"I thought you knew what you were asking for," Marthy replied. "Anyway, it's time to go now. The boys have their buckets full and so is mine."

I looked down at my bucket and moaned. It wasn't even half full. Clabbert came over, took it from me and in a few minutes had it full. Then we set out down the road in the blazing sun.

"Marthy, how far are we from home now?" I asked.

"Well, the tomato patch is a good mile and a half from the house," she answered.

"A mile and a half," I groaned, trudging along with my heavy pail. *This'll be the last time I'll choose the tomato patch over housework,* I determined, *picking tomatoes makes dishwashing look good*!

Yes indeed, farm life was different and an education in itself.

The Pine Pole Sled

In the backwoods of Alabama in the early '50s, there was not a lot going on to entertain children. If you found amusement, it most often was of your own making. Since necessity is the mother of invention, Aunt Flossie's boys were always figuring out new ways to have fun and occupy their time. That summer their latest brainchild was a joy ride they called the pine pole sled, and they were eager to share this adventure with me.

Marthy and I followed them through the woods behind the house to the base of a steep hill. Those strapping boys, like playful, overgrown puppies, were so excited about their new invention that they even had me excited. When we finally came upon it, I stood gazing in wide-eyed wonder as they busied themselves making ready for the ride.

It was an ingenious devise that they had painstakingly made from young pine saplings. Many of the same size were cut down, and after the bark was stripped from them, they were laid end to end as tracks that ran down a very steep incline. From old boards they had also made a kind of sled that fit down over the rails. And that's not all! Axle grease was then applied underneath the sled to insure top speed.

While we watched, they dragged the cumbersome sled up the hill, placed it on the tracks and one of the boys quickly hopped on to show me just how it worked. In a split second it was over; and he, sled, axle grease and all had dug a trench in the ground at the end of the tracks, peeling more bark from shins, elbows and knees.

It simply amazed me that no provision had been made for a better landing and that the splinters, rocks and jolting stop seemed to be of no concern to them. Needless to say, they never got me on that frightful contraption, though I don't believe it really mattered, for when Marthy and I left them, they were still having fun! Even though I never rode it, the pine pole sled taught me a strong, amusing lesson. Through the years I have seen many people live their lives in the same manner, enjoying the ride with no thought of the landing.

After three weeks of invigorating farm life, The Family came for me and I returned to Wingo, full of exciting tales and adventures. Although I enjoyed visiting relatives and summer road trips, I was always glad to return home to Kentucky.

Many changes were taking place. Uncle Howard met a lovely eighteen-year-old girl from Sand Mountain, Alabama who stole his big heart away. It wasn't long before he married Vestal Freeman (sister to Cat Freeman) and brought her home to Wingo.

That same year, Ruth was swept off her feet by a handsome and dashing Merchant Marine and soon they were married.

As if these occurrences had not given me enough to think about, Mama Goodman decided it was time I became a lady. No drill sergeant had ever taken his charge more seriously, and I'm sure a less determined person would have failed the task. I can still see the anguished look on her face when I came in from playing with the sash of my dress ripped and dragging the ground.

Since Mama Goodman couldn't keep me out of trees or off my head, she reluctantly agreed to let me wear blue jeans to play in. It was a wise choice, for I spent a big part of the time with my feet in the air. Even Bobby and Jimmy had trouble with me, for if a softball game was going too slow, I was apt to begin turning cartwheels on first base.

Mama Goodman patiently drilled me on how to sit, stand and walk in public. And chewing gum became an unpardonable sin. Well, I didn't care much for the public if they were unable to take a little chewing gum.

Every so often I was sent to Betsy's Beauty Parlor, about a half-mile from our house, for Betsy to trim, shampoo and set my hair. I enjoyed the long bike ride and the time I spent with Betsy. On one such occasion I found Betsy all excited about a new invention called the cold wave. Betsy had just purchased her cold wave machine and was eager to try it out. I was one of her first victims. My hair had a little natural curl and was easy to manage, but this machine was supposed to create a miracle that kept hair looking beautiful at all times. The procedure took hours. The heavy lead curlers must have weighed fifteen pounds, but this was a small price to pay for eternal beauty, so I toughed it out.

Then came the moment of truth when the curlers were removed. To my dismay, my hair frizzed all the way to my scalp and stuck out four or five inches all the way around. I was ruined! There was nothing to do but wait for the miserable mess to grow out. For months, when I dressed to go anywhere, I had to wet my hair and try to plaster it to my head so it wouldn't stand straight out.

One day in a big hurry, we were about to be late for a singing, I was ready except for my hair. Everyone was in the car waiting for me, and as I rushed through the house, I spied a glass of water sitting on a small table in the living room. What a God-send! Now I wouldn't have to go all the way to the bathroom. I dipped my comb into the water several times and applied it generously to my hair. My head was soaked when I climbed into the car and we drove away. I mentioned how lucky I had been to find a glass of water in the living room on my way out the door, but my remark was answered with gales of laughter. The glass hadn't contained water at all, but 7-Up! My hair dried stiff as a board, but for once it didn't stick out at all.

Christmas came. This time there were real gifts under the tree. And what a tree! It was the biggest and prettiest one I had ever seen. Stella and Rusty had found it in a field near the house, chopped it down and brought it home. It was a perfectly shaped cedar that reached all the way to the ceiling. Under Stella's supervision, we all joined in and decorated it from top to bottom with shining ornaments, snow and icicles. Every few minutes one of us would run outside to admire it through the window. When completed, we turned off the overhead lights and watched the multi-colored lights flash off and on. It took our breath away! The whole family gathered in the living room to sing Christmas carols, and being much inspired by our beautiful tree, we sang to the top of our voices. Events such as these are delicious to my mind and leave happy, glowing memories.

Christmas will never have quite the same feeling as it did then, just as a double-dip ice cream cone or a bag of potato chips will never taste quite the same as they did when I was a child.

Chapter 4

Metamorphosis

.

A car pulled up and stopped in front of the house. I was gripped with excitement. The long-awaited moment had finally arrived. The giddy chatter of young voices and the shuffle of feet on the front walk told me that these were the very first guests to Bobby and my birthday party!

Rushing to the bedroom mirror for a final inspection, I stood gazing at my reflection and was, for the most part, pleased. I was thirteen now, and it wasn't easy for my mind and emotions to keep up with all the changes that were taking place in my body. Quickly I dabbed a little powder on my freshly scrubbed nose and gave a few last strokes of the brush to my thick, reddish-brown hair. As it bounced back into place, I bounded out the door of my bedroom to greet the guests who were, by now, pouring in.

When I entered the living room, I stopped and caught my breath. Bobby and I had done the decorating, but nightfall had added a touch of splendor to the old waxed floors and our well-worn furniture. Overhead hung brightly colored strips of crepe paper that had been caught in the center by a mass of balloons, giving the whole room a Mardi Gras effect.

Mother passed out little bags to the guests as they arrived. Then when Bobby and I blew out the candles on our cake we were showered with confetti. Stella and Mother had planned the games and Vestal had made the cake and refreshments. What a night to remember and what a way to be welcomed into the teenage world!

Bobby and I both have birthdays in February, so we chose February 14, Saint Valentine's Day, to have our party.

It was neat being "Queen for a Day." All during the evening I'd turn and find admiring eyes following me. I felt like the ugly duckling who had chanced to look into a pond and found a stately swan staring back at her. I felt beautiful and pranced around all evening with my head held high like a thoroughbred filly. That night I tried to put into practice all the things that Mama Goodman had taught me about being a lady, but I also remembered Mother's words of wisdom: "Honey, be your own sweet self, and everyone will love you."

Evansville

The Family's decision to leave Wingo and move to Evansville, Indiana disappointed me greatly. Wingo was *home*. We had lived there longer than in any other place—four wonderful years. I hated to leave my friends and that sleepy little Kentucky town, but the die had been cast. Again we gathered all of our belongings and left for greener pastures.

Evansville offered so much more. It was a ripe, open field for gospel music, and there The Family began promoting our own monthly singings. We brought in such talent as the Foggy River Boys, who appeared regularly on Red Foley's nationwide TV shows. Other guests included renowned songwriters such as Stewart Hamblen and the famous singing governor of Louisiana, Jimmie Davis, plus most of the popular gospel groups of the day. In the 1950s, the gospel music industry was still very young and had little or no organization. There was no such thing as an appearance contract drawn up to protect singers or promoters. The Family (like all other singing groups) would drive hundreds of miles to a singing on a *promise* from a promoter, hoping the promise would be good. Sometimes the promise was reliable and sometimes the promoters didn't follow through. The work balanced out just enough to keep us afloat, but all those worries and disappointments soon caused Howard's hair to turn gray and also plowed furrows into his brow.

However, since the move to Evansville, things had been looking up. Prior to the move, The Family had purchased their first limousine, a brand new 1952 Chrysler. Now they were able to travel in one car. This was not nearly so dangerous nor expensive. In Evansville we bought a nice two-story frame house in town, thus providing much more room than we had ever had before.

But, as always, the wolf eventually found our door. On the gospel music scene several incidents occurred involving unscrupulous promoters, and consequently Howard refused to work for them again. Soon The Family became isolated from the mainstream all-night singings. They only held concerts as far as their local radio broadcast reached, in schools and in churches. It didn't take long to overwork such a limited area, including our hometown promotions.

After a couple of years in Evansville, The Family began migrating toward the South again and landed in Swainsboro, Georgia to work from a radio station there. To make matters worse, Rusty had to leave for the army, so The Family came for Bobby. He had to quit school to take Rusty's place in the group. Jimmy and I were left behind in Evansville with Mama and Papa Goodman to continue our schooling. I was in the eighth grade.

There was a great void in that big old house once The Family was gone, but mostly I missed Bobby. We had been together almost constantly for the last four years. Things were not looking good. Laughter and good times were replaced with the uncertainty of not knowing if we had enough money to live from one day to the next. Depression began to weigh heavily upon me. I could not enjoy school nor my friends because of my extreme loneliness. Also, things that I thought were necessities, such as lotions, face cream and sometimes even toothpaste and deodorant, were now luxuries. Coming home from school, I would walk very slowly and many times would go several blocks out of the way to avoid returning to all that emptiness.

One day as I rounded the corner and was still two blocks away, I thought I saw a black car parked in front of our house and broke into a run. Maybe it was Mother and Bobby. I couldn't stand another day away from them. Sure enough, there sat the big Chrysler. I never slowed down until I fell into Mother's arms, crying hysterically. This outburst shocked Mother, but still she didn't realize what the separation and insecurity were doing to me. I didn't even realize it myself.

In a few days they all piled into the big limousine and were gone again. This time the loneliness was worse than ever. Mama and Papa were so old that there were two generation gaps between us, and besides, they were wrapped up in their own miseries. Poor little Jimmy was failing school, and my heart ached for him.

The old wounds of being separated from Mother as a child broke open with a profound freshness, and my heart began to bleed for her. Without her I had no anchor: I belonged to no one. Without my mother there was simply no love in my life and absolutely no joy. When my spirits had plummeted to the lowest ebb, we heard about a gospel meeting being held in our town at the Coliseum. Mama Goodman and I scraped together cab fare and attended the day services. When we entered the building, it was packed. I found Mama Goodman a seat, but along with many others, I had to stand near the door, which had been bolted by the fire marshall so that no one else could come in.

At the meetings there was a woman named Betty Baxter who had been a hopeless cripple as a child. The Lord had completely healed her and she was traveling about, giving her testimony. I was mesmerized by what she had to say and strained to hear every word. I believed in miracles; but to see a woman who had been drawn and twisted from birth and who had never known a moment free from pain standing in perfect health was awesome. Then something happened to me that was inexplicable. One moment I was standing there engrossed in this testimony and feeling fine, and the next moment I felt myself falling. The last thing I remember was reaching for something to hold on to.

When I came to myself, I was being held up by a couple of strangers. The doors had been flung open to give me air. I felt sick and weak. Two ladies took me to the restroom and washed my face. My hands were numb. Then in a few minutes I felt fine and concluded that I must have fainted.

The following day was Monday and I attended school as usual. First period found me sitting at my desk, busy with pencil and paper with yesterday's incident forgotten. I raised my head to say something to a classmate and felt myself slipping away and sliding out of my seat onto the floor. I was as helpless as a baby. This time I did not completely black out. Away, off in the distance, I could hear a lot of commotion, and then someone was holding ammonia under my nose while someone else opened a window. In a few minutes, as before, I was OK. But this time I began to wonder, *What is happening to me?*

The next period was art class and the same thing happened again. I wound up on the floor. The school nurse came to take me home, but I was weak and shaking so badly that she had to have help to get me to the car and then into the house. I was put straight to bed, and by then I was terrified.

Swainsboro

Mother took the first flight she could get from Georgia and arrived the next day. A physical examination by a local doctor revealed nothing wrong with me other than anemia and extreme unhappiness. Mother went to the school, checked me out and took me back to Swainsboro with her. There I enrolled in school to finish out the eighth grade.

To combat the anemia, the doctor put me on heavy doses of iron, and Mother fed me liver almost daily. Liver and onions, liver and gravy, fried liver. I got sick of liver! But it worked and life started surging within me again.

Swainsboro was a warm and friendly little town and I was welcomed with opened arms and immediately included in most of the high school social functions. Moving from state to state made it difficult to get acclimated. For instance, where basketball was the main event in Kentucky and football in Indiana, it seemed that Georgia was more interested in *dancing* than anything else. I wasn't comfortable with these events. I had never seen alcohol nor had I heard of drugs back then; but I did know that my old-fashioned upbringing threw up a red flag when it came to dance parties.

What I didn't realize then was that in the mid to late 1950s, dance hops were becoming the rage and were springing up everywhere. I just happened to be in Georgia at the time. My fun-loving nature wanted to participate in all the hullabaloo, but my conscience warned me against it. This tug-of-war inside caused me to bow out of the school's social scene in Swainsboro, forfeiting popularity for the comforts of home. My emotions were too fragile to deal with it all, and more importantly I was too young.

Today as I look back, I can see that the hand of God was working strongly in my life, guiding me through difficult times, steering me around potential pitfalls and honing my awareness of right and wrong. Being with Mother and Bobby was like a tonic. My whole family was very loving and supportive during those days, and before long I was my old self again, with the wounds of insecurities firmly closed, leaving behind nothing but a scar.

Summer Vacation

The ringing telephone demanded attention in our compact Swainsboro apartment. When I answered, the operator said in a nasal tone, "Long distance calling for Miss LaBreeska Rogers."

"This is she," I said, wondering who could be calling me long distance.

"Hello, honey, this is Daddy!" came that familiar voice from the other end of the line. "Lila, Jane and I are coming through Georgia in the morning on the way to Florida for summer vacation. We'll be there early for you, so get packed."

Excitement rushed over me like a tidal wave. My goodness, school had only been out a few days, and here I was, about to go on a Florida vacation with Daddy and my other family!

All day Mother and I rushed around getting my things together. I went to bed exhausted. Daddy arrived the next morning before I even got out of bed. In a flash I was ready with my luggage in the trunk of the car and heading toward the Florida sunshine.

It was good to be with Daddy and Lila again. How Jane had grown! She was seven now with a year of school already behind her. Her love for me had not waned in my absence. She still wanted me right by her side every moment, and it felt good.

It was easy to slip back into Daddy's world. The change of pace was good. As we rolled along, I felt as light as a feather, the wind in my hair and a peace in my soul. I never had a worry when I was with him.

We finally arrived in Jacksonville and went straight to Uncle Herman and Aunt Ginny's home. Uncle Herman, who was Daddy's younger brother, was much like Daddy, except that Uncle Herman talked faster and had auburn hair. He and Aunt Ginny were wonderful hosts and saw to it that we had delicious meals and plenty of ocean, and ocean was just what Jane and I wanted.

What a vacation and what healing! The sunshine, salt water and the relaxed way that Daddy and Lila lived was just the medicine I needed. The roses returned to my cheeks and the sparkle returned to my eyes. Although that vacation came to a close much too soon, we all had a beautiful, rich tan to take home with us.

Home was a nice little four-room house nestled in the suburbs of Birmingham in a borough called Fultondale. Inside, the house was sparkling clean, with everything in place. The furnishings were some of the finest, and Lila kept everything polished so that you could see your reflection in the surfaces.

The closer the time came for school to start and for me to leave to go back to Mother, the easier it was to decide to stay. The routine of early to bed and early to rise, with meals served at the proper time, was the kind of normalcy I needed. So, for the first time since the third grade, I stayed with Dad and Lila and entered my ninth year of school.

Another reason to stay in Fultondale was to be with a new friend I had made, who was affectionately known to everyone as Snooky. Snook was short, freckled and very outgoing. She and I were the same age, and the two of us would be attending Fultondale Junior High, in the same grade. Snooky not only knew everyone but also seemed to be related to half of Fultondale. Because of her, I was invited to all the summer activities, including hayrides, wiener roasts and skating parties.

Consequently, when school started, I was no longer a stranger, which was always the hardest part of changing schools. The year started off with a bang when Snook and I both made cheerleader. A special thrill was added when the other girls elected me as *head* cheerleader. That school year was filled to the brim with fun and action. I also became a part of a female quartet that performed at school plays and minstrels.

School had proven to be an outlet for my singing aspirations from as far back as the third grade, when our music teacher picked me to sing a special in the Christmas play. Then in the fourth grade I was in a quartet that entertained those left in class each afternoon after the first bus made its exit. In our group, we held hands and swayed from side to side as we sang "Lucky Old Sun," "Moonlight Bay" and "Side by Side."

In Fultondale, our junior year sped by. The crowning glory came when I was voted Most Popular Girl in school. It was a red-letter day for a girl who, not so long ago, had felt rejected and alone. I was surrounded by friends. Daddy owned an insurance agency, with his office in the house, and often joked that if his phone rang as much as mine, we would be quite wealthy.

For some reason, I was content that year without Mother. Of course I missed her, but this time was different because I was finally growing up.

Lila and Daddy both worked and I began to shoulder responsibilities that I had never had before, such as cleaning the house on a daily basis and getting Jane, as well as myself, ready for school each morning. This gave me a feeling of accomplishment and heightened my sense of belonging. I was making a place for myself and standing on my own two feet, and it felt good.

I enjoyed working around the house and even tried my hand at cooking now and then. When Daddy and Lila came home from work in the evenings, I would sometimes have dinner waiting for them, and they loved it. Being able to give as well as receive taught me that I could be content almost anywhere under almost any circumstances. Then, just when it seemed that my problems were solved and that I could lead a fairly happy, normal life, something else happened. . . .

The Bible

It was a lovely day. Daddy and Lila were at work and Jane was playing outside. I was busy with my daily chores: dusting, making beds and washing a few dishes. When I had finished, except for dusting the living room furniture, I decided to clean out the magazine rack, which had become overloaded with old newspapers.

As I pulled the papers and magazines from the rack, a Bible, hidden beneath the accumulation, slipped from my hands and fell to the floor, catching me totally off guard. I just stood there, looking at it as if God had dropped his Holy Word from the portals of heaven at my feet to say, *What are you going to do with this?* It is awesome how the sovereign hand of God works in our lives. It was a routine day, an unsuspecting time, when the awesome hand of Almighty God jolted me out of my complacency with a thud that said, *Remember Me?*

It was the moment of truth, and of course I remembered!

In fact, a subconscious knowledge of His Presence had haunted me from my earliest recollections, along with an acute sense of right and wrong. I don't know just how I came about acquiring this almost sixth sense, but it was so keen that I could never *enjoy* wrongdoing. I'm not trying to say that I was sprouting wings on my back instead of shoulder blades—far from it!—but I am saying that, when I did or said something wrong, the guilt was so intense that I tried to stay as far from it as possible.

My two God-fearing grandmothers had a lot to do with sharpening my spiritual awareness, but this sense of His presence went beyond their guidance. It came as a result of my early suffering. It is something that God had allowed from my beginning: a crushing that made me *know*, without a shadow of a doubt, that nothing in this world is permanent.

It was a harsh lesson and one that must have caused my Heavenly Father much pain as He taught me, but I learned it well. I also realized that, when I felt the bitterness and rejection of my parents' divorce, *He was there.* When I wept silently in the night, a little girl yearning for her mother, He comforted me and wrapped me in gentle arms of love. He saw and understood my childish resolve when I determined in my heart to be pretty and sweet, and to smile so that I would never be rejected again.

And it was *He* who rescued me.

He and He alone.

But He didn't bring me through all of that to stop there. He simply was not going to stand by and allow me fulfillment without Him. So on a regular, mundane day He dropped a reminder in my path and got my attention!

There was no way around it. It was a matter that had to be dealt with right then because, in view of His Holy Word, I stood guilty. And for the first time in my life I knew that I was a sinner.

The thought that impacted me with compelling force was: *There's the Bible and you know so little about it; you don't even know how it begins or how it ends.*

In response, I quickly picked it up and thumbed to the very first chapter and read out loud, "In the beginning God created the heaven and the earth" (Genesis 1:1).

Then I immediately flipped over to the last page, and again read aloud, "The grace of our Lord Jesus Christ be with you all. Amen" (Revelation 22:21).

After that I closed the Bible, laid it aside and went to the only room in the house with a lock on the door—the bathroom. There I got down on my knees and, with tears of repentance, prayed and asked the Lord Jesus to forgive my sins.

Then I started asking the Lord to speak to me. It seems odd now, but I wanted the assurance that He had forgiven my sins. I had a yearning to really know Him: I needed to hear His voice. At this point, I would like to be able to say that a thunderbolt came from the sky and hit me or that I saw a great light or a vision; but unfortunately, none of the above happened. When I finished praying, I dried my eyes, unlocked the door and stepped back into the calm of the day, deciding that maybe I had overdone it a little.

What in the world came over me? I thought, as I straightened my hair and smoothed my clothes.

Then I went back into the living room, and the first thing I saw was that Bible, just as I had left it. Again tears welled up in my eyes and started streaming down my face and neck onto my blouse, and again I turned and ran back into the bathroom, locked the door and prayed all the more earnestly. It was as if I could hear Mama Goodman saying things like, "You'll know when you get saved; no one will have to tell you," or "Don't quit praying until you are completely satisfied." Still, when I stopped praying, I felt no different from before.

It would be a long time before I understood what took place in the spiritual realm that day. How could I know or understand that God, in His own way and in His own time, was knocking at my heart's door, saying, "May I please come in?"

Today I fully understand and know that that is exactly what happened. He was tilling the soil of my heart to impregnate it with the seed of His love, and I responded.

His seed bears His nature and His likeness. But, as in the natural world, when a seed is planted, there is always a time of germination before it manifests itself. A farmer knows that if he plants corn there will be a waiting period before he sees evidence that the seed is there; and he also knows there will be a much longer period before he will partake of it.

God assuredly planted His seed in my heart that day, and when I got up from my knees, there was a new nature lying hidden within me, no different from an expectant mother who had just conceived new life but was not aware of it. It goes without saying that the magnitude of that planting was incomprehensible to my fifteen-year-old mind.

Like most teenagers I was self-centered and, to some extent, enjoying a certain amount of self-pity, too carnal to know much about the spirit world. I was praying for something that had already happened. I was praying for the Lord to speak to me, and I was listening with my ears. That is not God's way most of the time. He speaks to the inner man so there can be no ignoring Him, and He spoke to my heart and conscience loud and clear that day.

The change that evolved as a result was incredible. A craving to be in the house of God and a desire to know more about Him emerged. Since Daddy and Lila did not attend church, I started going with Snooky on Sunday mornings. In fact, I went to many churches of various denominations with my friends while trying to satisfy my insatiable appetite. Most of them were very formal and, at times, I would find myself anxious for services to end because the sermons almost put me to sleep. At one point I remember thinking: *I can tell the story of Goldilocks and the Three Bears with more enthusiasm than this.*

There is a verse that says, "Those that hunger and thirst after righteousness shall be filled" (see Matthew 5:6). That was a description of me. I longed to hear someone *pray* a prayer rather than read from a prayer book. I wanted to hear a choir sing with exuberance and joy rather than sing with stilted reserve. Nevertheless, I kept going to the churches that were available to me and receiving all the good I could from them, but I was making no headway.

One afternoon, Snooky and I were standing outside the school, waiting for our bus. In six weeks the school year would be nothing more than a wealth of memories. We were making plans for our upcoming graduation. Lila and I had picked out my formal for the grand occasion and had it on layaway. We were excitedly trying to describe our gowns to each other when I glanced toward the curve in the road expecting to see the yellow nose of the school bus.

Instead I saw the hood of a very familiar black Chrysler limousine and my heart gave a wild leap! I'd know that car anywhere—it was Mother! The family was on a singing engagement and came by to check on me. Sorry to say, Snooky and all my friends in Fultondale did not see me again that year. As always, when Mother showed up, nothing else mattered. No plans were ever too important to abandon; no friends were ever too dear to leave behind. That's exactly what happened. In no time at all I gathered my things, threw them in the car and was headed for parts unknown.

Chapter 5

A New Happy Goodman

Asheville, North Carolina was brilliantly arrayed and bursting with color when we arrived. The hot pink azaleas and rhododendrons that lined the crisscross streets and boulevards were in full bloom.

In all my travels I was sure that I had never witnessed such beauty. This, along with cool summer nights and lush greenery, made me understand why the rich and famous would choose this part of the Great Smokies for their summer retreats. It is hard to say when the mountains are most compelling. Some say it's autumn when the leaves are changing colors, but it was spring in all its glory when I first saw it.

The Family was already settled in a suburb called Fletcher, renting two houses only a few feet apart. I was to stay in the ranch-style cottage with the biggest part of the family while Mama and Papa Goodman and Stella and Jimmy stayed in the "little house" next door. Sam and Rusty were still serving their final year in the armed services, and Ruth was happily married with a family of her own, in Fulton, Kentucky.

With those exceptions, it was good to find that everyone had made the move to Asheville together, and once again prosperity seemed to be smiling on my maternal family. They had launched into a brand-new media—television. Radio had been a part of our lives for many years, but a daily program on WLOS-TV with a wide viewing audience was more than we could have hoped for. Its popularity brought larger crowds than ever to the concerts. The day after my arrival, I went along with The Family to the television station and made my first appearance. It sure felt good when Howard introduced me as his niece and a *new member* of the Happy Goodman Family!

For the remaining six weeks, I enrolled in Fletcher High, a small country school not far from where we lived. The greatest occasion for celebration occurred that summer when Sam returned from the air force. He made his grand entrance while we were on television and while Howard was announcing the next song. We had no idea he was within a thousand miles until he walked right in front of the camera and shouted, "Hello, everybody!" We had a family reunion right there, hugging, kissing, laughing and crying all at the same time.

Many changes had taken place in the last four years while Sam was away. We had moved to Evansville, Swainsboro and finally here to Asheville. The children had grown immensely. I was eleven when he left and fifteen when he returned. That was hard for him to accept. Also, The Family's stage performance had changed, and a lot of adjustments had to be made to include him again. Those were trying times for Sam. He was a gifted singer, but his greatest talent was his ability to make people laugh. Consequently, he was known to our fans as the "funny man."

I recall one painful incident that occurred during those readjusting days. We were all on stage before a large audience, and Howard was trying to lead Sam into his funny lines, without success. Because Sam's timing was rusty, when he came to the punch line, no one laughed. There are no words to describe how deathly silent an audience is when they are supposed to laugh and they don't. Howard kept giving Sam lead-ins and Sam kept fumbling the ball. Then from somewhere in the balcony came a male voice yelling at him through cupped hands, "Why don't you tell about the Three Little Pigs?" Poor Sam.

Happily, those rough days were short-lived and Sam, being the true professional he was, slipped back into the role of being "funny guy" on stage and stealing the hearts of our audiences with his quick wit and humor.

Elvis

We found that Carolina people not only loved gospel music but country as well. When a big country show came to town, headlining such stars as Martha Carson, Kitty Wells, Hank Snow and others, I decided to accept an invitation to attend with a young man from school that I had been avoiding up until then.

When we arrived at the auditorium, there was a large crowd of people milling around the box office to purchase tickets and standing in line to enter. A feeling of expectancy filled the air. As we slowly inched our way inside, I had time to study the advertising poster. Every name was familiar to me except one. Down at the bottom of the list of entertainers, in small letters, was printed "Elvis Presley." I had no idea who he was, but I thought he was doing well to be in the show with such a great array of stars.

The usher led my escort and me to our seats, which were in the left floor section and close to the outside aisle. This was great. Not only did we have an excellent view of the stage, but we were also in direct line with the backstage door that opened into the main auditorium. Each time this stage door was opened we could see a great deal of activity as the stars rushed back and forth, preparing for the show. Another fascinating aspect of the door was the guard who stood by it, determined that no unauthorized person would get past.

I sat waiting, along with the rest of the crowd, allowing my emotions to be swept up with the excitement of the evening. Then suddenly the backstage door swung open and there in plain view was *Mother*, sitting in a chair, laughing and talking. It just couldn't be! I blinked my eyes, thinking my mirage would disappear, and looked again. She was still there, big as life, conversing with what appeared to be an old acquaintance. I had no idea that she even knew these people!

Excusing myself to my escort, I jumped up, moving transfixed toward the stage door, and found the guard to be just as strong-willed as I had thought. Finally, when he saw my determination, he gave me secret instructions as to how to get backstage. He pointed to the side exit and said, "Take that door, then there will be double doors to the backstage."

I followed his instructions and, to my horror, found myself standing in a dark alley just as I heard the door click behind me . . . I was locked outside! What was I to do? I had no proof that I had already been inside. It was pitch dark with no sign of a door anywhere. With shaky knees, I made my way a few feet toward the back of the building as my eyes slowly adjusted to the darkness. It was a great relief when I spied the double doors with BACKSTAGE written in black letters across them. Trembling, I tried to open them only to find that they were securely bolted from within. There was no visible sign of life anywhere.

As desperation settled on me, I began beating the door with my fists. After what seemed like an eternity, one of the doors slowly opened and I was face-to-face with a tall, handsome, black-haired young man. For a moment we simply stood staring at each other. I had never seen such wild taste in clothes: a chartreuse dress coat with melon-colored pants and a pink shirt with the collar turned up, showing the top two buttons unfastened.

He looked equally astonished to see me coming from the dark alley with no escort. The sleeveless dress, which had seemed just right for the occasion when I left home, was not much protection against the night mountain air. Chilled to the bone, I quickly stepped across the threshold, past my knight in shining armor. I smiled, thanked him and rushed off to find Mother before he had time to say a word.

As I walked away, I could feel his gaze follow me, and I was glad I had worn my favorite dress. It was light blue polished cotton with a close-fitting bodice and a much-in-style, three-tiered skirt with yards and yards of material that flowed about the ankles. To accent the dress I wore rose-colored, high-heeled slippers, a clutch bag and beads that were knotted and hung to my waist. Hurrying away, I fleetingly wondered if this would be my last encounter with "Lochinvar."

Only a few feet away, to my astonishment, I ran into Bobby!

"Well, who else is here?" I demanded, feeling my temperature rising.

"Gussie and Eloise," he said with a shrug.

"Where is Mother?" I said, my fuse getting shorter by the minute.

"She's in that dressing room with Martha Carson," he said, gesturing toward an opened door.

By now I was thoroughly disgusted. Had I known they were coming, I could have been here with them, on the inside of things, but not a word was said about plans to come. Now I had an escort who had paid a good price for my ticket *and* my attention for the evening, and I was going to do the right thing if it killed me!

Sure enough, I found Mother where Bobby had indicated. She introduced me to her longtime friend, Martha Carson, and a few more of the country entertainers. She explained that these were some of the "Opry" folks that they were packaged with last year when they did a tour of Canada. I remembered her writing me about it at the time, but it had completely slipped my mind. Much too soon, it was time to get back to my date. This time I came from the inside backstage door, and it gave me great satisfaction to march past the guard as I reentered the auditorium and took my seat. By then the program was well underway, and the building was pulsating with the rhythmic sounds of country music.

As the show progressed, the announcer eventually introduced "Elvis Presley." When he came self-consciously to center stage, carrying a guitar in one hand and having a hard time finding something to do with the other, my jaw dropped. There were that same chartreuse coat and melon-colored pants! Elvis's three-piece band looked very small following all the big acts with a stage full of musicians. I became tense for him, afraid the audience would get up and walk out before he could get started. Then like a flash, he hit a chord on that old guitar and started singing,

One for the money,
Two for the show!

As he continued with "Don't You Step on My Blue Suede Shoes," a change came over him, and he immediately became at home on the stage. The audience was electrified! When he finished his first song, they stamped their feet, whistled and yelled for more. It was phenomenal! Never had I seen this kind of response for any performer.

Afterward it was hard to calm the fans and make them settle for anything less than Elvis. He was swamped with admirers and autograph-seekers. Stars who had been enjoying fame for years were saying, "Don't you want *my* autograph?"

The next day I learned that Bobby had spent the entire evening with Elvis. He and Eloise sang gospel songs with him most of the night. Elvis even wanted Bobby to go on to New York with him. He was creating such a whirlwind with his new method and sound that he was looking for a friend to go along and help steady him. Bobby said he and Elvis had taken a couple of girls out after the program, but they could never get very far from Elvis's manager, Colonel Tom Parker. He kept Elvis in a separate booth in the restaurant most of the time, talking over business plans.

Parker planned to take Elvis to New York City for a few weeks and expose him to influential show business personalities. As Bobby talked on, I had my doubts that New York was ready for a country boy like Elvis Presley. Being a hit in Asheville was one thing, but entering the fierce competition on the "big time" scene was quite another.

Then, as abruptly as my chance meeting with him, Elvis Presley faded from my consciousness and was replaced with the reality of everyday living.

Weeks later, Bobby and I, along with several of our friends, were in the living room one Sunday evening watching *The Ed Sullivan Show* on television. Sullivan was introducing a new talent who was causing a sensation everywhere he went. "And now, ladies and gentlemen," came the famous drawl, "El-vis Pres-ley!"

Bobby and I sat straight up! We couldn't believe our eyes when Elvis stepped from behind the curtain. Turning, he pointed his finger at the television camera and assumed the Presley stance.

Hysterical screams went up from the crowd. Then he strummed his guitar and began to sing, "You Ain't Nothin' but a Hound Dog." In a few minutes the song was over, but the crowd was as wild as they had been in Asheville.

By now Bobby and I were on our feet, jumping and shouting, "He made it! He made it!" Papa Goodman, sitting in his favorite television chair, was smiling through tears. "That boy made it," he choked. You'd have thought that Elvis was a long lost relative!

Eloise spoke from the doorway. "Bobby, just think! He tried to get you to go to New York with him, and you wouldn't go!"

Bobby turned to me, grinning sheepishly, "Yeah, and he asked me if I knew who Breeska was. He wanted to take her out that night but I told him she already had a date and fixed him up with another girl."

That did it! I exploded. "Oh, Bobby! How could you? You knew I was home long before Elvis was through with that show! And why didn't you tell me before now?" I was still a little touchy about that whole episode.

"I guess I knew you would get mad," he replied.

"Well, I guess you're right! I thought he was really great, and look where he is now!"

After that night, Elvis's career exploded, and the rest is history. When we went out to eat, his records played on the jukebox, and every radio station was spinning the Presley platters. But no matter how successful he became, there was an indelible imprint in my mind of a lanky lad in a chartreuse coat, framed in the backstage door of the Asheville City Auditorium.

The Tent Revival

Howard, Vestal, Mama Goodman and I found an exciting, spiritual church in Asheville that we enjoyed and attended as often as our schedule permitted. That summer the pastor decided to have a tent revival on the outskirts of town and asked if we would help with the singing. We readily accepted. The revival began and the services were great. It was just what I had longed for back in Fultondale: old-fashioned heartfelt preaching and singing.

At this point, I really didn't know where I stood as a Christian. Since that episode with the Bible, I had done a lot of soul-searching, along with silent tears and whispered prayers in the night, and was convinced that I had done all that was in my power to do. The rest was up to the Lord. Yet something was missing. I still felt empty and lacked the strength to overcome my human nature. What I needed was that "joy unspeakable and full of glory" (1 Peter 1:8) that I had read about in the Bible.

The meetings went by swiftly and proved to be successful, with good numbers in attendance each night. All too soon it was Saturday evening. As we entered the tent and took our seats, the sweet smell of sawdust rushed up to meet me. It was hard to believe this would be our last night under the tent. I hated to see the revival come to a close. Each service seemed to be better than the last, but the next day was Sunday and we would be going back to the church to end the series of services officially. My thoughts were interrupted when Pastor Connors and the evangelist came around to shake Howard's hand and thank us again for our help. Then the evangelist turned to me and said, "LaBreeska, I feel impressed to tell you that you are going to receive the baptism of the Holy Spirit tomorrow night." His comment took me by surprise.

As odd as it seems, I hadn't even thought to ask the Lord to fill me with His Spirit. In all honesty it had seemed out of reach for me. That was an experience, in my mind, for people like Mama Rogers, Mama Goodman and Howard and Vestal. I guess without realizing it I had counted myself out.

Sunday came and it was finally time for the evening service. I went to church that night full of hope. According to the man of God, this was my time to receive all that I needed from the Lord. It never occurred to me to doubt Him, yet I had no idea what to expect.

A "glad to be alive" sensation swept over me as I entered the sanctuary, and I soon found out that I was not the only one with those happy feelings. The air was charged with expectancy.

Revival fires were ablaze!

Then before the service started, Pastor Connors stepped behind the pulpit, and in a voice shaken with emotion said, "I want everyone here, under the sound of my voice, whether you call your self saint or sinner, to raise your right hand toward heaven, close your eyes and sing this chorus along with me, 'He's All I Need.' "

Immediately hands were raised all over the building, and in one accord we began to sing:

He's all I need
He's all I need
Jesus is all I need.[6]

With the words of that song, I was confessing with my lips and heart my great need of the Lord and, at that moment, I was overcome with desire for Him. With my right hand held high, I made connection with something I had never before experienced, so I raised both hands. That's when I completely surrendered my will to His. With no forethought, I slipped to my knees beside the pew where I had been sitting, oblivious to my surroundings, and I was swept into another realm. An invisible current flowed through me, surging, cleansing, penetrating.

Vaguely, I remember being led to a side room. Before long, my cup did indeed run over as I began to utter sounds I had never heard before. Strange syllables were flowing from my lips and my soul as I communed personally with my Maker. I had no idea what I was saying (1 Corinthians 14:14), but I was definitely drinking from the well that would cause me never to thirst again (John 4:14)!

The days and weeks that followed were happy ones. My Heavenly Father and I shared a love greater than any I had ever known, one that put a glow on my face and a twinkle in my eyes.

I was surprised to find that being baptized in the Holy Spirit heightened my senses. When I went outside the next day, it was as though I had stepped from a fog. The earth had been bathed by a mid-morning shower and sparkled beneath the June sun. The clean fragrance filled the air and caused my heart to swell with thanksgiving. The sky was bluer, the sun brighter and a prevailing joy flooded my being as I basked in His profound love and total acceptance of my person.

More Dark Days

Even though the Lord was doing wonderful things in my spiritual life, it didn't take long for hard times to catch up with us in Asheville. Like an ugly creature lurking in the dark, failure kept sniffing at our tracks. When it found us this time, there was no fight left in The Family. Everyone was weary with the miserable struggle for survival and lost heart to continue any further.

I was fortunate to have a new friend to share my troubles with and found myself calling on Him often during the next few months.

As our audiences dropped to a mere fifty to twenty-five people, we did well to come away from a singing with gas money. It was a blessing that the kiddie show that came on just before our daily telecast was sponsored by a local bread company. We were free to take the bread used in the advertisements home with us, though we didn't have much to go with it. Across the road from where we lived was a vacant lot. One day Stella spied poke salad, a wild edible plant somewhat like mustard greens, growing in abundance. We felt that the Lord had put it there just for us, so we lived on it for weeks.

During those days, if we drove up to a school where we were to sing and found a large number of cars, there was no need to get excited. It would only be a school basketball game going on in the gym or a meeting of the local PTA. Yet every time that happened I would get my hopes up and think maybe this time they were here to hear us sing. It was very disheartening to walk into an auditorium and find thirty people scattered about. We had no choice but to swallow our pride and sing for those who came.

At one such singing, two of our group members discovered several gallon cans of commodity-issue beef and gravy stacked in the back room of the cafeteria, adjacent to the auditorium where we were performing. I'm not saying who, but one of our gang stood on the shelves and pitched the cans down to another who then took and stashed them in the trunk of our car. So, for a couple of weeks we had beef and gravy to go with our bread and poke salad.

That is, *they* had beef and gravy. As hungry as I was, I could not bring myself to eat the stolen food.

One day Daddy called. "Sugar, what do you want for your sixteenth birthday?"

"Oh, Daddy, I'm so glad you asked! I have been going to church a lot, and I would love to have a Bible. The one I'm using now doesn't look so good. I found it here in the house, and the back is off. A rat or something's chewed the corners and I can't tell what book I'm reading in!"

"You're sure that's what you want?" I could hear the surprise in his voice.

"Oh, yes, Daddy. A pretty white one. Please hurry and send it!"

Sure enough, my first Bible came through the mail from Daddy and Lila, just as I had ordered.

After my sixteenth birthday, I began to think of leaving school. I didn't want to quit, but it was becoming harder and harder to go on. The Family had come to the end of its endurance and was making plans to return to Evansville to "hang it up" in gospel music.

In ten school years I had already gone to eleven different schools and didn't have the heart to change again. So with four months left in my sophomore year, I became a statistic: a high school dropout.

In desperation, we rented a U-Haul trailer, loaded everything we could into it and left the rest. Then we hooked the trailer to our old broken-down Chrysler and, with broken spirits and broken pocketbooks, headed for home. The car almost dragged on the ground. The tires were slick and thin, but with the help of the good Lord and about $30, we arrived at the big house on the corner of Blackford Street. That house was the only thing left that we could call our own, and it had never looked better to us than when we drove up to it that day!

From that day forward the Happy Goodman Family, as they were known back then, ceased to be. They all left gospel music in search of new horizons.

All, that is, but Howard, Vestal and me.

Looking back, it is easy to see that God had brought about the division. It is as if He had drawn a line in the sand and said, "All that's on My side, step across." It was commitment time, and the dawning of a new day.

His blessings on our music and our efforts from that time on would depend on our relationship with Him, our motives, our actions and our lives.

When God decides to move, things begin to shift swiftly, and God was orchestrating our affairs and directing our footsteps. Mother, Stella and Eloise rented space uptown and opened their own business, the Three Sisters' Upholstery Shop. Sam and Bobby went to work in a local TV repair shop, and Rusty joined Martha Carson's band when he came home from the army.

Howard, Vestal and I turned our attention completely to church work. We began to hold revivals in the surrounding areas with Howard preaching and the three of us singing.

Our large number of nine on stage was reduced to a measly three. We did a lot of improvising and rearranging but went right on as though that was how it had always been. It reminded me of what I read in the Old Testament about Gideon's army. God said to Gideon, "The people that are with thee are too many. . . . That of whom I say unto thee, This shall go with thee, the same shall go with thee; and of whomsoever I say unto thee, This shall not go with thee, the same shall not go" (Judges 7:2-4).

Later God added a couple more family members to our number, but for a while it was just the three of us. The rest of the family, no longer sharing a common goal as a cohesive unit, soon scattered and went their separate ways. We were still living under the same roof, with the exception of Howard and his family, but seldom saw each other. Mother worked all day, and when she came in, I would be at church. If I happened to be at home for a night, she was usually there only long enough to get dressed for a date.

Bobby developed friendships with people I didn't know. At times I longed to have things as they were when our mutual friends were always around. I missed those fun times with Bobby when we needed little to entertain us: just a few Cokes and potato chips to munch on while enjoying TV or a gang to go play miniature golf with.

Not being able to see into the future and unaware of God's purpose in all of these changes, I had trouble bringing into focus what was happening. Why was all the change coming about? What was going to happen to everyone?

One night, as Bobby was getting dressed to go out, I naively asked him to take me along. He was reluctant but finally agreed. That night was a real eye-opener. I received a clear picture of Bobby's new interests when he drove me by the place where he and his friends had been going to have their fun. It was a *nightclub*, with a party going on inside a huge fenced-in patio. He and I got out of the car and walked to the fence. The band was playing, drinks were being served and people were laughing and dancing. Someone was standing at a microphone singing and Bobby explained that he sang there also.

As I stood there listening to him, nausea swept over me. I reached for the fence to keep from swaying. I saw several familiar faces, kids I had gone to school with, friends of ours whom I had wondered about. In stunned disbelief, I clung to the fence suffering from the shock of reality. This kind of life was totally foreign and repugnant to me. Every fiber of my being rejected it with an overwhelming repulsion.

Like fitting the remaining few pieces of a jigsaw puzzle, the picture was completed. Bobby and I were no longer bound together by innocent childhood.

The two of us stood in the darkness, beyond the circle of light, with the sound of laughter, music and tinkling glasses driving a wedge between us. We had reached an age where we might each choose our own path, and we were going in opposite directions. Bobby was eighteen; I was sixteen. We had been raised by the same standards, but each of our spirits heard a different call, and our measured steps were set to the beat of different drummers. The pain of that knowledge pierced my heart.

Bobby sensed my sorrow that night and never offered to take me inside. Instead, we walked to the car and drove home in silence.

The days that followed were bleak ones: I felt beaten and alone. Why did I keep losing touch with those that were dearest to me? First Mother, now Bobby. What was wrong with me? Why couldn't I enjoy the things that others did? These questions brought on self-doubt and a depression that weighed heavily on my emotions and my will to live. At times I even found myself praying to die.

The one thing that I was sure of was God's love for me. He'd accepted me totally and unconditionally when I reached out to Him. Now I longed to be in His presence forever and begged Him to take me home with Him. It seemed that I had nothing to hold me in this world any longer.

Those were difficult days, but it is true that the darkest hour does come just before dawn.

Chapter 6

Love Is Strange

Howard, Vestal and I continued to hold revivals. Madisonville, Kentucky, a town about sixty miles from Evansville, provided several open doors for us, one being with a pastor named David Epley. David, a young, energetic preacher, and his wife Sue, a talented organist, had started a new work there and were having church in an old theater building. We preached and sang for them often. After we had worked with them quite a bit, David had a brainstorm: we could form a group and really branch out. Howard, Vestal and I could sing, Sue could help with the music and he would do the preaching.

Howard was all for it, and so were the rest of us.

Our first scheduled meeting was way down in the bayou state of Louisiana, in a small town called Winnsboro. It was March of 1957. I had just turned seventeen and was happy to be involved in church work. The revival was a success and proved to us that we had made a wise choice. We sang every night to a packed house. David delivered dynamic sermons, and eager souls responded to the invitations.

Other pastors from the area began to attend the services to look us over to see if they would like to have us come to their churches. One such pastor was Reverend W.T. Hemphill, who had a large assembly in West Monroe, a paper mill town, about forty miles away along the banks of the Ouachita River. Brother Hemphill was a neatly dressed, elderly man with a firm handshake and a gentle voice. He had with him his lovely wife Beatrice and teenaged son Joel. After the service Brother Hemphill approached us to come to his church for a week when we left Winnsboro.

We readily accepted his invitation and, in a matter of days, were off to West Monroe and settled into a furnished apartment that Brother Hemphill had rented for us. I well remember the first night of that revival. The church seemed vast, yet simple. One thing that I had noted about Louisiana churches that was different from others was their extremely large platforms, and this one was no exception. To the right sat a baby grand piano and a band of musicians. There were electric guitars, a steel guitar, an upright bass, accordions . . . the whole works.

Our group entered through a side door leading onto the platform and took our seats as the band played and the congregation gathered. Excitement was in the air. I was pleasantly surprised to find Joel, the pastor's son, among the musicians. He looked dashing in his light blue suit and was certainly in his element playing the electric guitar. With one foot propped on a small amplifier, he held a shiny black Gretsch guitar that had the tassel from his graduation cap hanging from the neck. At that moment I decided that this might prove to be a very interesting revival. As the week progressed, the crowds grew larger until there was hardly a place to sit.

On Friday I was dressing for church and realized that we were only two nights from the end of the revival. To my dismay, Joel Hemphill had kept his distance. He had not so much as asked me for the time of day. It really had me puzzled. I had caught his gaze several times and knew he was interested, but I couldn't figure out what was holding him back.

After church I was in the main auditorium, shaking hands and making light conversation when Joel's younger sister, Anna Gayle, came up and asked if I would like to go with her and Joel for ice cream. Of course I would. It would be great to be with someone my own age for a change. We went to a busy little drive-in soda and ice cream shop and, in no time at all, were chatting comfortably as though we had known each other for years. They were good company and we became friends quickly.

The next day was our final day in town, and Joel dropped by the apartment to see Brother Epley about a guitar. He asked if I would like to ride out to where they lived. I was delighted. There I became better acquainted with him and the rest of his family. At this time he told me that he was going steady with a minister's daughter in a neighboring town.

That was not good news but it answered my questions. It also didn't stop us from enjoying each other's company. We had an immediate meeting of the minds, laughed and talked and had a great time. I teased him and said if we ever did come back he'd probably be married, but I secretly hoped I was wrong.

That night when church was over, I was standing in the aisles exchanging greetings with others when I looked up and saw Joel coming toward me. In a second he was at my side and asked if he could take me home. My heart skipped a beat as I said "yes" and then hurried to tell Vestal. Soon we were on our way, this time just the two of us.

The car radio played softly as we drove through the summer night. For some reason neither of us said very much. What was there to say? I was about to leave and we had barely had a chance to get acquainted. We pulled up to the same little drive-in and ordered something to drink, both preoccupied with that thought and trying to hang on to the moment at hand.

In a short while we hurried on to the apartment, expecting everyone to be waiting for me. It had been decided that we would travel all night, and I knew they would be in a hurry to leave. But no one was there yet, so Joel and I sat in the car and listened to the radio while we waited. The sky was brilliantly alive with millions of stars. A gem-like radiance dusted the heavens and spilled down through the car window onto Joel and me. Mickey and Sylvia were softly crooning "Love Is Strange" and our lips met for the first time.

Then like ships passing in the night, we said our good-byes with nothing to bind us together but the memory of a lovely evening and an unforgettable kiss.

Something painfully sweet had happened: painful because the circumstances which had brought us together were about to put between us both time and distance; sweet because there was a mutually magnetic attraction that, under normal circumstances, would have declared this the beginning, certainly not the end.

Soon after Joel's departure, the rest of our group arrived, and in less than an hour, we were on the highway. As I settled back for the long ride, I tried to clear my mind.

I had been dating for a couple of years now and had turned down two marriage proposals and headed off more. I reasoned that my feelings that night were not simply the excitement of a first date. Nevertheless, I knew that I could not spend my time thinking about someone I might never see again, no matter how right he seemed to be. And if by chance we did meet again, what about that other girl?

Right then and there I used my lifelong survival tactics and firmly put Joel Hemphill out of my mind and emotions. The day had been long and exhausting. I wearily laid my head back on the seat as we breezed down the highway in the darkness. The tires made a steady, clicking sound as they crossed the tiny trenches in the pavement and lulled me into peaceful oblivion.

Evansville greeted us on our return with many changes. Sam had married. Rusty had quit Martha Carson's show and was home, and Mother was engaged. All this had taken place in the six short weeks we were away.

After only a short stay in Evansville, which I used to make a few new dresses and do some shopping, it was time to leave again, with Rusty as an addition to our team.

Those early weeks of spring were taken up with a few other engagements while preparing for our meetings in the upcoming summer months. These included Brother Epley's purchase of a large gospel tent and an old truck with which to haul it and Sue's Hammond organ. I was glad to learn that our first tent meeting was to be held back in Winnsboro, Louisiana.

This time when we set off for Louisiana, we were in three vehicles. In the lead was a new Buick that carried David, Sue and their small baby. Next came a well-worn pink and gray Packard with Howard,

Vestal and their two children, Ricky and Vicki; and laboring behind, in the old beat-up truck, were Rusty and me.

It was great to have Rusty with us. On his return from the army, even though he had changed some, I found him to be the same gentle spirit I had always loved. While he had been in the service, I was the only member of the family who had written him regularly. I tried to keep him abreast of the happenings at home, and he would answer and send me photographs of himself from faraway places. Once while in Korea he sent me a pair of Korean shoes, and I even wore them.

Our journey began on a lovely May day, warm and sunny, and the further south we went, the greener the scenery became. Rusty and I laughed, talked and sang throughout the day. But when the sun went down so did our spirits. In the bright sunshine even the shabby old truck seemed grand, but we soon realized that without the sun we had no source of heat.

Not only was the truck without a heater, but there were also numerous holes in the floorboards, letting in the chilling night air. Poor Rusty! This was his first trip with us, and it was getting off to a bad start. That rickety old truck reminded him of all the poverty we had suffered as kids, and he hated those memories.

At long last, to my delight the cars ahead of us stopped for gasoline. Aching all over from the cold, I fully intended to get into the warm car with Howard and Vestal, but when it came time to pull out again, I just couldn't leave Rusty alone in that miserable old truck. Howard had a couple of white shirts hanging in the car, and I put one on and gave the other to Rusty. The shirts gave very little protection from the cold night air; nevertheless, we endured and finally reached our destination: Winnsboro.

David rented rooms in a not-so-modern boarding house for the remainder of the night. The next morning found the men at the fairgrounds erecting the tent, then hunting for an inexpensive apartment to house us for the duration of our stay. In a couple of days we were settled, with the revival underway and everything looking up.

Louisiana was beautiful at that time of the year. Spring flowers were in full bloom and the moss-hung trees were sporting new dresses of green. My spirits were high because I knew we were not very far from West Monroe and the Hemphills.

Several days passed with no sign of them. Then one night just before the start of service, Brother and Sister Hemphill walked in. It was so good to see them again. I rushed over to speak to them, expecting to see Joel any second. When they said that he had to work late and sent word that he would come when he could, I decided that he was using that as an easy way of saying we had better not see each other again. Whatever the case, I could live with it. Joel Hemphill was definitely not the only fish in the pond! Having arrived at my own conclusions as to why he had not shown up, I was surprised a couple of nights later when, during the service, Joel walked in. When church was over, I greeted him somewhat cautiously and introduced him to Rusty. Then the three of us went to get something to eat. Rusty and Joel hit it off great. They laughed and talked as if they were old friends. Later we dropped Rusty off at his room in town, and Joel took me back to the apartment.

When we were alone I had no idea what he might say. I thought that perhaps the other girl was still in the picture and, being the gentleman that he was, he had come to tell me in person. Then it happened again—he kissed me good night.

This time there was no doubt about it. Joel Hemphill *was* different from other boys. All the doubts that had filled my mind, and possibly his, quickly dissolved. Joel said he would be back as soon as he could and I knew he would. Then he turned and began to walk toward the car. *He was leaving!*

Without thinking, I blurted out his name into the darkness, "Joel."

He stopped, turned and started toward me. "What is it?" he asked. Then I realized I had nothing to say. My heart shouted, *Please don't leave! Now that I've found you I can't stand to let you go!* But wisdom prevailed. I could never make bare my soul without first receiving a commitment from him, and it was all too soon.

I answered back, "Oh, it's really nothing. Good night." And he was gone.

Full and exciting days followed. Joel came as often as he could and even spent a few nights with Rusty. The more I learned about him, the more I liked him. Joel was not a showoff. He was not a smooth talker. He was simply himself without apology and without phony trappings. Though Joel was ruggedly handsome, he was not the tall, dark type of which girls sometimes dream. He stood only a few inches taller than I and was a mixture of Choctaw Indian from his mother's side and Irish and German from his father's. His ancestry may have had some bearing on his character traits, but most of the credit was due to how he was brought up. He had a firm but gentle father and a loving and wise mother. These two created an environment that molded their children into wholesome, dependable, God-fearing adults. Joel had character and high morals, and besides all that, he was fun to be with!

Our courtship was unusual. The nights were taken up with church, so we did our dating during the day, indulging in my favorite sport, fishing. All that I had learned from Bobby on a creek bank in Kentucky surely came in handy. Rusty, Joel and I spent many happy hours in a boat at a nearby lake, catching white perch and establishing a solid friendship.

After six weeks in Winnsboro, it was time to take down the tent and move to another location. That was long enough to stay in any one place. The revival had been wonderful, but David and Howard knew it would not be wise to stay longer.

Joel and I had been seeing each other day and night for five weeks now. I was seventeen and he would be eighteen in less than two months. It was simply too early for us to become serious. Joel didn't even have a regular job. He helped his older brother Daniel, a painting contractor, when he was needed and had other part-time jobs, which were sufficient for a single boy living at home. As the time drew near for us to pull up tent stakes and leave, it became harder for Joel and me to part, even for a day.

Then Brother Hemphill called David and asked if we would come to West Monroe and set up our tent for a couple of weeks. After much deliberation as to whether this was the hand of God or the hand of Joel, David and Howard consented to go. What a relief. There would be no sad good-byes just yet.

The next morning, bright and early, the men began taking down the tent in preparation for the move to West Monroe. When Joel came in his dad's pickup truck to help them, I was at the apartment with Vestal and the children, packing. Howard told me I could stay and ride over with Joel. Then they left. Soon the two of us were merrily bounding down the highway with the wind in our hair and Fats Domino belting out "It's You I Love" on the radio. Time was on our side again. We both felt light and happy as we drank in the warm June air that whipped through the open windows of the truck.

When we drove into the churchyard, the men were waiting to help set up the tent in a vacant lot nearby. It was decided that Rusty and I would stay with the Hemphills. Joel's sisters, Rita and Gayle, had a big room and seemed happy to have me share it with them. Howard and Vestal and their children moved into a little house Brother Hemphill had built in his yard specifically for evangelists. And David and Sue stayed in an apartment uptown.

The revival started on Sunday night. Again there was a great deal of music and singing and old-fashioned preaching. The crowds responded enthusiastically.

Staying in the Hemphill home was a delightful experience. I found them to be quite different from anyone I had ever been around. They lived a simplistic lifestyle, yet there was an abundance of everything, especially food. There were two big refrigerators in the kitchen crammed full of food. On the old-fashioned, screened-in back porch was a cooler, filled to the brim with cold drinks and fresh milk, gallons of it, so cold it would hurt your teeth when you drank it.

One morning I walked into the living room where Joel sat reading the paper with his younger brother David and his three sisters: Gayle, Rita and even little Brenda. The whole Hemphill clan loved the newspaper. I had never seen anything like it. Everyone was absorbed with the morning news when suddenly "Love Is Strange" started playing softly on the radio. I saw it hit Joel and he looked up from the paper to find me standing there. It was a sweet moment. Here we were in a crowded room, yet a song, *our song,* gently transferred us to another place in time.

Those happy days flew by, and once more we found ourselves nearing the end of the revival. The next meeting was to be somewhere in West Virginia. This time I knew the chances of my coming back soon, or at all, were slim. By that point both Joel and I had lost our appetite, and it was very apparent that we were in love. Again we were racing against time. The alternatives were to marry much too soon, or wait, with the possibility of losing each other.

The Wedding

I know now that Joel thought it over very carefully before that Tuesday night the twenty-fifth of June. He drove me home after church. Those were the days before air-conditioning was prevalent. We were sitting in the car with the windows down. It was sultry and hot, as only Louisiana can be, and the mosquitos were relentless.

None of the above provided a romantic setting when Joel hurriedly popped the question. "Will you marry me?"

"Yes. When?" I responded without hesitation.

"Friday," he came back.

"You know, that paper mill sure smells good," I said with a grin. Up until then I'd held my nose and gagged as we passed it and wondered how anyone could ever get accustomed to the horrible odor. Now I was more than willing to try.

"Will you make banana pudding for me?" he asked, indicating his favorite dessert.

"Sure, will you take me fishing?" was my comeback.

Here we were in the innocence of our youth making plans and trying to imagine a whole lifetime together. What an awesome quest for anyone, especially us! We hardly knew each other and came from entirely different backgrounds. His was stable, rooted and grounded; mine, insecure and very mobile.

When we told our families, no one was surprised at our decision, and even though they were concerned, they supported us wholeheartedly.

Mine and Joel's decision to take that leap was not the only change coming about. Joel proposed on Tuesday. Then on Thursday morning, one day before our wedding day, hurricane Audrey blew in and demolished the tent, the organ and our sound equipment. In one sweep all was lost. Howard, Vestal, Rusty and the Epleys were heartbroken and full of questions. What was the purpose of this? How could any good come from such a horrible loss?

After much soul-searching, prayers and tears, there was nothing left to do but just trust the Lord. His ways are far above ours, and He certainly doesn't make mistakes.

The following day, on Friday the twenty-eighth of June, 1957, Joel and I exchanged vows and pledged our troth. We were both too young to marry in Louisiana, so we drove to Greenville, Mississippi, and there in front of the courthouse beneath the big oak trees, Joel's dad pronounced us husband and wife.

Howard signed for me. Rusty stood as Joel's best man and Anna Gayle was my bridesmaid.

After the no-frills ceremony, Joel and I left to spend a honeymoon weekend in historic Vicksburg, arriving back home in time for church on Sunday night. This would be the last time that I would sing with my family's team.

During the preliminaries, I noticed Vestal thumbing through an old songbook until it looked as if she had settled on a certain song. Then Brother Hemphill turned the service over to us. When we were about to go to the podium to start singing, Vestal stepped up to the microphone. She looked over at Howard, who was already seated at the piano, and said, "This is something I have never done before, but I have a song that I want to sing because it says exactly how I feel. Now, this is completely unrehearsed. I don't even know what key to sing it in, so, Howard, your guess is as good as mine."

Howard found a key and ran his fingers down the keyboard, not knowing what to expect next. Then, cautiously at first, Vestal started singing the song, "I Need No Mansions Here Below."

Somewhere between the lines of that song a holy boldness overtook her and the anointing of heaven fell on her voice, making it stronger and stronger. Clear and deliberate, it split the air and pierced the hearts of all the congregation. There was hardly a dry eye left in the building when she finished, and the entire congregation stood with hands raised heavenward, praising God.

It was phenomenal. We had just witnessed a miracle. It is a beautiful thing to watch the sovereign hand of the Lord orchestrate our lives. To learn that He does have a purpose and plan for each of us. Yet the only way He can execute *His* plan at times, is to bring *ours* to naught.

When Tuesday morning arrived, the rest of the family was packed and ready to go. It was time for me to say good-bye, not only to my family, but to a way of life.

In my mind's eye I can still see that cumbersome old pink and gray Packard as it bounded out of the yard. Ricky and Vicki were hanging out the back window waving and shouting; Howard was behind the wheel blowing the horn; and Vestal's handkerchief fluttered from her window. Then they were gone.

I would miss them—that went without saying—but as I stood there watching them fade out of sight, there was not one doubt in my mind that I had done the right thing. I was where I belonged; from now on wherever Joel was would be home for me.

The ideal is for couples to get to know one another before they marry, but that was impossible for Joel and me, since we had only dated six weeks. Thus, the ensuring weeks and months became a time of learning about one another and adjusting to the idea of being *one* instead of two.

Mother hadn't met Joel yet. She had wanted to attend our wedding but was unable to. Louisiana seemed like the other side of the world from Evansville, and funds were still a major problem.

Daddy was not quite so far away, but I hadn't let him know that I was getting married because, knowing how fathers can be, I was afraid he would try and use his authority to stop us. I knew he would like Joel once he got to know him, but sometimes it is easier to get forgiveness than permission. Also, I had been looking out for myself for some time, and no one knew what I wanted out of life but me. If I made a wrong choice, no one but I would suffer for it.

I had determined that when I did get married, it would be to a Christian. He would have to love the same things I did: the Lord, church, music and children. Joel met all those qualifications and more. It was three months before we could go to see Daddy and six months before we could visit Mother. Their approval of Joel meant a lot to me and, of course, both of them loved him on sight. They saw immediately how happy I was, and what more can parents ask for their children?

Chapter 7

*To Build
a Life*

For the first few months of our marriage Joel still did not have a regular job, so we moved into the evangelist's quarters in Brother Hemphill's yard. We called it the *little* house. This made things easy for us. A place to ourselves, yet no bills. It was a delightful period in our lives as we continued to learn more about each other. His part-time jobs provided enough money for us to go fishing, swimming and out to dinner. Joel had a large family and their acceptance of me was wholehearted. They were genuinely glad to have me. Life was beautiful.

The hot summer months passed and were replaced by crisp autumn days. The smell of burning leaves and snuggling up in a wool sweater were invigorating; and the thought of impending holidays made my heart sing. I had never experienced being in love in autumn until now. It was wonderful!

That fall Joel and I attended our first circus together. Since it was outside, we bundled up and sat high in the bleachers to watch the aerial artists perform their amazing feats. It was fun just walking around, looking at all the colorful displays while stuffing ourselves with popcorn and cotton candy. Then Joel surprised me when he walked over to one of the stands and bought me a big pink and white teddy bear. Since he wouldn't gamble for it, he asked the man to quote him a price. This was a first for me! *Just what kind of guy am I married to?* I wondered.

During our period of adjustment there were tears as well as laughter, like the day that Joel came home for lunch and refused to eat the bean salad I had proudly made for him. I was furious when he wouldn't even taste it, and informed him bluntly that I never wanted to cook for him again! He remained firm. At that time I found out how much he hates bean salad, which happens to be a favorite of mine. To this day he won't touch the stuff and even dislikes the look of it! That bean salad was definitely a milestone in our adjustment.

Then there was the time I left him. We were only about six weeks into our marriage when we had a dispute about something. I didn't like the tone of his voice, so I grabbed my coat and marched out into the rainy night. Joel thought I had gone over to the "big house" and was surprised when he went over and learned that they hadn't seen me. He jumped into the car and found me walking down the street, soaked to the bone. My head was uncovered and my hair was dripping wet. Tears mixed with rain ran down my face as I walked along, hoping he would come and find me. I was so glad to see the glare of the headlights coming from behind, and much relieved when Joel opened the door and ordered me into the car. Soon we were back at the house warm and dry with the feud forgotten.

Those lovers' quarrels, which later seemed frivolous and even silly, were very important at the time. By them we were setting boundaries, making statements and digging the foundation on which to build a life together. At no other time are we so completely vulnerable and our emotions as exposed and testy as when we are hopelessly in love. It's as if you want to keep reminding your partner, "Hey, that's my *heart* you're dealing with! Be careful, it's breakable!!" Then of course there are those sweet moments of making up. A continual cycle of stormy weather, rain and sunshine makes love grow.

In less than a year Joel announced his call into the ministry. This came as a pleasant surprise to me. During our dating not a hint was made that he had been struggling with a call on his life. And I was perfectly content with the idea of leading a normal, settled, churchgoing existence, but it was not to be.

In fourteen months Joel and I were blessed with a six-pound, three-ounce baby boy. We named him Joel Wesley, Jr., but by the time he arrived home from the hospital he was known as Joey. Fifteen months later Joey had a baby brother, William Trent. We named him so that his initials would be the same as his Grandfather Hemphill's. There have been W.T. Hemphills in the family for generations.

Joel had a regular job by then in an automobile parts store in Monroe. His salary was moderate. We rented a small two-bedroom house three blocks from his mom and dad's. By the time Joey came along, we were already branching out and getting our feet wet by going around to small churches in the area singing and preaching. Every Saturday night found us in some church not too far from home. Then on Sunday mornings, we arose early to help Brother Hemphill with his radio broadcast. We would wrap the boys in big blankets on cold mornings and drop them off with their grandmother while we went to sing on the radio. Then we would grab a bite to eat from Mom's table as we ran out the door to rush home and dress for Sunday school.

On one such hectic Sunday, we had the car radio tuned to a gospel station on the way to church and The Statesman's Quartet came on singing "Everyday'll Be Sunday By and By." Joel looked at me, grinned and said, "I sure hope not."

Our work on the radio began a month after our marriage and continued until we left West Monroe to go into full-time evangelistic work. We didn't let the services we conducted out of town interfere with our attendance to our home church. We only missed services for some serious reason such as the time that Joel was ill with Asian flu and the times when I went to the hospital to have our babies.

We loved our home church and were very active in it. Joel bought me an old upright piano and I learned a few homemade chords, enough to play a little when the church pianist was away. Joel taught the young adult Sunday school class, and we helped with the Christmas programs and all the special events.

When Trent was only five months old, we began to feel that we were ready for full-time evangelistic work, having already preached several revivals round about. Secretly we set the date for leaving West Monroe: the first of June. We'd worked hard to pay off the few bills we had and bought and paid for a fairly new Pontiac.

No one knew that we had set a date to leave except Joel and me. Then one afternoon, three weeks from our chosen day, we received a call from Pastor Edward Kelley, Joel's brother-in-law, whose church was in Birmingham, Alabama. He phoned to see if we'd consider coming for a revival beginning the first of June. That was our confirmation! The next three weeks were spent sorting our belongings, selling our secondhand furniture and storing a few things we wanted to keep. Then the last several days were spent in fasting and prayer.

When we left for Birmingham, Joey was not quite two and Trent was six months old. Since Birmingham was close to Fultondale, several of my relatives attended the revival meeting, including Mama and Papa Rogers. We also spent time with Daddy, Lila and Jane and the new addition to the family, Buddy. He was born to Dad and Lila just six weeks before Joey came into the world. While visiting in Fultondale, I phoned my friend Snooky and she came too. It was a good revival, and many souls were saved, including several young couples.

More revivals followed that first one. We held meetings in Alabama, Florida, Texas and Arkansas. We were having a great time, doing exactly what we wanted to do when we were brought up short. Another little one was on the way. As the time grew nearer, we returned to West Monroe to wait for the blessed event.

We parked our two-bedroom house trailer on a vacant lot beside Brother Hemphill's house. While we waited, we held a few nights' services at neighboring churches. We held the last few nights of special services before the baby's arrival in the small town of Bastrop, about thirty miles from Monroe. It was a good meeting, and at its close, we settled down to wait. Joel had heard that the fish were biting at a nearby lake, and though I was big and bulky, I insisted that he take me fishing.

Pastoring a Church

We were in the middle of the lake that sunny morning in a boat when we saw a car pull to a stop on the bank. Two men got out and began waving to us. I couldn't tell who they were, but Joel said one was his dad. As we drew closer, we saw that the other man was the pastor from the church in Bastrop, for whom we had held our last services. He had driven down to have a talk with us. He was retiring from the church, and his congregation had asked to have us as a replacement. Joel and I discussed the matter at length and decided that pastoring a church would be the best thing for us since our growing family. A few nights later we drove to Bastrop and accepted the pastorate officially. The vote had been almost unanimous.

We sold our house trailer with a nice profit, bought furniture and then happily moved into the small parsonage, only a few steps from the church. Our move was completed on Friday. At 8 o'clock on Saturday morning, June 10, 1961, we rushed to the hospital in Monroe for the birth of our beautiful baby girl.

Carmel Lynn was the name we chose for her, but her dad started calling her "Candy" before we ever left the hospital. She had a big dimple in her right cheek and a head full of dark hair that the nurse had brushed into a Kewpie doll curl on top of her head.

I was blessed and I knew it.

Things had moved swiftly for us. We were both twenty-one, the parents of three children and were pastoring a church. That was a lot of responsibility for anyone, but we accepted it unflinchingly.

Having three small babies can create an infinite number of problems. There was a space of time in my life when I wondered what it would feel like to sit down to an uninterrupted meal. I was constantly in demand, during mealtime, bath time, bedtime or any other time. It seemed that those times when I was the most tired and desperate to crawl into bed, one of the children would cry all night with a tummy ache or an earache. Joel was awakened many times to find one of the babies crying and me crying right along. He said there were occasions when he couldn't tell who was crying the loudest.

The two of us managed to survive our hectic schedule of howling babies, runny noses and dirty diapers while other young people our age enjoyed college life or whiled away their time partying and dating.

Joel was a great dad. Since he didn't have to punch a time clock as most men do, when something serious was wrong with one of the children, he would help by taking turns with the night vigils. It was Joel who played doctor when it came to extracting splinters or bandaging up stubbed toes. The two boys followed their dad from the time they could toddle. Often he took them along on his rounds to town, which included a daily visit to the post office.

Punishment of children is never a pleasant chore, but I loved Joel for the way he handled it. I think the children dreaded the big "to do" of finding out who was to blame more than the actual punishment. Joel held court and each child had his turn to testify and tell his side of the case.

It pained my heart to watch the tiny fellows standing there before their father, tears mixing with the dirt on their fat little cheeks, gulping as they told their story. Amazingly, at the conclusion, it always seemed that neither admitted to any fault. In order to catch the culprit, the judge many times had to sentence each to two or three wallops across his backside.

These unpleasant sessions were designed to bring dread and hopefully to cause our children to stop and think of the consequences before they acted. Our children were never allowed to make such statements to one another as "I hate you" or to call names, even though they seemed harmless. And passing licks was strictly taboo. It was well understood that if any licks were to be passed, Dad or I would pass them and would make them count. But actually, their restrictions were few. They could wrestle and tussle all they pleased, and so they did.

Our boys were all-boy, and Candy, being the only girl, had to be tough to keep up with them. Watching her interact with her brothers reminded me of myself following after Bobby and Jimmy, climbing trees and turning cartwheels. At last I knew how poor Mama Goodman must have felt as she watched in vain for some small sign of ladylikeness in me.

All the commotion of raising a family was exhausting but rewarding. Only a mother can understand the feeling of accomplishment at the end of the day when the little ones are fed, scrubbed and pajama-clad. One by one you kiss them good night. With the fresh smell of soap still clinging to them, they slip their little arms around your neck and whisper, "I love you, Mommy." To lie down to sleep and know that they are in the next room, safe and sound, is one of life's most wonderful feelings. All my life I had wanted only to belong and now I had four people who really needed and depended on me. Joel would tell me in those days that I was not merely a housewife but a homemaker. That was a real compliment.

Since we were only thirty miles from Mom and Dad Hemphill, we saw them often, and at times they would come and take the three children home with them for two or three days. This respite gave Joel and me time to regain our sanity and enjoy lovely outings, and on occasion we would even travel to Vicksburg to stay overnight in "our room" at the Magnolia Courts where we had spent our honeymoon.

Oftentimes I would slip off to town for a couple of hours to shop while Joel puttered around the house and baby-sat. It was a tonic to be alone. Afterward, I was ready to tackle again the never-ending job of being mother and housewife.

And so my husband and I, youth still fresh on our faces, worked together, played together and watched our children grow as the years passed.

When we accepted the pastorate of the little country church in Bastrop, it had only about sixty members. Immediately we started to work, having Sunday school contests and drives for the youth services on Wednesday nights to introduce others to our church. At the end of a contest, the losing side served the winning side an ice cream supper or a barbecue. The numbers on the attendance board began to climb rapidly.

Joel burned the midnight oil, studying and searching for answers to problems and challenging our members to a higher standard of Christian living. Watching my husband work with that church reminded me of the man who took a stony field, removed all the rocks, broke the ground and planted seed. That is exactly what Joel did, spiritually. He dug, planted, pruned and watered, and God gave the increase. Before long we were enjoying the fruits of our labor with a flourishing church.

The people of Bastrop were not wealthy. The main employment there came from the two paper mills, and most of our male members worked there. But these fine people were liberal with what they did have. Most of them raised their own gardens, and in the summer months we had an abundance of fresh vegetables. During our first summer there, we purchased a deep-freeze. I learned how to put food up for the winter months. Many times when one of our members slaughtered a cow, we were given a portion of the beef. During the ten years we were there, we were constantly invited to their homes for lunch or dinner. We gave our people spiritual food, and in return, they gave us natural things.

I often recall with a smile or a tear those early days at Bastrop. Pastoring was a new experience for both of us. It was certainly different from evangelizing. Our job still included winning the lost and encouraging the discouraged, but now so many more duties had been added to our roster. Working with people and helping them to iron out the problems of everyday living brought us face-to-face with situations we had not even known existed—things in people's personal lives that stagger the mind. Yet God gave us wisdom as it was needed to help heal marriages and patch up homes that previously had been held together by only a thread. We rejoiced with our members over their triumphs and suffered with them in their tragedies.

Evangelizing had been glamorous and even shallow compared to this: it was more like boot camp training. In pastoring we were engaged in hand-to-hand combat as we helped our people through the unending skirmishes and conflicts of life. The comparatively few hours we had with them each week in the regular church services were filled with leading them into a higher realm. We learned together as Joel taught them the Holy Scriptures, and they in turn taught us about human nature.

It would take volumes to relate the many things we all learned in the ten years we spent together. We wanted them to understand that ours is a continual struggle against the flesh. Like salmon going upstream, it isn't easy. Sometimes we gain ground; sometimes we lose. Sometimes we get a little bruised, but the idea is to keep trying. Don't give up. Don't quit! We pointed out to them the importance of forgiveness: how bitterness and unforgiveness are like acid—each destroys the very container that it's held in. We encouraged them to rule their tongues. Harsh words cut and wound and are like feathers in the wind; once they are spilled they can never be retrieved.

Not only did we address these issues and many, many more, but we taught them the cure. God, the Great Physician, has the formula in His holy Word for whatever ails mankind. All we have to do is come into agreement with Him and follow His instructions. We change our *minds*, He changes our *hearts*.

From those pastorate days Joel and I possess a ten-year degree in sociology and psychology that cannot be bought and is not taught at any seminary or university in the land. In our dealings with people, we found that the most outstanding need in young and old alike was an insatiable desire to be loved and accepted. Yet strangely enough, people seldom learn how to get what they need and desire the most. We want love but we don't want to bother with being *loveable*. Unfortunately it doesn't work that way this side of heaven. The only place to find that kind of love is to come to Jesus. If we are to find love and acceptance with our fellowmen, we must *be loveable*.

When the Lord said, "Give, and it shall be given unto you" (Luke 6:38), He was not referring to a commodity such as money. The very life of Christ and His example of giving Himself, right down to the final sacrifice on the cross, is a rich and beautiful lesson. The happiest and most fulfilled people in the world are those that have learned this lesson and have given of themselves. They strew love and kindness like "bread upon the waters" (Ecclesiastes 11:1), and it comes back to them . . . buttered!

And so my husband and I continued our ceaseless work. We saw results, but it seemed that as each new challenge was met and conquered, another arose to take its place. Our work lay before us, unending . . .

Chapter 8

The Way Is Made

One summer evening Joel and I were lying across our bed, relaxing in the quiet house while the children played outside. My thoughts were contented ones. I was thinking of the lovely home Joel was building for me just a couple of blocks away. We had admired that acre of ground studded with giant oak trees since we had first come to Bastrop more than three years ago.

I had never dreamed we could afford it, but Joel had a talent for stretching a dollar, and somehow he managed to save money when it didn't seem possible. Slowly but surely our dream began to material-ize.

Now, in a matter of weeks, we would be moving into our first real home. We had been so patient, paying as we went and taking our time, but sparing nothing to make it beautiful and lasting. The four bedrooms and the two tile baths would seem like a mansion com-pared to the cramped little four-room house we now lived in. But I certainly was not complaining. The parsonage had served us well. Be-cause of its location I could go home right after church and tuck in my little brood. Joel was always the last to leave, making sure everything was locked up and turned off.

Joel startled me when he spoke, and more so when I realized what he was saying, "You know, honey, we could wake up old in this little town someday and realize how very little we have accom-plished."

What was he talking about? That was exactly what I had in mind: moving into my lovely new home with my beautiful little family and watching as the days turned into months and years. This was the clos-est to heaven I had ever been. I had everything I ever wanted. His statement clouded my happy thoughts. I sat up to search his face for a sign that he was only joking. When I saw his grim countenance, my heart skipped a beat. He was serious!

At that moment I saw Joel in a different light. I studied his features and realized that, when we married, he had only been a boy, but one with a bright future. All through school he had been among the head of his class, with a keen interest in government and history. From as far back as grade school, he had involved himself in politics. At local, state and federal elections he had studied the platforms and had chosen his man. During campaigns he was in and out of his candidate's headquarters, helping in any way he could. He put up posters, handed out cards and on occasion would make a sandwich sign to hang over himself and walk into a public gathering, proudly announcing his man.

By this demonstration of interest and enthusiasm, he came to know many high officials of the state of Louisiana. When he graduated from high school, one of the most powerful United States representatives, Otto Passman, a family friend, tried to persuade him to look toward a future in politics and offered to secure him a scholarship to West Point or Harvard.

All these thoughts raced through my mind as I sat there looking at that face that had turned from boy to man overnight. For the first time, I felt like I had held him back. He was saddled with the responsibility of a wife, and if that were not enough, three small children.

A silent cry came from my heart, *Oh, my darling, what have I done to you?* "If it's continuing your education that's bothering you, you can enroll at the university," I said, when I finally found my voice. "It's only twenty miles away and you could drive back and forth easily. Study law. You've always loved it. I'll study music and become a teacher." What could I say that would erase that troubled look on his face and restore the contentment that I was accustomed to?

We sat there looking at each other. Then slowly he answered while deep in thought, "I don't know if that's the answer. But I do know something is missing, and I don't want our youth to slip away and leave us with regrets. If we are ever going to make a mark in this world for God and ourselves, we are going to have to do it now."

What did this mean? I felt so utterly helpless, like a baby bird watching its mother pluck the soft, downy lining from its warm nest, revealing the ugly, bare sticks and thorns that held it together. I knew this day and this conversation would be a turning point, but I didn't realize that *God* was "stirring up our nest."

Right then we decided to start praying and fasting for direction for our future. From that day forward I knew that our lives were headed for dramatic change. We both agreed that the most important thing was to be in the center of God's will, whatever it was. A departure from His favor would leave the both of us unfulfilled.

All that we had ever done and were doing now was accomplished with vigor and sincerity, but most of the time we had stretched ourselves pretty thin. We still loved evangelizing and had never completely given it up. At intervals we would have minister friends come and take charge of our services for a couple of weeks while we went cross country to preach and sing. We held several revivals a year in this fashion. Pastors had never stopped calling us to come. Our singing was a plus and Joel's thirst for knowledge kept him digging in the Word and finding inspiring messages of faith and deliverance. Every summer we received calls to be the special guests at camp meetings, youth camps and conferences. Carefully we picked a few and spaced them so we did not neglect our church by our absence.

But where were we headed now?

Neither of us had a clue.

What we really desired was a miracle ministry, with the gifts of the Spirit in operation. We wanted gifts of healing, the word of knowledge, the gift of discernment, etc. We had concluded long before that it would take nothing less than the uncontested power of God to move people to repentance in our day, and we wanted results.

We also knew that God had the answer. All we had to do was fast and pray until it was revealed. Days passed without either of us put-

ting a morsel of food to our mouths. As we fasted, we spent hours at
the church in prayer, most of the time lying facedown on the floor.
Someone came to help us with the children and the household chores
while we gave ourselves fully to seeking the will of God. Up until then
I had been perfectly content for Joel to be the one with a divine call
on his life. I enjoyed the role of housewife, mom and pastor's wife.
But as I continued to pray, I was reminded of my own personal en-
counters with Him and began to desire something more for myself. It
went beyond a *team* thing and became an individual pursuit.

Lord, what would You have me do? What do You want from me?

My mentioning this private part of fasting and prayer is in no way
meant to imply that what came out of our petitions was earned or de-
served. God's gifts are freely given, but we are told in Scripture not
only to desire them but to seek them as well (1 Corinthians 12–14).
God's imparted gifts are freely given, and like salvation, they cannot
be earned. A gift that is worked for ceases to be a gift, but He did say,
"Ask, and it shall be given you; seek, and ye shall find" (Matthew
7:7).

After a while we broke our fast and things returned to normal. In a
few weeks we moved into our new home and that was a happy day!

The Gift of Songwriting

Then one evening I realized that Joel had been down at the church
longer than usual. When he came in through the kitchen door, his
face was wreathed in smiles. He said, "Honey, come to the piano, I
want to sing you a song I just wrote." I followed him into the living
room and he sat down and started singing:

The Way Is Made

> *There was once a mortgage on ev'ry soul*
> *That could not be repaid with silver or gold*
> *But there is One who paid the price*
> *Oh how great His sacrifice*
> *That ev'ry soul from sin might be redeemed*

I saw the King upon His throne
And one before Him stood alone
Saying, "Father, for the lost these wounds I plead"
I did not hear the King's reply
For heaven echoed with a cry
The way is made that ev'ry captive can be free

Mighty men have their great armies led
Conquered nations and left millions dead
But greater conquer'r never trod
Than Jesus Christ the Son of God
He holds the keys of death and hell for you and me.[7]

While he sang his song, I was thinking, *Why is he wasting his time doing this?* There were so many good songwriters around and Joel, at twenty-six, had never shown an interest in that direction. However, there were times when we were learning a new song that he would change a few words to make it more biblical. This would frustrate me. But for him to out-and-out write a song caught me completely off guard. It left me speechless. When he finished, I just stood there trying to assimilate what was happening.

Did he actually presume to enter the arena with the likes of Vep Ellis, Ira Stanphill and Albert E. Brumley? Besides, that new song of his had such a wide musical range that I'd never be able to sing it with him. The words were poetic and good, but he would have to sing it as a solo.

I regret to say that this was my reaction to the beginning of Joel's songwriting endeavor. I was less than excited about the whole thing and was afraid that he was getting sidetracked from who he was and what he was about. I was aware that there were some new songwriters coming on the scene like Dottie Rambo, Bill Gaither and even Rusty, but it appeared to me that the field was well covered.

How was I to know that Joel's song was in the plan of God?

Even the title itself was a statement: *the way is made*! Blindly, I had been looking in the distance at how God might manifest His will for our future. It had never occurred to me that He would use what we already had, the little bit of singing we could do. Because it was so close to us, we had both overlooked the obvious.

It's comforting to know that I'm not the only one that has had this problem. When God called Moses to send him on the mission of his lifetime, Moses protested. He needed something to give him confidence. The Lord asked him, "What is in your hand, Moses?" Moses responded, "Just a stick, Lord" (Exodus 4:2, paraphrased). I know exactly how inadequate Moses felt. But he didn't take into consideration what God can do with just a stick. And neither did I.

From the day that I married Joel, the whole gospel music scene had been a dead issue for me, and I never intended to look back. Even Howard and Vestal had left the road and settled quietly in Madisonville, Kentucky to pastor a church. The Epleys and Rusty had all gone in different directions after their trip to West Virginia. Rusty had married, and he and his wife Billie were living in Baton Rouge. There he joined the Plainsmen Quartet and was working with Louisiana's singing governor, Jimmy Davis.

From time to time Joel and I had exchanged revivals with Howard and Vestal. We went to Madisonville and preached for them and they came to Bastrop to preach for us.

When Rusty came anywhere in our area he'd call day or night and we'd get together. All in all, things were pretty ordinary for all of us. Then something happened on the world scene during President Kennedy's term of office that cast a giant shadow across our nation. Trouble erupted with Cuba, which was backed by the strong arm of Russia. Would the United States find itself plunged into World War III? It had been a foregone conclusion for many years that any confrontation between the major world powers would result in partial or complete nuclear destruction. As Rusty watched the unfolding events, he felt terror strike his heart and felt the need to rededicate his life to the Lord. At this point he called, and Rusty, along with Billie, came to Bastrop several times. We had some wonderful sessions of prayer and soul-searching.

After that experience Rusty didn't want to go back to the same environment and enticements that he had been delivered from, so they packed up and headed for Madisonville. Rusty and Billie would help Howard and Vestal with the church in whatever capacity they could. Sam and Barbara were already there. It was just the right thing to do. Rusty needed to be with his family. "I don't know what I'll do when I get there. I just know I'm going to work for God, and if they starve, I'll starve with them." He didn't know it, but with those words Rusty had finally defeated his greatest fear—poverty. He was now in a position to be used by God.

His timing was perfect. Nothing is better than an idea put into action when its time has come, and the time was certainly right for Rusty. When he had sung with the Plainsmen, I had never heard such perfection. Their harmony was the best; their arrangements were soothing to the ear. In fact, gospel music as a whole was selling perfection. But Rusty had an idea. "I'm sick of perfection," he confided to us. "It would feel so good just to sing from the heart and not worry about complicated arrangements." He had learned many things about recording, management and the singing business as a whole while in Baton Rouge.

Governor Davis, who is a shrewd businessman, also taught him much about songwriting and publishing. This knowledge, along with Vestal's new anointing and the varied talents of Sam and Howard, was a combination that would bring them success in gospel music that far exceeded their wildest dreams.

It goes without saying that the Cuban crisis blew over, but it helped put the Happy Goodmans back together again. This time their purpose and goals were right.

Rusty was with them only a short time when they decided to record an album. When I first heard the finished product, I was surprised by their new sound. They came on like gangbusters, and their singing was about as smooth as a Chinese fire drill! This concept had an appeal that no one expected. It revolutionized gospel music overnight.

Perfection was out. It was *spirit* that took precedence over everything else, and the only way to get that was on your knees.

The Family had finally made it. Their delay reminded me of the children of Israel who wandered in the wilderness for forty years when they were only three days' journey from Canaan in the beginning. That wilderness trek had been for them a humbling experience, plus a time of purging and rededication.

The Goodmans' new approach was different, but one thing could not be denied: it spoke to the soul. It was a joyous, happy sound that went straight to the heart. That first album made quartet music with only a piano for accompaniment almost obsolete. Their new stage approach was fresh and unique with no prescribed pattern to follow. Most of the time you couldn't tell who was singing what. They never ended a song together. One would end, then another, and another, then perhaps the first one to end would pick up the note and carry it further than the rest. If one member wanted to tell something the Lord had done for him, he told it. If another wanted to sing a song over and over for twenty minutes, he did. Each one did what he or she felt like doing, and the audience response was overwhelming.

The Goodmans not only came on the scene with a new sound but also with new songs. Some of them were written by Rusty. And now for the life of me I couldn't understand why Joel decided to try his hand at it. Since Joel's first song did not have the desired effect on me, it was bound to have slowed him down a little. But it wasn't long before he wrote another entitled "Point of No Return." Again, the song had such a wide range that it was practically impossible for me to sing it with him.

Then a couple of weeks later, we were returning home from Birmingham, where we had preached a week for Brother Kelley. Joel was driving and the children and I were asleep when we pulled into our carport. It was 4 a.m. Sleepily, I started gathering the kids from the car when Joel said excitedly, "Hurry, honey, and come to the piano. I want to sing you a song I just wrote." To say that I was not as

anxious to listen as he was to sing would be an understatement, especially at 4 o'clock in the morning! But I mustered all the enthusiasm I
could with a wistful glance toward my bedroom and followed him
down the hall to the living room like a lamb to the slaughter.

Then he began to sing, "Well, my time is short, my way is narrow.
A heavy cross I have to carry . . ."

As he finished the first verse of the song destined to be called
"Not in a Million Years," *I* got excited! This was a good song!
Then I forgot the time as I began clapping my hands and singing
along with him.

A few weeks later, the Goodmans were to be in Monroe for a concert. We were looking forward to seeing them again. I was only able
to see them on rare occasions when they happened to be coming
through or were in the area to perform.

That night we rushed to get to Monroe early for a visit. The auditorium was packed. I was so proud of them. Just to have a few hours of
fellowship with them really gave me a lift. Sam always saved up his
new jokes to tell us, and we loved it.

When the singing was over, we all went out to eat. Then they
boarded their big bus, and we headed back to Bastrop. On the way
home Joel said to me, "I told Rusty about my songs."

"You did?" I said in a breathless whisper. "What did he say?"

"He said to put them on tape and send them to him. I would have
sung them to him backstage," he continued, "but I'd have felt like a
Little Leaguer trying to pitch before Mickey Mantle."

We were silent the rest of the way home, each filled with a strange
anxiety. What if Rusty liked Joel's songs? But we could not speculate
too largely on that possibility. It was too far-fetched, and the letdown
would be hard. The next day we taped the songs and put them in the
mail to Rusty. Then we waited . . .

The waiting was the worst part. We knew the Family was always
home on Monday and that would be the day Rusty would have time
to get the mail and listen to the tapes.

By late Monday afternoon the suspense was too great to bear. Joel put in a call to Rusty. One way or another, we just had to know what he thought. Rusty answered the phone and said that he had not been to the office yet to pick up his mail. He assured us he would go right away. We hung up the phone and the waiting began again. Joel and I both tried to stay busy around the house to work off some of the mounting anxiety. However, we stayed well within hearing of the phone.

An hour later, the phone rang. Instead of Rusty's being on the other end of the wire, it was Billie, his wife. "Joel, Rusty is here listening to your tape and he is having a fit. He can't believe you wrote these songs! He says they are great!"

Rusty took the phone from her. "Bubba, did you really write this stuff? This is great! We are going to record both of them on our next album."

Joel was speechless and I was trembling. This could not be happening to us. Surely we would wake up to find that we were dreaming. Rusty continued, "I can't believe these songs are so commercial. With no work on them at all, they'll sell."

For the next few days, Joel and I walked on clouds. Could this be the new calling for which we had fasted and prayed? A ministry of songwriting? Would we be permitted to make our life's work something that we both loved and enjoyed so much? The excitement was almost too much as we waited to see what would happen next.

A few weeks later The Family was to perform at the Jimmie Davis Tabernacle in Jonesboro, Louisiana, a town eighty miles from our home. We started to dress early, anxious to get there to see them, and to see if Rusty was really as excited as he had sounded on the phone.

I had just finished bathing when I heard the loud blast of an air horn in our drive. I grabbed a robe and rushed to the door in time to see the big pink and purple Silver Eagle pull to a stop in our yard. Goodmans began pouring from the open door.

They only had a few minutes to spare, but they wanted to hear us sing Joel's songs. Feeling slightly embarrassed, Joel and I led them to the living room to our badly out-of-tune piano. We began to sing, not only the songs Rusty had liked so much but also two others Joel had written in the meantime, "He Filled a Longing" and "The Eyes of Jesus." They loved all four of the songs.

We had a wonderful time that night with The Family. After the singing, we were invited out to pie and coffee with them and Governor Davis. We did not get home till the wee hours of the morning. But how exciting! Now we were sure that Rusty was genuinely enthused about the songs. Promotion by the Goodmans would mean the difference between Joel's talent for songwriting languishing or its flourishing.

The next morning the alarm went off early. After getting the children off to school, I crawled back into bed and woke up later to find Joel busy at his typewriter. I followed the sounds to his study to tell him about an odd dream that I'd just had.

The dream was about an elderly man and his grandson. Somehow I had known that the man was very wealthy. He was down on one knee, clutching the boy by the shoulders and gazing desperately into his face. As I watched the scene unfold, I realized that the old man would soon pass away and that he was counting on the boy to see after the great wealth that he'd worked all his life to accumulate. He was still trying to hang on to his money through the child. It was a fleeting yet a revealing scene that stirred my emotions. I couldn't understand why I'd have such a strange dream. When I finished telling him about it, Joel smiled and said, "Honey, you're inspired. Why don't you try to put it into a song?"

"Me, write a song? I could never do that—that's your calling."

"You'll never know until you try," was his answer.

"Well, maybe I could try," I said and returned to the bedroom with pen and paper to see if something would come to me. In a few minutes, I began to write.

Treasures that I feel and see,
Things that are so dear to me,
Shall with life's shadows be . . . gone evermore.
And I know this house of clay
Will fade as light of day,
And be gone . . . gone evermore.

I look into the face so sweet
Of a child who'll someday meet
The fate of Man, life incomplete and be . . . gone evermore.
Beauty shall return to dust,
Lest in God he's placed his trust,
And be gone . . . gone evermore.

I went to the piano and started putting the melody to it, but it was incomplete, for I only had two verses. Then Joel came from the study and added the chorus.

How foolish are the ways of Man,
To hope, toil and plan
For things of earth that will soon pass away.
But I know God has made a way
That we might have eternal day,
And life . . . life evermore.[8]

There it was, my first song, "Life Evermore."

Without Joel's help and encouragement, I could have never written a song, but the inspiration had come from the Lord. It was a happy day to find that I would share in this exciting new ministry of songwriting. And an even happier day when Rusty decided to record it.

The year was 1965. We had been pastoring the church for four years now. Ever since we had come to Bastrop, we had envisioned a new church building. The one we had now was a little frame structure mounted on concrete blocks. There were no restrooms inside, no nursery and only four small Sunday school rooms that had been tacked haphazardly on to the rear. In the winter the heating was insufficient, and in summer the ventilation was poor. If it rained (and rain it does in Louisiana) the parking lot became a "lob-lolly" of mud.

All of these inconveniences should have been enough to discourage anyone from coming to church, but it never stopped our congregation. They came right on, rain or shine, and the number grew steadily. Now we were cramped for space. We had to expand and soon began to make plans to build.

Joel purchased the materials as he had the money to buy them. When the money ran out, construction was halted until more could be raised. Labor was donated by church members and their friends. On the days that the men worked at the church, the women cooked lunch and fed them there on the grounds. It was a group effort and everyone shared our enthusiasm. The beautiful new brick church, surrounded by a concrete parking lot, featured all the conveniences that the old one had lacked and was finally complete. We furnished it throughout with new furniture. When we held our first service, we were only a few hundred dollars away from being debt-free.

My husband had worked long and hard on this project, but the end result was gratifying. As he worked on the church, he continued to write songs. They poured from him in a remarkable way. We were happy and thankful for his talent, but still we failed to realize the importance of this new gift and where it would eventually lead us. On moving into our new church, we broke all records with 255 in attendance. It was hard to believe that only a short time before, the attendance board had read only 60.

Chapter 9

Take One!

The telephone was ringing. When I picked it up, Uncle Howard was on the other end of the line. "Breeska, we have a recording session in Nashville next Monday. Do you think you and Joel could meet us there? We are going to cut 'Point of No Return' and 'Not in a Million Years' for our next album and we'd love for you to be there."

Could we come? Wild horses couldn't keep us away!

Monday morning found us in Nashville, Tennessee, excited and eager for an "inside" look at the recording facet of gospel music. In all my association with the singing industry I had never been privileged to have a firsthand view of a recording session.

When we entered the building where the session was about to begin, we found ourselves at RCA in studio "B" on the celebrated Sixteenth Avenue. At this place on Music Row, Elvis Presley had recorded many of his greatest hits. Singing stars from the country, pop, blues, gospel and bluegrass fields had entered these doors with high hopes that the song they were about to cut would be that really big one. There were microphones, wires, instruments, chairs and gadgets I didn't recognize cluttering the room.

Each musician was comfortably stationed in his own little cubicle divided from the rest of the room by a movable half-wall. This, I learned, was so that each instrument could be "miked" directly into the control room where the engineer would keep his ear tuned to each sound and could control the volume in order to give the proper mixture of music.

In fact, I found as the session progressed that nothing escaped the ear of the highly skilled engineer. With him in the control room behind the large plate glass window sat the producer. His job was to come up with an overall plan as he directed each song and got the feel of it. The producer is the key to a good album and the genius behind it. He lets each musician know if he is giving too much, too little or just the right amount to the song. The final say was given from that control room. Everything possible was done to complement the singers and the song.

Joel and I were awestruck. It was amazing to watch these professional Nashville musicians catch the mood of a song they had never heard before, then put themselves into it, working hand in hand to create a hit. The atmosphere was charged but, at the same time, relaxed. If a suggestion offered by one wasn't accepted by a fellow musician, no one became ruffled. This was a world of creative genius where each person respected the ability of the other. Sounds that would be heard all over the world on stereos, radios and even television were being produced right there in that room by the simple method of trial and error.

As I stood and watched the prerecording bustle, I knew this was for me. I wanted to be right in the middle of the action. Having The Family record Joel's songs was quite an honor, but it wasn't enough. I wanted Joel and me to record too! If only I could sing one song on that precision microphone that picked up even a breath! I had never heard such a magnificent sound. Each person involved in the recording listened closely and passed judgment on the quality of his performance, musician and singer alike.

When The Family finished "Not in a Million Years," I was elated and maybe a little beside myself when I made a prediction to the man sitting next to me. He was Marvin Norcross, vice-president of Canaan Records, a division of Word, the largest gospel and sacred recording company in the world. I leaned toward him, placed my hand on his arm and said, "Mr. Norcross, I predict you will be recording Joel and me in the very near future!" He just smiled graciously and said, "Is that right?"

As we were leaving the studio that night, exhausted and wrung out with emotion, Joel reminded me of my wild prediction. "Dear, do you realize what you said to Mr. Norcross tonight?"

"Oh my, I don't know what came over me. I just couldn't help my-self. It was out before I knew it!" I exclaimed.

We both laughed it off and hoped that Marvin Norcross wouldn't think I was too much of a nut. Little did we realize that in less than six months my prediction would come true. I still don't know how it happened, but it did. I do know it had a lot to do with the new songs that we were writing. Rusty called with our session already set up. Since we were fresh new artists, Canaan wanted us on their label. Sure enough, our first recording was back at RCA studios with those same Nashville musicians. Thus came a new sound to gospel mu-sic—the Country Gospel Style of Joel and LaBreeska.

When our record was released, it was sent by Canaan to radio sta-tions all across the country, and astonishingly it was played. This brought a dilemma as we began to receive calls for concerts. It seemed as though we had the cart before the horse. Here we were with a pro-fessionally recorded album playing on the radio which could be bought in many religious record shops around the nation. However, it was still just Joel and me. We had no musicians and no money to hire them. The demand for our singing became greater, so we trav-eled with Joel's guitar, borrowing musicians at each place we went.

For one of our first appearances, we flew to Phoenix, Arizona and sang at a large auditorium. Although we knew we were not set up for concert tours, we felt that we had to go for the sake of our songs. Rusty had said to Joel at one point, when they came to the house for material, "Bubba, your songs will never do what you want them to until you and Breek are out there singing them yourselves." We were now firmly convinced that we were headed in the right direction. Joel continued to write songs, and the Goodmans, as well as others, were singing them.

Those were exciting times as it was becoming clear to us that the success of our songs had all come about as a result of our fasting and prayer.

Rusty and Joel became closer than ever in their relationship as they called each other from time to time with a new lyric. When Joel wrote "Pity the Man," Rusty couldn't wait to cut it. Then when he wrote "Who Am I," he just had to call and share it with us.

One day Rusty called, "Bubba, if 'Pity the Man' wins the Dove Award, do you want me to pick it up for you?"

"What is a Dove Award?" was Joel's response.

"It is an achievement award given by the Gospel Music Association for the song of the year," he said, "and I'm going to the awards program." Of course Joel wanted Rusty to receive the Dove if his song won! But the fact that we had a song eligible for such an honor was wonderful. The song that year was chosen from the top five as opposed to the top ten (which later became the rule).

From there our musical career accelerated, and after our second duet album, it was apparent that we had to have full-time help. Joel's brother David had been going with us at times, singing and playing the bass, and Jimmy Pierce, a young man from Little Rock, played guitar. But they were not always available. Now we must have someone that could go anywhere, anytime. At this time Tim and Dixie McKeithen came with us.

Tim, who was Joel's nephew, possessed rare musical abilities on the electric guitar, and his voice blended well with ours. His wife Dixie played piano and organ. They were exactly what we needed. We hired Bill Tharpe as our bass guitar player, and our son Joey, now ten years old, played the drums. No longer could we be called Joel and LaBreeska, so our new group became "The Singing Hemphills."

Had *God* called us into a singing ministry? This puzzled everyone. In fact, a few believed that God had no part in it at all, that He would never do such a thing. We had a nice little church in a nice little town. Some who were closely associated with us and others who hardly knew us at all felt we were leaving our ministry and selling out for fame and fortune. Actually that never fazed us. Once we were sure that the songwriting gift was from the Lord, we became single-minded in our efforts to get our songs to the masses.

We scheduled concert dates only when we were not having services at our home church. When we returned to Bastrop, we devoted our full time and attention to our church and its needs. Our members were in a sense our children. They looked to us not only for spiritual guidance but also for help in making decisions for everyday living. Some of the problems brought to us were important and some were insignificant, but all were time-consuming. As we traveled and broadened our world, the more trivial many of these problems seemed.

After a while, our members began to feel that we were not giving them sufficient attention. This was the beginning of divided interests that eventually brought about a parting of the ways.

I was caught in the middle, torn between our new calling, which I found completely satisfying, and the calling of the church. I struggled with the idea of leaving security and trading it for something that had been a source of pain for me as a child, the instability of singing for a living. But let's face it, gospel music was my heritage. I was born into it. It was as much a part of me as my nationality. It didn't take long for me to understand that the inevitable would happen.

So after ten full and happy years of pastoring people who will never be replaced in our hearts, we gave our resignation, and the church was turned over to our assistant pastor. Though we remained another year in our Bastrop home, in almost every sense we were already gone.

It was a lovely spring morning. I had already gotten the children off to school and Joel was peacefully sleeping in. The house was quiet as I went about dressing for the day. Since I had awakened, I'd felt a curious sadness that I could not understand. I thought if I indulged in my favorite pastime, shopping, the melancholy would vanish. Besides, I had to purchase Mother's Day gifts.

It was nearing the end of the week and Sunday was Mother's Day. On Monday we would be going to Madisonville to see Mama Goodman and The Family. Mother and Stella had taken extended vacations from their jobs in Dallas and were already there. Mama Goodman had lived in a beautiful mobile home in Howard and Vestal's yard since the passing of Papa several years before. I had phoned Charlene, my friend and shopping companion, and asked her to meet me at Ira's, my favorite dress shop, at 9 o'clock. But try as I may I could not shake the sadness that had invaded my otherwise happy demeanor. An old song came to mind and I started singing it. When I did, the tears began to pour.

> *I'll meet you in the morning*
> *With a how do you do*
> *And we'll sit down*
> *By the river,*
> *And with rapture old acquaintance renew*
> *You'll know me in the morning*
> *By the smile that I wear,*
> *When I meet you*
> *In the morning,*
> *In that city that is built foursquare.*[9]

I sang it over several times, crying all the while as I slipped out to the carport to keep from disturbing Joel. I certainly didn't want him to see me in that condition. He'd want to know what was wrong and I couldn't tell him. When it was time to leave the house, I pulled out of the drive still crying and singing. *What is the matter with me?* I thought as I brushed the tears away and tried to straighten my face. I would be at Ira's in minutes and Charlene would think I had a problem.

By the time I had joined Charlene, I'd finally overcome the strange feeling. We shopped a while, said our farewells, and I went back home. Soon I pulled into the drive, but before I could get out of the car, Joel came out of the house. The minute I saw him, I knew something was wrong. His face was ashen. "Honey, your mother called. Mama Goodman passed away this morning about 6 o'clock." His words just hung in the air.

"How? No one told me she was that sick," I said hoarsely.

"No one knew. It was her heart," was Joel's reply. "When she got out of bed they heard her fall. By the time they reached her, she was already gone."

I stood there, holding on to the car door, trying to make it register. It just couldn't be. In a couple of days I would see her and hug her again. In my mind I could see those tiny worn hands that were always doing something constructive. She never let them be idle. Every time we'd go to see her she'd show me dress after dress she had made. Many of them she had never worn, but she was continually creating and ever busy. Now that great little lady was gone.

That explained my sadness that morning. I never knew it was possible to grieve over someone's passing before learning about it. But in my spirit I had already bidden good-bye to Mama Goodman and had promised to meet her again someday. I prayed and asked God for the strength to help me give her up and I thanked Him for memory, for in my memory Mama Goodman would always be alive: loving, scolding, teaching and most of all, being a part of all that I am and will ever be.

On the Road Again

The year our group formed we were still traveling by car. We had a well-worn 1962 Buick and pulled behind it a luggage trailer that Joel had made. The trailer was painted white and resembled a dog house more than anything else. We knew this, but hoped that no one else did. One sunny afternoon as we were on our way to a singing in the backwoods of Mississippi, we stopped at a Dairy Queen in a small town to get something to eat. When we got back into the car, we noticed several old-timers sitting under a tree, jaws bulging with tobacco, watching our every move. Before we could leave, one of the old-timers' curiosity got the best of him and he ambled toward us. As he approached the car, with one thumb hooked in the galluses of his overalls, he spat on the ground, then leaned toward the window and asked, "What kinda dogs y'all ahaulin'?"

We traveled in this fashion for more than a year. Then one night the Blackwood Brothers were to be at the Civic Center in Monroe. We had heard that they were trying to sell their bus, so Joel, Tim, Dixie and I drove over to talk to them. The Blackwoods' bus driver, Bundy Brewster, took us out to see it. A close-up view of that bus made me catch my breath. It was so big! When we stepped inside, it looked even bigger! *What would we do with a monster like this?* I wondered, aware of the fact that Joel couldn't even drive it. Or at least he never had!

While Dixie and I were admiring it, Joel was attending to business. Soon the deal was made. This was Friday night, and on Monday morning Bundy was to deliver the 1962 high-level Flexible to our door. We only had one more trip to make in that worn-out Buick with the dog trailer.

The following day found us back in Mississippi. On our way home through the humid delta night, we became tired and road-weary. At 4 a.m. we were only twenty miles from home when suddenly the poor old Buick gave up and died. What a miserable plight. We pulled off the road in front of the post office in a little one-horse town. What were we to do?

If we rolled down the windows, the mosquitos would destroy us. If we left them up, we would suffocate in the heat.

While Bill, our bass player, and Joel went to look for a phone to call for help, Tim went for a stroll and came back with a can of insect spray. We couldn't believe it! We came to find out he'd found it sitting inside the window of the barber shop. It surprised him to learn that the window wasn't locked, so he borrowed the can of spray and gallantly came to the rescue of Dixie and me, two wilted, half-dead, aspiring stars of gospel music. Then Tim returned the can, and before long help arrived to see us safely home.

Monday morning came and so did Bundy with our first bus. He took us all for a ride and made Joel do the driving. He learned quickly—he had to.

The following year was full of exciting events. We were invited by Les Beasley of the Florida Boys Quartet to be on his popular syndicated television program, the Gospel Singing Jubilee. Television exposure proved to be an outstanding boost. At the taping we met John Matthews, president of Sumar Talent Agency of Nashville. A few months after signing with the talent agency, we found ourselves on stages all over the country. John had the contacts, knew how to book and had us right in the middle of the action in no time.

The first singing he booked for us was to be in Mount Airy, North Carolina. Never having been there before, Joel and the boys picked what appeared to be the shortest route on the map. After our Friday night concert in northern Arkansas, we boarded the bus and headed for North Carolina. Before we had gone very far, we realized we had made a mistake. The route the boys had chosen was over steep and winding mountainous roads like we had never seen before. That slowed us down tremendously.

We traveled all night and the next day, stopping only for fuel. We ate nothing but junk food. It was 9 o'clock that evening when we finally came to a stop in front of the auditorium, hungry, tired and full of anxiety. As fast as we could we dressed in our finest, hopped off the bus and entered just as the group before us was leaving the stage with a bang. The Downings were an exciting new group. The audience showed their enthusiasm by giving them thunderous applause and two standing ovations.

Now it was our turn. Our guys had to set up their equipment in full view. As they worked, the audience became distracted and began to mill around. This was our first Sumar date and everything was going wrong. By the time the spotlight hit us, we were so disoriented we hardly knew where we were. I felt as if I were miles from the audience. We weren't accustomed to singing in places that big, and neither were we prepared for the competition that was running rampant in gospel music.

Besides that, we were pioneering a new sound that was unfamiliar to the ears of mainstream gospel music fans. Ours had a country flavor. Besides, we were the only group at that time with a steel guitar on stage. All of this received a less than satisfactory response from the audience. When we finished our performance that night, their applause was out of courtesy. We knew because we had just heard it otherwise.

When we checked into the motel after the program, we were exhausted and beaten, in body and spirit. Early the next morning found us again bounding down the highway to our next engagement. It was to be in Richmond, Virginia, at the Mosque Auditorium. We were with the same groups for the same promoter: The Florida Boys, The Downings and The Singing Hemphills.

That was the night that we got our first real taste of victory on stage. We were stirred up about our bad performance the night before and were determined to give this audience their money's worth. We were also rested and ready for a challenge. We prayed, pulled out all the stops and hit the stage with our best songs with a renewed fervency. Not only did we receive several standing ovations but the applause brought us back for two encores.

Experience is the best teacher. That trip taught us two valuable lessons: stick to the interstate highways in areas you are unfamiliar with; and give your best, no matter what the circumstance. These were two basic rules of survival that we learned the hard way.

I found out that being in gospel music could be fun. Even though we were dependent on it for our income, it was much different from my childhood experiences. First of all, Joel was a good manager. We didn't launch out in debt, expecting to find a pot of gold at the end of the rainbow. Our home was paid for, and for the most part we paid cash for our bus. Also, we had our songs that brought in steady royalties. We were blessed and we knew it.

On the all-night singing circuit, our tours became more extensive. We worked not only in the United States but also in Canada.

By spring of 1972 our group was doing quite well. We had money in our bank account even though all the members of the group had just had the entire month of December off with pay.

Early one morning after traveling all night, Joel watched the sun rise as he drove the bus and waited for us to stir. I was up first, but before long everyone awoke and came to the lounge at the front of the bus. He waited until we all were there, then he began to share what he had on his mind. "I hear that Continental Trailways has a new shipment of Silver Eagles coming from Belgium in a couple of weeks. Do you suppose we ought to buy one?"

We all just looked at each other as he went on. "If we get a new bus, we may have to work a few extra singings to pay for it. Is everyone willing to do that?"

"Of course we are!" everyone shouted. By then we were jumping up and down and clapping our hands. Joel pulled to the side of the road at a pay phone, put in a call to Dallas and ordered our first new bus, a 1972 Silver Eagle.

LaBreeska Rogers Hemphill
Photo by Ken Kim, compliments of Benson Company

"From this day forward. . . ." Wedding Day, June 28, 1957.

Our first picture together.

Mother, Dad and
me as a baby.

My first
grade picture.

Gussie Mae Goodman
Rogers, my mother.

Mama and Papa
Rogers, paternal
grandparents.

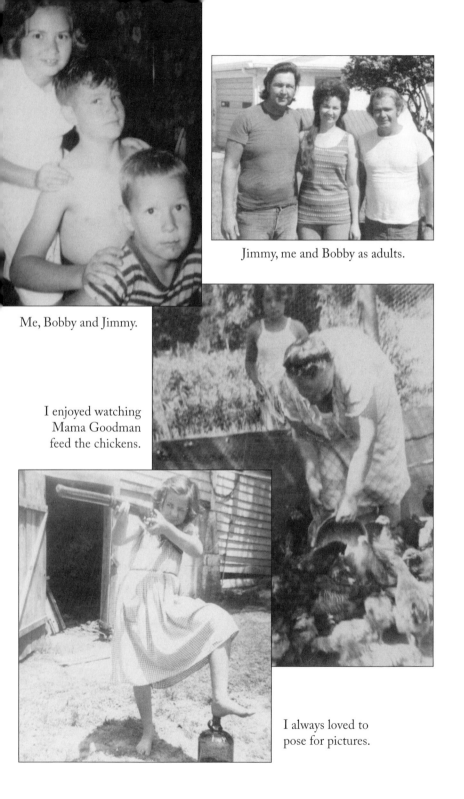

Jimmy, me and Bobby as adults.

Me, Bobby and Jimmy.

I enjoyed watching
Mama Goodman
feed the chickens.

I always loved to
pose for pictures.

Posing with Uncle Rusty.
I am eleven, and he is seventeen.

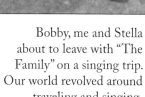

Bobby, me and Stella
about to leave with "The
Family" on a singing trip.
Our world revolved around
traveling and singing.

Having refreshments around Mama Goodman's table in Wingo.
The whole family is in this picture. Mama and Papa are
in the foreground, Mother and I at the top left.

The cheerleaders of Fultondale Junior High (I am on the ground).

A new "Happy Goodman"—Asheville, North Carolina, 1956. L to R: Howard (seated), me, Vestal, Stella, Mother, Eloise, Jake (drummer), Bob and Sam.

L to R: the Hemphills, me, Uncle Howard, Vestal, Sue and David Epley.

These pictures were taken in the revival in West Monroe, Louisiana church—Pastor and Mrs. W.T. Hemphill (Joel's parents).

Me, Vestal and Howard.

From our album, "He's Still Working on Me."

Taping television show for TNN.

From our "Excited" album.

From our "God Likes Kids" album. We both received a Dove Award for it.

Taping one of the many "Homecoming" videos for television.

At a concert in Alabama. L to R: Candy, Joey, Dad, Lila, Kristy, me and brother Buddy. Joel and Trent behind.

My sister Jane, Lila, Joey and Taylor.

A big church wedding, celebrating our thirtieth anniversary. L to R: Bethni, Rita, Sue Ann, Candy, LaTasha, Brittney (in front), Mandy, me, Leah, Charlene, Gayle and Brenda.

Photos by Bobby Bentz

At the White House
with Jimmy Carter.

Taping "Hemphill Family Time" in our front yard, with guest Roy Acuff.

A family portrait. Back, L to R: Kent and Candy, Joey and Sue Ann, Joel, Trent and Bethni (Josh Christmas between them). Seated L to R: Sarah, Madeleine, Taylor, me, Jasmine, Nicholas and William.

Photo by Ralph Barrett

"Partners in Emotion" as the years go by.

Catching King Salmon in Alaska.

Mimi, William and Madeleine
having fun with the baby goats.
"Tinkerbell" in the background.

Enjoying the latest
arrival in Papaw's menagerie!

Joey looking on as Jasmine and Sarah Kate ride "Ed" and Taylor rides "Misty."

Jasmine and "Jackie Boy" on set taping a commercial for the homecoming kids video.

Taylor, William, Jasmine, Madeleine, Sarah and Nick in Papaw's 1933 Caddy. The children call it Chitty Chitty Bang Bang.

Our fortieth wedding celebration—a surprise from our children.
Photos by Victor Bruce

Some of the guests
at the party: L to R:
Me, Connie Smith,
Marty Stuart,
David Hemphill
(Joel's brother),
Don Light, Joel
and Jerry Hicks
(brother-in-law).

Chapter 10

The Silver Eagle Rolls

Our singing group came to be like a special kind of family. We spent a lot of time together and shared a variety of experiences. Some were funny and some not so funny, like our first trip to Chinatown in Chicago. It was a new and exciting adventure for us. One night after a singing we went to a restaurant for some Chinese food. When we sat down to order, we had a difficult time communicating with their staff but didn't think too much about it until they presented us with the bill. It was more than triple what we understood it to be! But the food was great and the education priceless.

Another experience not soon forgotten happened after a concert in Baltimore, Maryland. This one had a twist of irony. We were part of an all-night singing with several other groups that sang to a packed house. However, when the promoter came around to pay us, he shorted us $100. When incidents such as these happen, there is little you can do, especially if you're a new group without a lot of clout, except to chalk it up to education.

Another group was planning a surprise birthday party after the program for this promoter and had invited all of us to a local restaurant to participate in these festivities. We had a long trip ahead of us that night. Since we didn't feel much like celebrating, we "bowed out" graciously, then left without finding out where the party was to be.

After several miles, Jerry McGuire, who was driving, spoke up. "Joel, I believe that bus is following us." He pulled to the shoulder of the road and the bus behind did the same. Jerry stepped out, and in a minute was back, grinning with amusement. The group following us had the birthday cake and all the goodies for the party but hadn't bothered to find out where the restaurant was. They had simply followed us, assuming that was where we were headed. The mistake was not intentional on our part, but as we continued on our trip, we were smiling and feeling that somewhere in this incident perhaps justice had been done.

Coming through Atlantic City, New Jersey late one afternoon, we realized that the Miss America Beauty Pageant was to be held there that night, so we decided to go down the boardwalk and have dinner. We could feast on fried clams, which that area is famous for, and might, by chance, get a glimpse of some of the contestants.

The town was so crowded that, in order to park the bus, we had to drive down a narrow alley to a parking lot. Joel inched the bus forward until he reached the lot. There he saw that he would have to back up and turn several times before he could enter. During these maneuvers we had failed to notice a house that faced the alley. Suddenly we heard a loud commotion.

It was a little old lady who had burst out of the house shouting and shaking her fist at us. We couldn't understand her frantic behavior until Joel pointed to a couple of big flowerpots. They were filled with an array of sweet petunias in her "yard" of solid concrete that just happened to butt up close to the alley. She was going to keep us away from them if she had to do it barehanded. We all felt sorry for her, and Joel, wanting to ease her mind, opened the door and told David Robbins to run over and assure her that we were being very careful. David started in her direction, but he didn't get far. She ran to meet him with fists flailing.

David wasn't expecting her to actually get physical and started backtracking immediately. But he couldn't escape her anger. She backed him over the flowerpots as he held his arms up to shield his face. Still she managed to land several solid blows. By now we were all convulsed with laughter as we watched from the safety of the bus.

With a red face and wounded pride, David finally hopped on board and quickly shut the door. He had gotten the bad end of that deal, and we never let him live down the fact that a little old granny beat him up one day in Atlantic City, New Jersey!

Some of our happiest traveling experiences have been in the state of Florida. One Sunday afternoon we finished a sing in Lakeland. As we were driving away, Joel announced, "We have a benefit to do in Alabama Tuesday night for Smitty Gatlin's widow. It's on our way home, so why don't we just stick around here tonight and tomorrow? I've checked the map and we are only about an hour and a half from Daytona Beach. We could get there before dark." At that we all started cheering! This was a rare treat. We would have the rest of this evening and all day Monday to play on the beach without a singing that night. It was like a mini vacation and we were ready for it.

Being cramped up in a bus for hundreds of miles and spending hours dressed in our finest would soon be rewarded with leisure and freedom. When we got to Daytona we drove the bus right down onto the sandy beach that was hardened by all the beach traffic. It was perfect. We had our own private place to change, our own bathroom and everything. We ate hot dogs, rode rented Hondas and swam the surf until we were exhausted.

By late afternoon of the next day, it was time to go. We were parked near a motel that had an outside shower for guests to rinse off the sand before entering the lobby. Dixie and I put it to good use. We got our shampoo, lathered and rinsed our hair and wrapped it in a towel. Then we set out for Alabama, red as lobsters and happy as larks!

Our travels, which took us over most of the North American continent, educated, honed, stretched and challenged us as we stood before audiences of every description. We sang at street carnivals, in skating rinks, fairs, school gymnasiums, business parking lots, coliseums and churches of many denominations. We worked hard in every imaginable kind of weather and played every chance we got.

Joel and I decided from the beginning that we would see and show our family all the wonders that this country has to offer as opportunity presented itself. We marveled over Mount Rushmore in South Dakota and thrilled at the wild herds of antelope on the plains of Wyoming. We stood speechless at the grand display of beauty and power of Niagara Falls and wept over the Alamo. From the North Pacific shores to the Everglades of Florida, we took it all in. We dined overlooking the Great Lakes and were dwarfed by the magnificent trees of the Redwood Forest.

From the windows of our bus, we beheld the majestic beauty of Canada from British Columbia to the seaboard of Nova Scotia, where we enjoyed the delicacies of the sea and even stopped once to watch a moose cross a stream. We experienced the diverse customs of others as we presented the gospel in song at their celebrations and feasted on their culinary specialties. On the streets of Illinois, we ate "burgoo," cooked in a pot for hours and stirred with a boat paddle, and sampled shoofly pie in Pennsylvania.

All this was a wide swing from where we had started. A small town with a small congregation can produce limited vision and understanding. Our travels were educating us, and we were young and eager to learn. We witnessed the vastness of God's creation, which intensified our awareness of His infinite wisdom and boundless love. Without a doubt God had us in school and was paying the tuition as He continued to anoint Joel to write songs.

I'll never forget our first tour of Canada. It began at the western tip of the map in the city of Vancouver, British Columbia and ended in Toronto, Ontario. It was a 5,000-mile trek that lasted several weeks.

We held concerts in Ottawa, and in Stratford at the lovely Shakespearean Theater. Our last stops were in London and two nights in Toronto, not far from the American border. Just before our final performance in Toronto, I was suddenly overwhelmed by where we were and just how far we had come.

I watched from the bus as the people came filing in and came to realize that I was a long way from home in every sense of the word. As Joel and I stepped from the bus and walked toward the backstage door, I said, "Honey, can you believe we are here at Massey Hall, the Carnegie Hall of Canada, and all those people are actually paying to hear us sing? It's a miracle, nothing less! Not only are they coming to hear *us* sing, but they are coming to hear Southern Gospel music!"

That night as I sang "An Unfinished Task," the words took on a deeper meaning and summarized what we were endeavoring to accomplish.

> *If I carry the gospel to the lost,*
> *Near and far,*
> *I won't stand empty-handed*
> *at God's judgment bar.*
> *But I dare not relax*
> *Until I've done all He's asked,*
> *Lest I should leave behind*
> *An unfinished task.*[10]

I still hold in my mind a picture of the dome of that great structure, as I threw back my head and sang with His anointing.

Pennsylvania is another area that loves and supports gospel music. Our first several concerts were held in Lancaster County. There we found their demeanor to be much like the Canadians—controlled emotionally. However, we discovered their enthusiasm to be outstanding in attendance and purchases. It took several trips to that place of unmatched beauty, with its rich farmland, horse-drawn carriages and Pennsylvania Dutch cooking, to understand them.

We were accustomed to singing to Southerners, who are usually more open with their show of emotion. To stand before an audience that responded very little to our songs, or anything we said, was disheartening as well as frustrating. I remember coming from the platform after our first performance there and telling Joel, "I don't believe those people even know who Jesus is." We were still judging by lack of outward display.

Little did I know we were singing to folks who would become some of our most ardent fans and best supporters. At the end of the concert that day, they swamped our record table and tried to buy everything we had.

In the beginning that part of Pennsylvania was quite foreign to what we were accustomed to. The Amish and their conservative attire of black, white and gray were fascinating. The men sported Abe Lincoln beards and the women wore sweeping dresses and old-fashioned bonnets. To see such a large number of people unaffected by modern conveniences such as automobiles, running water and electricity has a soothing effect on the soul and gives one the feeling of having stepped back in time. The men plow the open fields with their big teams of horses. Beautiful hand-sewn quilts of the finest quality can be found hanging for sale in just about any business establishment.

Many of our singings there were held outside, under what we call tabernacles. To the Pennsylvanians they are camp groves. These are excellent places to have gospel singings because the summer nights are usually cooled by a gentle breeze.

I recall one particular night when we had such a singing and waited for the breeze that never came. As we sang, I could feel the perspiration trickling down my back. Soon our clothes began to stick to us as the night wore on with stifling, sweltering heat.

Following the singing, when the last fan had left the premises and most of the lights were turned off, Joel and I searched for a hydrant outside while our guys packed up the equipment. We found one that was tilted upward to make it easy to drink from, and there in the darkness we took turns under the spigot enjoying a refreshing, makeshift shower.

Why not? I had bathed in streams and creeks all over the country as a child traveling with my mother's family. I even recalled a time in a small Texas town when Joel and I had held one of our first revivals. The house where we stayed had no running water, so every afternoon we bathed underneath a water hose in the backyard. We dressed in old clothes and made a game out of what could have been considered a hardship.

Our First Prison

Speaking of hardships, the most rewarding yet heartrending experiences of all take place in our prison ministries.

Our first one was the Terre Haute Indiana Federal Penitentiary. I was extremely nervous while we waited to be cleared to enter, and even more so when I heard the loud clang of that fifth door as it locked behind us. It had a ring of finality as it echoed through the corridors. I couldn't help but shudder as I thought about the menacing razor wire on top of those thick surrounding walls.

I was locked up with every kind of criminal that the mind could imagine, and with some that were unimaginable. Yet according to the statistics, there were also some in that prison being punished for crimes they did not commit. Our system of trial by jury is the best in the world, but at its best, legal experts say we can only hope to attain a ninety-five percent accuracy. This means that five percent of the people convicted in America each year of everything from traffic violations to felonies are actually innocent. The last survey I studied stated that over 200,000 are convicted a year in our nation, so it is reasonable to assume that up to 10,000 of those are innocent. That is a staggering number!

Also, there are those who have learned by their mistakes, and if they had a chance, they could live within society's boundaries; but only God knows who they are.

Yet, if none of the above were a factor and if everyone inside the prison walls were all hardened criminals, who would have a greater need to hear about the saving grace of Jesus? Our Savior's last act of mercy while He was dying on the cross was extended to a prisoner being executed for a crime for which he was guilty. But Jesus reached out to him in compassion and changed his sentence from death to life, with the promise of *paradise* on that same day.

If Jesus cared so much about prisoners, could we just ignore them and still be His faithful followers? This was the motivation behind our being in Terre Haute that day. Here lived a community of 1,500 men of all ages and nationalities with backgrounds ranging from preacher's boy to nobody's boy. When we walked down the halls that divided the cells, it was a relief to find it clean and completely warm. I had not known what to expect since I had never been inside a prison before.

While our musicians and a few trusties hustled the equipment down the hall to the chapel where we were to perform, I stood glued to the floor.

There were at least a score of men scattered down the long hall, watching us. No smiles, no frowns, no expression at all, just watching. The thought of my being the only woman there caused a chill to sweep over me, and I self-consciously pulled my coat a little tighter.

The chaplain, Brother Lindsey, ushered us into the chapel, where only a handful of men sat scattered about. Joel opened the program by letting them know that we were happy Christians who had come to spread a little sunshine their way.

By the time we began our second song, I noticed other prisoners had started slipping in, and before long the chapel was full. As we continued to sing, I saw that the faces of the men softened a little and that a few even began to smile. The music was lifting their heavy hearts and hopefully making them forget for a few minutes where they were.

Joel's introduction to his song, "Preacher's Boy," a ballad about homemade haircuts, patches on pants and hand-me-down clothes, drew a great response. I'm sure it carried many of the inmates back to happier days of childhood.

They loved the instrumentals and encored old favorites like "The Great Speckled Bird" and "Life's Railway to Heaven." We all sensed the need in those men and tried to do our best. Their favorite songs for the evening were "I'll Soon Be Gone" and "Thank God, I'm Free." The prisoners gave us a standing ovation for both of those!

The program came to a close all too soon, and after Tim's touching rendition of "I Want to See Jesus," there was an overwhelming response when the invitation was given.

We stood and shook hands with the men as they filed from the room. I was thankful that we had been able to help them face another day and hopefully leave them with something for days to come.

That was our first prison trip, but it certainly would not be the last. We found it so refreshing to minister to people who knew they needed help and weren't ashamed to admit it. That is a far cry from many in the free world who are just as bound in chains of self-will and diverse addictions and aren't even aware of it.

In those early days one of our biggest thrills occurred at an electric cooperative in Sumterville, Florida, when we were called on to entertain some 15,000 people who came to hear Vice President Spiro T. Agnew speak.

Since this was a grand event, we dressed for the occasion. Joel and the boys wore white tuxedos and Dixie and I, floor-length gowns of black and white crepe. As we stepped from the bus at the huge pavilion, helicopters circled overhead making a disturbing noise, while men with walkie-talkies meticulously combed the grounds. Security was tight. The Secret Service was on the job.

We made our way to the stage with television cameras from all the major networks pointed in our direction. Reporters rushed back and forth and photographers with flashing cameras were everywhere. Our adrenalin was pumping, thus bringing out our very best.

In all these varied situations we were challenged to find the key to every audience. Mediocrity was an ugly word to Joel. He was never satisfied with a questionable performance but always wanted us to give 100 percent. Often he would make the statement that an audience can be played like a fine instrument, if you find the right key. He never consoled himself, or us, by saying, "That was a hard crowd," if they didn't respond. He always put the blame where it belonged by admitting that we failed to strike the right note to turn them on.

No one has to tell us if we have performed poorly or if we have done well. That day we did great! So much so that we were asked to come back the following year!

The Move

By September of 1972, we knew it was time to leave the little town of Bastrop, Louisiana. It had been over a year since we had given up our church, and we really needed to be more centrally located for our travels.

Louisiana was too far south. We were spending an estimated average of one and a half to two extra days on the road each week. Many times on our way home from a tour we would arrive in Nashville before dawn on Monday morning, but still had nine grueling hours to go before we reached home. Not only were we spending precious time away from our children, but the wear and tear on our bus was expensive and the cost of diesel fuel was mounting up.

The undisputed choice by every member of our group was Nashville, Tennessee.

When the final decision was made, we stayed over in Nashville one Monday to look for a house. The group had decided that Joel and I should find a place first, since we had more to move, and they would try to locate near us. Before the day was over we found and rented just the place we wanted and returned to Bastrop, eager to complete the transition.

But it wasn't as easy as it sounded, especially for me. It is one thing to talk about leaving but it's another to do it. I loved Bastrop and I loved my home. It was a great place to raise kids. We were tucked away in a relaxed little neighborhood that had been our home for over eleven years. And I feared the unknown. What would it be like to live in a busy city? What would it do to my children to uproot them and take them from family and friends?

All my questions and fears were eventually overruled by the reality that if we lived in Nashville, I could spend more time with my children while they were being schooled. Still, when the last piece of our furniture had been loaded on that big truck and the door locked, we could not lock from our hearts the sweet memories that our home and that little town held for us.

Early that Friday morning as dawn was erasing the shadows on our peaceful street, we pulled out of the drive for the last time. Joel drove a rented truck filled with our belongings and Joey and Trent, now teenagers, rode with him. I drove the Cadillac and eleven-year-old Candy sat with me in the front seat as we slowly watched the city limits fade out of sight. Knowing that it was a final farewell, my heart was heavy. For all the reasons we had to move, I could think of none at that moment. Candy and I were both silent, still saddened by the scene that had taken place in our driveway minutes before.

Laddie, a neighbor's dog who lived across the street from us, was an English Shepherd that had grown up with the children. On the day we moved into our new home in Bastrop, Laddie came over to introduce himself, and from the beginning was happy to receive any crumb of affection that came his way.

As time passed, it was Trent who most often supplied Laddie's thirst for attention. He tussled with Laddie often while the gentle dog sat there with his great tongue hanging out looking as though he were smiling. Through the years the children had several puppies of their own, including two poodles and a German Shepherd, but invariably something fatal happened to them.

Laddie, on the other hand, wise with years, possessed a strong constitution and had weathered each storm of his dog's life. He was a survivor. Most nights when we went to bed Laddie was there, lying on the patio under my swing or huddled under the carport if it were cold or rainy. The next morning, if he wasn't still there, at the first sign of life over our way, you could count on him to come bounding down the path that he had worn between his house and ours.

When we loaded our car or the bus for a trip, Laddie would supervise the job, see us safely off then make for home in a slow, easy stride.

Year after year it was Laddie who, on each return, was our welcoming committee of one. His sensitive ears would catch the whine of the diesel engine long before we were in sight. No matter what time of day or night, he would meet us happily, wagging his tail and barking as we wearily pulled into the drive. It was a wonderful feeling to be greeted with such sheer joy. Laddie made our homecomings always special.

Yesterday we had carefully loaded everything, including mine and Laddie's swing into the truck. The house was locked securely and nothing was left but the big U-Haul truck sitting in the drive. Joel and I and the kids had driven the thirty miles to West Monroe to spend our final night in Louisiana with Grandma and Grandpa Hemphill; then we returned at daybreak to begin our journey. We noticed right away when we drove up that Laddie was nowhere in sight, but we had to find him. We had to say good-bye. We called and called. And we waited, as the early dawn was being replaced by a few faint rays of sunshine, filtering through the giant oak trees, causing bright and dark splotches on the lawn.

As we called, I could not help but feel that Laddie was somewhere listening. He had already sensed the emptiness of the house and knew that we were leaving, this time for good. We just couldn't leave without seeing him, and kept calling. Finally he came bounding down the path, making a sound I had never heard from him: a doleful, mournful cry of pain.

When he came into view, he circled us several times before collapsing at our feet still moaning. The kids put their arms around him with tears in their eyes. It was plain to see that he was consumed with grief. I sobbed because I thought surely he was dying. Then I knelt beside him and patted his old gray head. Joel said, "We can't leave him here. We've got to take him with us." At that, Trent ran to his owner's house, an elderly couple, and told them the story. Knowing how much Laddie loved us, they tearfully gave permission.

We were delighted, but when Joel and the boys tried to load him into the truck, he refused to go. He sadly walked away, stopping every few feet to gaze back at us. He was too old to start over in a strange, new place. This was his home, and even without us, he would have to stay here.

It was then that our two vehicles slowly pulled away, carrying five people with heavy hearts and tear-stained cheeks.

Chapter 11

By the Banks of the Cumberland

I have loved the state of Tennessee for as long as I can remember. Every time we passed through, pleasant sensations stirred within me. Maybe it was something that was transmitted through the genes, since it was the birthplace of Papa Goodman and home to my ancestors from as far back as the 1800s.

Whatever the reasons behind it, I drink in the beauty of its lush farmlands, cedar-covered hills and mountains, and abundant lakes and streams. The climate, with four distinct seasons and the winters with enough snow to go sledding, was very appealing after having lived in marshy Louisiana with its near-tropical weather and ever-present rain.

Of course, no one makes such a drastic change without having to adjust. I found that there was much to be said for the slow, easy pace we had enjoyed in Bastrop; consequently, I slipped into a state of depression for at least six weeks following our move. To give us time to find a permanent location where we could build, we'd rented a house just off a main exit from Interstate 65 in an established residential area on the north side of town. The traffic poured from the interstate and passed our house bumper to bumper.

I felt that my life was in danger just to drive to the grocery store for a loaf of bread. I had never driven in such traffic. Soon I learned the rule of the road was to get in, get out or get run over! Also, I have a poor sense of direction, and to Joel's amusement could sometimes get lost in Bastrop, as small as it was. Now I wondered how I would ever learn my way around in this crowded, congested town.

I don't know who coined the phrase "you can't teach an old dog new tricks," but I firmly contest it. It is amazing how quickly one can adapt to a different lifestyle. There is an unseen element in the human spirit that has no fancy medical term, but is known as grit, and I soon put mine to work. Before long I was going anywhere I wanted to like an old pro.

As if the exasperating changes of moving were not enough, Dixie, after seven years of childless marriage, had to give up her place in the group to play another role—mother. Not only did I face the problem of her leaving, but I also encountered a dilemma over Joey's schooling. He, at fourteen, was already taller than his dad and had been our full-time drummer since the sixth grade.

In Bastrop I had no problem finding a tutor for him. There was always a teacher who was not teaching school that year for some reason or another. They were happy to teach him in their home a few hours a week for a small fee. When we moved, I thought that in a city the size of Nashville I would have no trouble finding the right setup for Joey's education. I was wrong. I scanned the yellow pages for a tutor. There were scores of them willing to help, but when I explained our situation they all gave the same answer. "I only tutor one or two subjects, not an entire grade."

Seeing that I was completely off course, I tried to find another way. Someone suggested I call the colleges. With so many in Nashville, surely I could find a student teacher who needed both the experience and the money. I finally found someone who would tutor him for a king's ransom. The price she quoted was a staggering amount at the time. It looked as though Joey's education was going to cost a small fortune. I tried calling several Christian schools to see if they could offer some suggestion. They simply were not willing to allow him to miss school every week and try to educate him.

By this time we had been in Nashville for five weeks and Joey's schooling still had not begun. At thirteen years old, Trent was happily situated in junior high, making new friends, and Candy was equally satisfied with her new school. It just wasn't fair. Joey had no opportunities for making new friends and was missing the old ones that he'd left behind.

After sending Trent and Candy off to school one morning, in desperation I decided it was time to take it to the Lord in prayer. There in the kitchen I quietly kneeled before Him and cried, "We must have help, Lord! I have exhausted every idea and have come up with nothing." As I prayed, the tears poured. This was serious. Just then, while still on my knees, a new thought struck me: *Why not call Brother Jimmy Snow?* His church was less than a mile from our house. Also, I thought that I had seen a sign out front that said "Christian School." Jimmy, the son of country singer Hank Snow, was a pastor and doing a great work among the Opry entertainers by leading many to the Lord. Believing this to be the answer to my prayer, I immediately got up and rushed to the phone.

In minutes I was talking to Harry Yates, the principal of Evangel Temple School. Harry was a congenial, Christian man and a highly educated teacher. He was also, I later found out, married to Johnny Cash's sister, Joanne. I gave him a brief outline of my dilemma and finished by saying, "Do you think you can possibly help?"

"Meet me here at the school at 10 o'clock this morning," he said. "Bring the boy and his books. I'm sure we can work something out."

It was amazing how quickly things changed when I finally gave my problem to the Lord. Excited and feeling sure I had my answer, I put the receiver down, rushed to the bedroom and woke Joel. "Get dressed, honey. You'll have to go with me. The Lord has answered my prayer about Joey's schooling."

At 10 o'clock we walked into the office. Harry said that he would take Joey any school day that he could be there from 10 a.m. to 2 p.m. He could sit in class with the rest of the students his age and Harry would also personally tutor him. Joey could have lunch at the school and even play ball with the rest of the kids.

My heart was light as a feather! But one more thing had to be discussed: money. I had a set amount in mind that I felt we could afford. If we could agree on the fee we would be in business. Joel spoke up: "This sounds great, but we haven't discussed the fee yet."

Harry answered, "Well, this is the first time we've ever tried any-thing like this, so I don't really know, myself. How about $25 a week, if he comes all week, or if he doesn't come at all." That was it! That was just the amount that I had in mind!

Joey stayed at the school that very morning and loved it from the start. Harry Yates was as good as his word and did a great job with Joey's education—so much so that the following year we enrolled Trent and Candy. From then on we never had to leave them again. That was one of the greatest blessings that the Lord ever granted me.

The acute pain of leaving our children behind during school months casts a shadow in my memories that tends to cloud my remi-niscence of those days. It had been a tremendous sacrifice for the chil-dren, as well as for their dad and me, but somehow we made it through those trying times. Joel and I had called them daily from ev-erywhere while we were on the road! We stood outside at pay phones in all kinds of weather, sweltering heat or rain, ice and snow to try to communicate our love for them. I'm sure it helped some, but nothing could fill the void left by our absence. I knew this firsthand.

There is no way to describe the peace of mind that resulted for our entire family when that came to an end. As the children matured, they filled the positions in our group that became vacant by personnel change.

When Joey was seventeen, he left the drums and became our bari-tone. It was an easy change because he already knew the songs and his voice added another dimension to our family harmony. About the same time our bass player quit and Trent took his place. Candy was already showing promise with her vocal ability, so we started work-ing her in on a couple of songs right away. These changes were made possible because of the prayer of desperation about Joey's schooling that I had prayed that morning down on my knees on the kitchen floor!

As soon as we had the children settled in school, Joel and I were free to start looking for land to build on. We wanted several acres to have "elbow room," yet not be too far from downtown, the hub of the music industry. This was not an easy task. Even though we found Nashville to be a big country town, there wasn't a lot of acreage available within the city limits and within our price range.

One day while riding along Dickerson Pike, I spotted a tiny "for sale" sign, barely visible, on a very steep and wooded hilltop. Joel turned the car around and pulled into what had once been a driveway. It was all grown up and had deep trenches washed in it, so our car could only go about a third of the way. We then got out and walked to the top. When we reached the peak, we were delighted to find ourselves isolated from the traffic below and centered in the midst of several acres of sprawling oaks, giant walnuts and other lovely shade trees. Then down on the opposite side stood a small lake filled with clear mountain water.

As we explored further we found that it had once been an old home place. There were enough antique bricks lying around to help decorate the inside of a new house, for things such as fireplaces, hearths, half walls, etc.

When we left that day, we were also happy to find Evangel Temple School to be only one-half mile from the property and downtown Nashville only eight miles. Within days the deed was drawn up and signed to those five beautiful acres that were soon to become *our* new home site.

Soon a two-story antebellum structure began to emerge, visible evidence of the roots that we had firmly placed into the soil of our adopted state.

The day that I saw the first brick being laid had a profound effect on me. Brick and concrete speak of permanence. The overwhelming thought, *Someday I'll play with my grandchildren on this very spot,* moved me to tears. Of course, our children weren't nearly old enough for me to be thinking in those terms. In fact, it would be approximately fourteen years before that came to pass, but it surely did!

Back at the Ryman

Being residents of Nashville had countless advantages for those in the field of music. Joel often said more can happen to you by *accident* there than *on purpose* somewhere else. For instance, he came home one day from town with exciting news. He said, "Honey, I've just come from our booking office, and guess what, in six weeks WSM Radio is starting a Grand Ole Gospel Opry, from the Ryman, to be aired every Sunday night! We can be on just about any Sunday we are in town. You know the Grand Ole Opry is sold out every Saturday night and the Friday night Opry is full most of the time, so I guess they want to have the Gospel Opry for tourists that are already in town, as a kind of church service for them."

"Do you mean that I'm going to get to sing at the Ryman again?" I said.

"That's right," Joel went on. "I thought we were doing the right thing by moving to Nashville and now I'm sure of it. This could be to gospel music what the Opry is to country, and let's face it, WSM put country music on the map." As he talked on Joel's voice seemed far away, for I was deep in thought wondering how many years had passed since I'd first walked out on that stage with Mother.

Then I heard him say, "When they move the Opry to the new auditorium at OpryLand, the Gospel Opry goes too. And that is only a few months away!"

"When will we be booked on one of the programs?" I asked.

"The very first one!" Joel exclaimed. "They already have the talent lined up and we are on the first show."

Sure enough, it all happened just as he said. In a few weeks we found ourselves at the famous Ryman Auditorium as part of that first program.

When I stepped from the bus and onto the walk, just a few feet from the backstage entrance, it hardly seemed real. Twenty-four years was a long time. I was trying to find something recognizable.

Well aware of my nostalgic mood, Joel slipped his arm around me and asked, "Well, honey, how does it feel to be back at the Ryman?"

I laughed nervously. "Well, I don't really know. Right now I can hardly believe it is happening."

As we entered the building and passed the guard, I was all eyes. I could see there had been some changes backstage. There were many lighted pictures of Opry stars along the wall to the left. To the right, I was sure there had been some remodeling around the ladies' restroom.

Aside from that, things looked much the same. There was the same descending walkway leading to the stage and, as usual, friends and relatives of the entertainers were milling in the wings.

Joel left my side, saying that he had to attend to some business, but I was sure he wanted to leave me alone with my thoughts. Slowly I made my way down the walkway to stage level. There I searched for the exact spot where Bobby and I had sat that night so many years ago. I could not be sure.

My thoughts were soon interrupted when Joel came for me. "We follow the group that is now on stage and this is their last song," he informed me. Then a few minutes later I heard the legendary Grant Turner announce, "And now, ladies and gentlemen, Nashville's own Singing Hemphills!"

The audience roared as we stepped up to the microphones and led out on a moving, up-tempo song that Joel had written especially for me: "He Filled a Longing."

Along the pathway of dark despair
All brokenhearted, bowed down with care
I met the Savior and knew Him there
He filled a longing down in my soul

I searched for Him
And knew not what I searched for
I longed for Him
And knew not what I longed for
When I found Jesus

I knew that I would search no more
He filled a longing down in my soul

If you've been bruised by the chains of sin
And you are searching for peace within
I know the Savior who'll make you whole
And fill that longing down in your soul.[11]

I cannot recall a more emotional experience than I had that night, to be back on that stage with my own family, singing the songs that my husband had written.

My heart swelled within me as I stood looking over the auditorium. As I was taller now, the lights no longer blocked my view. It all looked just as it had many years ago, except for one thing—*it had shrunk*! As I scanned the balcony, there imprinted in my memories were two small children going through the audience selling 78 r.p.m. Bible Tone records wrapped in brown paper for a mere fifty cents.

When Joel introduced the next song he said, "The *Singing News* charts are saying that this is the number one song in gospel music, and I sure hope they are right, because I wrote it." And we took off on "I'll Soon Be Gone."

That was a night long to be remembered; however, WSM's plan to include gospel music had to go back to the drawing board. As much as they wanted it to happen, there were too many things that just didn't pan out. Namely, most well-known artists with a following had to work on Saturdays and Sundays in order to make the payroll. And most of the time they were just too far away to make the Sunday night Gospel Opry, so the idea died after a few months.

It wasn't long after our move that some unexpected tests came our way. Gospel music began to shift in another direction, being greatly influenced by a new sound that had come on the scene, contemporary gospel. Almost overnight Southern gospel music, as we had known it, began to lose its appeal. Our crowds started falling off and promoters began losing money.

It was a very trying time. The frustration of not knowing the definition of gospel music any longer was like trying to build on shifting sand. I'm not saying that the new sound wasn't good. On the contrary, I believe it eventually challenged us all to a higher degree of excellence. But to be in the midst of all the change and not knowing what is actually taking place is frightening.

Record companies, including the one we were signed with, were intrigued with this fresh new sound and turned their attention in that direction. They began spending the bulk of their energies backing the new artists that seemed to be springing up everywhere. A cloud of uncertainty hovered over our music and our future. Week after week we sang to dwindling crowds. Of course there were exceptions; the annual sings with a big lineup of talent still seemed to be drawing a healthy number of fans. But as a whole, Southern gospel music was feeling the effects of tremendous change. We were caught in the middle. Here we were, newcomers trying to get established in an industry that was in a quandary as to just what its fans really wanted.

If we had not been in Nashville at the time and if we couldn't have definitely pointed to the time and place that Divine Providence had brought it all about, we would not have survived. Then God, being the faithful provider that He is, dropped a financial blessing in our laps to sustain us and see us through.

The Bus Business

It all came about through a bus that Joel purchased from a man and his wife in Atlanta who came to our concert. She was suffering from ill health and they were desperate to sell and couldn't find a buyer. Joel had compassion on them and thought he could bring the bus to Nashville where there are so many entertainers and get his money back, with possibly a small profit. It took a while for Joel to finally sell the bus, but the people who bought it never paid for it. It dragged on month after month, and when Joel would call, they would promise that the money was on its way but it never came. Because they were friends, Joel would implore them not to force him to bring the law into the picture. Again they would promise and again no money came.

I couldn't believe that Joel would be so patient with them. It exasperated me. *I* would have lost my cool much earlier in the picture, but I can truthfully say that he didn't. What happened next was unbelievable.

Joel found out that the bus was in town at a diesel shop being worked on. He went to see the county judge for advice and explained the situation. The judge asked Joel if he could drive the bus. He said, "Sure!" The judge said, "Son, just go down there, pay the repair bill and drive it home." And that is what Joel did! We came to find out the bus was *leased* to a well-known pop artist. His management didn't care who they leased it from; they just wanted to stay in the bus and finish their tour. They asked Joel if he would lease to them. Then Joel asked them how it was done and "presto"—we were officially in the bus-leasing business!

The transactions were made through a management firm out of Los Angeles, and when Joel found out how badly they needed buses, he took that lease money, added to it and bought more busses.

Every time we had another bus ready, there was an artist waiting for it. There seemed to be an endless clientele of rock, pop and country artists needing custom coaches to travel in. Soon we found ourselves leasing to such big-name performers as Linda Ronstadt, James Taylor, David Bowie, The Marshall Tucker Band and the list goes on. We even provided transportation for Paul McCartney's "Wings Over America" tour. And every bus went out with Bibles on board.

Bus leasing was a lucrative business and Nashville, Tennessee was the perfect location. Our whole family got caught up in becoming successful in music and in business. By sheer strength and determination, Joel and the boys built our home and a huge bus shop while at the same time building interiors in our lease busses.

I helped by running all over town shopping for fabrics for the sofas and drapes. I actually made all the bunk and lounge drapes for the first several busses before finding someone else to do the job for me. Then when the busses came in from a tour, I stripped the beds, took the linens to the laundry and later put them back on. It took all of our time and energy to keep up the pace, but it was exciting and the money was good.

There were times when our busses would be downtown in some specialty shop being worked on and I'd lug all my cleaning supplies and clean linens there in order to have the bus ready to leave town on time.

During those days I think the hardest part for our family was having to travel in unfinished busses. Just as soon as one bus was completed we sent it out on lease to bring in more income. I've seen the time that we rushed to take most of the seats out of a newly purchased bus, placed mats on the floor and hung sheets across the middle to divide a sleeping and dressing area. Then more than a few times I've rushed to tack up sheets over roughed in bunks, then hung mirrors for dressing, while the guys took the equipment from the bays of the previous bus and swapped it over to the one in which we were about to leave. All of this eventually leveled off to some extent. But as the business continued to grow, it brought more work and added stress, especially for Joel.

Many Monday mornings we would drive in from a long trip just in time for Joel to get off our bus, without a shower, and go straight into his office. Mondays were always the busiest because the lease drivers would be calling in to report or standing in line to settle up and get paid. None of this was easy, but we were young and determined, and the bus business was another great outlet for our zeal.

God is awesome and never ceases to amaze me by moving His hand in the affairs of His children. While gospel music was painfully trying to redefine itself, our family had a thriving business to focus on, one that would take care of our finances. At the same time our children were developing musically to flow with the tide of change. Candy started singing full time and was coming on strong.

Trent filled another important spot in our group when he assumed responsibility for the band. By the time he was seventeen he was hiring, firing and directing. He also worked out all the arrangements, trained new musicians, called practice, etc. The band was his baby and he took it seriously and gave it his very best. Then in 1979 when he lost one of his best keyboard men, he decided to apply himself to the piano so he would never have to train another one. He was so determined to learn that he sold his car, pooled his assets and had a brand-new black Kawai grand shipped to the house. There he practiced day and night all winter long and by spring started off at the keyboard, where he continued to excel.

As we persevered, time had a way of smoothing out the rugged terrain that jutted the path to our goal. Eventually, with the help of the good Lord and with a single-minded determination, we began to realize a greater measure of success with our music. Candy soon developed a style all her own that was influenced by a combination of country and gospel artists.

Her voice, along with Joey's rich baritone, was a great addition to the family blend. Our children's youth and a fresh approach broadened our appeal and ignited the second stage of our career. As a result, for several years we enjoyed riding the crest as one of the foremost family groups in our field. According to Harper and Associates, who were our booking agents, we were second in demand in their impressive roster of artists.

I am not boasting when I say that we became known to our peers for the talent and expertise of our band personnel and for the quality of the material that we sang, most of it written by Joel— songs such as "Master of the Wind," "He's Still Workin' on Me," "Consider the Lilies," "I Claim the Blood," "Let's Have a Revival," "Jesus Saves" and more.

We went on to receive six Dove Awards, the highest honor given by the gospel music industry. I was honored with five nominations as female vocalist of the year, and Joel was nominated ten times as songwriter of the year. With all the honors and blessings that came our way, Joel and I felt that our greatest blessing and appeal was the fact that we were ministering together as a family. That really seemed to touch people. A large portion of our audiences was made up of other families. To see us working together was a testimony that it could be done.

We had numerous number one hit songs from some twenty-five record albums. And in a twenty-year span, Hemphill songs stayed in the gospel charts with a number eight average. We spent sixteen of those years as contracted artists with the well-known Benson Company based in Nashville.

In addition to these activities, we decided to finance our own television show and taped it on location from our home. Every morning the crew had access to our house as if it were a public gathering place. The make-up artist was there by 9 a.m. to prepare us. Guests arrived daily to participate: Roy Acuff, Connie Smith, The Happy Goodmans, Walt Mills, Barbara Fairchild and Bill Monroe, to name a few. Also, every year we hosted an annual Christmas bash, turning our bus barn into a place of feasting and gospel entertainment. We had hundreds of guests, including some of the most prestigious names in town. And our friends, such as The Cathedrals, The Lewis Family, Wendy Bagwell and the Sunlighters, came to entertain us.

Also, for a number of years we had open house and a sit-down dinner in October for all the gospel DJ's that were in town for the quartet convention. We rented tables and chairs for the front lawn, spent hundreds of dollars on flowers to decorate with and hired caterers and live entertainment. One hundred to two hundred people flooded our home annually for this event.

To be sure, we were living in the fast lane, but all our success came with a high price.

From one point of view our family was the picture of perfection. We were seeing our dreams materialize on every hand. Life had become just one big roller-coaster ride. The thrill of success and our fast pace had somewhat numbed our senses and blinded our eyes to serious problems that were developing from within.

Passing the Test

However, I am happy to say that we passed a crucial test during this time. In 1984, our family was singled out by a wealthy Jewish businessman who made his fortune in advertising. He loved the fact that we were a mom, dad and three adult children, and he felt that we could be the next Partridge Family. Somehow he had heard one of Joel's songs called "God Likes People" that spoke to his heart. It says,

> *God likes people*
> *Any shape, any color, any size*
> *You don't have to be an angel*
> *To be really special in His eyes*
> *He said it in John 3:16*
> *And He proved it on Calvary too*
> *God likes people, ordinary people*
> *People like me and you!*[12]

Joel was trying to relay in the song that God knew He wasn't making angels when He made man. We are imperfect human beings with a free will and choice, and God *likes that.*

This man called several meetings with our record company and family before offering his proposal. He wanted to present us internationally with his advertising firm. He said all the ingredients were in place for worldwide fame: the talent, the looks and the family appeal. Of course when anything sounds this good, there has to be a "catch," and we sat waiting to hear what his would be. That's when he broke out in a cold sweat and started mopping his face with his handkerchief. He said, "You can sing about God, country, family values, but you can't sing about Jesus."

There it was. His one stipulation. We all sat there trying to digest what we had just heard and the silence was deafening. We waited for Joel to speak and his answer came without hesitation. "Ron, you have been open and honest with us and we are going to be the same with you. We are *Jesus* people. If we didn't sing about Jesus, we wouldn't have a song." That wrapped it up. The meeting was over in a hurry and we soon adjourned. The deal was off.

Even though we tried to do all that we did with integrity, it's easy to lose sight of purpose and goal when you are stretched as thin as we were. The first thing that gets neglected is fellowship with the Lord. There was very little time for that with our hectic schedule.

The next thing that suffers is relationships with each other. Joel and my relationship was left more or less on automatic pilot. The demands on Joel just ran into each other without let-up, and after a while he was totally depleted. He ran out of steam. I think the sight of me, even though he loved me very much, reminded him of all his responsibilities; and in his mind, I just became one more burden.

The Threat of Divorce

At this point I really needed to step in and help more by assuming a greater share of the responsibilities, but I didn't know how. I had absolutely no concept of how to run a business. Joel had always been so competent in that area and I'd just left it up to him. But the formula that made our marriage work in our youth was no longer sufficient. He needed something from me that I couldn't supply. When we recognized that our marriage was in trouble, we were both helpless to alter it. We didn't know where to start. Joel eventually got out of the bus business, but the damage was already done, and divorce threatened our future.

What amazes me is how a great marriage like ours could get to that place. We were locked into roles that needed to adjust with time, but we did not have a clue how to make those adjustments. It was as if it was chiseled in stone in our minds what worked for us, when in reality it wasn't working at all, and hadn't been for a long time.

The crash came in the winter of '85 while we were off the road from our singing engagements. A big part of that winter was spent separately. Joel went on hunting trips with friends, whoever was going, whatever they were hunting. It really didn't matter. He just needed to be away, to escape. Meanwhile, I stayed at our farm in Monroe or at home in Nashville. Divorce loomed before us and I recoiled from it with every fiber of my being.

Joel was so burned out that there was nothing left of the man that I had married but an empty shell. Nothing I said or did seemed to penetrate. By February 1986 he and I were tearfully at the crossroads. That was when I went running into the open arms of Jesus.

With a broken heart and bruised pride, I went into my closet, which now serves as my prayer closet, and on bended knees desperately called out to Him.

Overcome with pain and smudged with my share of the blame, daily I sought relief from my despair. It was as though I were talking to the wall when I tried to reason with Joel. I was totally helpless to stop this tragedy that would bring a blight on the gospel and affect so many lives. At least I thought I was helpless.

Day and night I cried to the Lord. I laid it out before Him and implored Him to come to my rescue. My heart was bleeding and, at times, I begged the Lord to let me bleed to death. I couldn't bear the rejection I was feeling from the man that had once loved me so completely. The only thing that seemingly held us together at that point was our surroundings, the children, our music, etc. Our marriage was like a big framed house that looked good from the outside, but the strength and the heart of it was completely destroyed, eaten away by decay.

It even came to the place that we called our three children for a family discussion in our living room. It was a painful scene, but they had to understand that it was *over* for their dad and me. With our children's wise counsel and Joel's overwhelming desire not to wound the body of Christ, Joel tearfully decided to stay and honor our singing contracts for the year. We were booked until the end of October. This was February.

With that plan, our booking agent, who knew nothing of our dilemma, wouldn't have to call all over the nation and cancel our dates while giving the tragic news that our marriage was over. In the meantime Joel and I would have to try and find a way to make it through each stressful day. I moved his things out of our bedroom to the one at the end of the hall. The atmosphere became thick and heavy in a home whose very foundation was poured in love and adoration. Music and laughter were replaced with silence and suspicion. I did not know how I was going to live through it all.

The feeling of being unloved stripped my soul bare. My countenance became drawn and bitter. One day I drove to the mall as a means of escape. While I was browsing, a song came over the intercom that I had never heard before. It was Michael Bolton crying out in anguish, "Tell me, how am I supposed to live without you!" The words of that song stabbed my wounded heart like a dagger.

One day I decided that I really had to get away. I told Joel I was leaving for a week but that I would be back. I just wanted to go somewhere near the water with the hope that the wind, sand and the sea might alleviate some of my pain. I packed a few things and headed toward Monroe, Louisiana to meet Joel's sister Rita and her husband James Maryo. From there I boarded their customized tour bus and accompanied them to their bass lodge in Old Mexico. No one other than our children knew that Joel and I were having trouble, but I confided in Rita for help. That was a wise choice. She was wonderful.

At the camp she insisted that I room with them on a third cot. That first night Rita started pumping me full of Bible scriptures like a nurse hooking up a dying patient to glucose. There in the darkness she softly quoted the life-giving Word to my famished spirit as silent tears streamed down my checks and soaked my nightshirt.

Rita reminded me of the sufferings of Christ in First Peter, how we are partakers of His suffering when we suffer as Christians, and how we will also be partakers of His glory that shall be revealed. The verse that she quoted that really spoke to me was:

> *Beloved, think it not strange concerning the fiery trial which is to try you, as though some strange thing happened unto you: but rejoice inasmuch as ye are partakers of Christ's sufferings; that, when his glory shall be revealed, ye may be glad also with exceeding joy.* (1 Peter 4:12-13)

Rita wound up that night with a startling question: "LaBreeska, have you thanked God for your trouble?"

"I've never heard of that," was my response. "But I am willing to."

Rita said that Dad Hemphill relied on the Scripture. He said, "In all things give thanks" (see Ephesians 5:20) when trouble comes our way. He said that God would surely turn our problems around if we did that and bring about His purpose from our suffering. I could hardly wait to get alone in prayer the following day.

There was a secluded road that ran adjacent to the bass lake that I found to walk along and pray early the next morning. There I cried out to the Lord. I didn't just say, "Thank You, Lord, for Joel's and my problems," but I spelled them out. I named every pain by name and thanked Him for it. Each time I did I would bend over and gag, choking on the words that were coming from my lips.

I knew that the Lord was the only hope in our situation. If this didn't work, *nothing* would. Then I straightened up and with a loud clear voice, looked toward the heavens and said: "Father God, in the name of the Lord Jesus Christ and by the precious blood of Calvary, I claim my husband's total restoration. I also claim a greater ministry for the two of us, greater than we could have ever imagined. Now, thank You, Lord, for rebuking Satan from my husband and our marriage, in Jesus' name." Then I went back to the camp.

Rita had read in the Bible where God had prepared a big fish for Jonah (Jonah 1:17). She knew how much I loved to fish, so she secretly started asking the Lord to prepare a fish for me. She was asking the Lord to make me smile again. Then the three of us went out in the boat that evening to see if the fish were biting. Rita was still praying this prayer under her breath without my knowledge. Just as we were about to go ashore because neither of us had gotten a strike, I hung one and Rita and James cheered while I reeled in a six-pound bass! God is wonderful! He knew what would bring joy to my aching heart.

The few days in Mexico with Rita and James helped to sustain me. But that trip ended all too soon. Once again I found myself at the steering wheel of our car going toward Nashville to face my heartache head-on. By then my pain had shifted somewhat and was turning into anger. *How dare Joel put me through this! I have loved him without reserve for twenty-nine years, giving my all to this marriage, and it means nothing to him!*

The more I pondered my situation, the more I was ready to tear into him. My trusting loyalty had even kept me from taking a paycheck from all of our concerts and recordings. I had just used our joint account and had always bought whatever I needed and most of the time whatever I wanted. Now I realized how completely vulnerable that left me. Everything relied upon him and his willingness to be fair with me. That really got to me, so I decided, *I know what I'll do. I'll go home and demand my rights. I want a good salary and a separate bank account. I'll show him that he can't do this to me.*

I was so worked up that I stopped and called him. I was curt and cold. "Joel, I'm on my way home. I've had a good trip but I've also come up with some things that I want to discuss with you that has to do with what is rightfully mine. I'll be home about 5 p.m." Then I signed off and hung up. That call made Joel think that I was going to ask for divorce proceedings immediately and he started thinking about a lawyer.

After having said my piece, I was satisfied and again turned my thoughts to the Lord. My sweetest relief came when I prayed in the Spirit. As I glided northward along Interstate 65, I poured out the anguish of my soul in my prayer language. It was like dousing warm oil on a raw wound deep down inside, while at the same time bypassing my troubled mind. Then the Spirit spoke forcefully back to me: "[A] house divided against itself shall not stand" (Matthew 12:25). Those words hit me like a thunderbolt and got my complete attention.

The Spirit continued: *What if he leaves? At least he is at home waiting for you. He could leave before you get back. Then what would you do?* That was a possibility that I had not taken into consideration and it gripped me with terror. The thought of an existence without Joel was the most desolate of feelings.

I was glad that he was still at home, no matter how turbulent our relationship had become. Without a doubt the Lord was speaking wisdom into my frustrated and irrational thoughts. He was letting me know that He was working things out and if I used force or tried to fight my own battle I would botch it up. Was I going to let my wounded pride drive Joel farther away? Did the thoughts of sweet revenge and vindication mean more to me than the restoration of my marriage? At that moment I opted to rely totally upon the Lord.

Feeling an urgency that Joel was about to leave for parts unknown, I began to implore the Lord to keep him at home until I could get there. With every breath I prayed that prayer, all the time looking for an exit and a telephone. When I finally came to a rest area, I phoned Joel and told him I loved him and was anxious to see him. I could hear the relief in his voice.

That same evening after my return, Joel asked me out to supper. We sat across the table from each other in strained silence, not knowing what to say or how to address our problem. Finally, when I gazed into Joel's tear-filled eyes, I knew what I had to do. I said, "I came home to make you pay for all that you've put me through. But I realize that you owe me more than you are able to pay. I'm just going to have to forgive you. From this moment on you are forgiven. This is a dead issue, never to be brought up again. The next thing is for us to sweep off a clean spot somewhere and start over." I don't think that either of us ate a bite of supper that night. But it looked as though we were making progress toward reconciliation.

That night I sat up with him into the early hours of the morning, pouring the Word into him that his sister Rita had given to me at the bass camp. Joel received the scriptures gladly, for his soul was as famished as mine. From there we decided to go to our farm in Monroe for a few days, hoping to begin rebuilding our broken marriage, but made little headway. On the way home I was driving. Joel was lying in the backseat, trying to get some rest, when Barbra Streisand came on the radio singing, "The Way We Were." We both started crying and came to the conclusion once again that ours was a hopeless situation. In my heart I continued to call upon the Lord. *Lord, I feel rejected and betrayed. I'm so helpless. Nothing I say or do seems to make a difference.*

As I poured out my feelings to Him and trusted in His grace, I honestly had no idea to what extent my tears were disturbing heaven. Then the Lord God Almighty turned His wonderful face in my direction. What happened next may be hard for some to accept. Joel's youngest brother David back in Nashville had several visions about Joel and me while we were in Monroe that shook him to his foundation.

The visions revealed to David (a minister of the gospel) the extent of our troubled marriage, how to help us deal with our problem and eventually surmount it.

The Lord stated, "This is not a situation between a man and a woman, this is a situation between a child and his father."

Then He said to me, "Lay before Me, hold onto My feet, do not be denied and I will heal you."[13]

God's visitation to David on our behalf included divine understanding as well as visions and prophetic utterances in a manner such as neither we nor David had ever experienced. During a six-week span of time David was used much like an Old Testament prophet and was moved on by the Holy Spirit to speak as an oracle of God. He trembled in the presence of the Lord as He spoke and, at times, was in great fear.

Through David, the Lord assured Joel that He was not angry with him and reaffirmed his calling, telling him that He had a specific job for Joel to do. He said that He had heard the cry of Joel's heart—that he did not want to wound the body of Christ by a divorce.

Those were painful days because of our problem and yet breathtakingly wonderful because of the presence and the wisdom of God. It was at this desperate point in my life that I began to get a glimpse of the heart of God and His compassion for those who turn their tears toward Him.

For thus saith the high and lofty One that inhabiteth eternity, whose name is Holy; I dwell in the high and holy place, with him also that is of a contrite and humble spirit, to revive the spirit of the humble, and to revive the heart of the contrite ones. (Isaiah 57:15)

These comforting scriptures seemed to have been written just for me. I found them while prayerfully reading my Bible and clung to them for added strength and assurance. I continued to find many faith-inspiring passages regarding other women whose prayers were answered, and it helped to make my faith strong. I read about Sarah, Rachael and Hannah, and how these women turned to the Lord in their distress. The Bible states that the Lord remembered each of these dear ladies and harkened to them (Genesis 21:1; 30:22; 1 Samuel 1:19-20). I can also say that the Lord remembered LaBreeska Hemphill. My miracle was one of biblical proportions and no less dramatic than theirs.

Chapter 12

The New
Covenant

Moving quietly, I tried not to disturb Candy, who was asleep in the bed adjacent to mine in the LaQuinta Motel in Monroe, Louisiana. Going over to the window, I just had to peek out to see what kind of weather we were having for our big day. It was absolutely gorgeous!

It was Sunday morning June 28, 1987, Joel's and my thirtieth wedding anniversary, which we were about to celebrate in grand style. At 2 o'clock we were renewing our vows at our home church, where hundreds of guests had been invited to attend.

Our marriage had been healed for over a year. The pain was over and the fires of love rekindled by the realization of just how close we came to losing each other. We were happy to have all that behind and were ready to shout it from the rooftop!

The event that was about to take place was the stuff dreams are made of. And, incidentally, a dream was what had set it all in motion. Joel had dreamed six weeks prior to this that he and I were back in Monroe, at his dad's church having a big, formal wedding. It was so vivid that it woke him that morning before daylight.

Of course, when Joel is awake, I'm awake. When I opened my eyes, there he sat, upright in bed in the dark. "Honey," he said, "I dreamed that you and I were back in Louisiana at our home church, having a big wedding. It was on a Sunday afternoon." He thought for a moment and said, "Next month is our thirtieth anniversary. Wonder what day that falls on?"

With that he bounded out of the bed and down the stairs to the office to check our date book. Returning with date book in hand, Joel announced that our anniversary fell on Sunday. Another surprise was that particular Sunday was not booked, even though we were well into our concert season. "We'll do it. We'll go back to our home church and have the wedding that I wanted for you the first time."

With those words, *I* leaped out of bed. I loved the idea and immediately started making plans. That day I called my sister-in-law, Leah (David's wife), to help put the event together. I wanted her as my matron of honor and Candy for my maid of honor.

David and Brother Kelley would officiate. Joey, our tall and handsome son, would escort me down the aisle while Trent would stand as his dad's best man. Bethni and SueAnn, our daughters-in-law, along with Joel's sisters, were to be my bridesmaids. Candy, Tim, Dixie and Joey, in addition to others, would sing the specials. In fact, it would be a family affair. They all were excited about our plans and jumped in and worked to make it happen as though it were their own. Brenda and Leah put their heads together and wrote a lovely ceremony around a scripture that I had chosen from Jeremiah, which states: "Behold, the days come, saith the LORD, that I will make a new covenant with the house of Israel, and with the house of Judah" (31:31).

"A new covenant" was our theme and was printed on everything, including purple napkins at the reception, where a feast of Guamian finger foods was being prepared. And the cake was spectacular!

Never in my wildest dreams could I have imagined that this would happen to me. Even as a child when my friends talked and dreamed of big, beautiful, wedding gowns, *that* was so completely out of reach for me that I never even allowed myself the pleasure of hoping. Formal weddings were something that just didn't happen in my family. Before I became a Hemphill, I doubt I had ever attended more than one in my life. Now I was going to my own, and nothing had been spared, no stone left unturned.

From the motel window that morning I glanced back at Candy lying there sleeping peacefully and my heart swelled. I remembered watching her play as a little girl, wondering what she would look like when she grew up. *Now I know,* I thought, as I smiled at my sleeping beauty, who had far exceeded my highest hopes and expectations.

Often I tell her that she makes me rich even if I didn't have two dimes to rub together: the greatest of that wealth being the heart that she has to serve the Lord. When Candy was nineteen, we came close to losing her to the world and its enticements. The enemy was out to destroy her and to steal her talents for his benefit.

During that time our family suffered much pain over her plans to marry a black-belt karate expert who was not a Christian, and who, we later learned, was making serious threats on his life and hers. We had several unpleasant confrontations about this. Her dad had firmly stated that he would not finance such a wedding, nor would he give his blessing.

This had been an ongoing source of distress for our family for several months when Trent came to us. He and Candy have always shared a close relationship and he was more aware of what was taking place in her private affairs.

Joel and I were backing out of the drive headed for Monroe to spend a few days at the farm when he intercepted us and confided with furrowed brows, "Mom, Dad, there are some things going on with Candy that you need to know. I'm not at liberty to say what, but I will say it's serious and you need to be aware that she's definitely headed for trouble."

Needless to say the trip to the farm was overshadowed with deep concern. When we arrived that night around midnight, Joel and I prostrated ourselves on the floor in prayer. There we wept and prayed for our darling Candy, knowing that the only help we had was from Him. When dealing with an adult, there's not a lot you can do except pray, but that works, for God is master of the heart as well as "Master of the Wind." After prayer we went to bed, and while Joel was reading his newspaper, I fell asleep. In a few minutes I raised up and asked Joel if he had said something. "No," he replied, "I'm just reading."

"Well, if you didn't say anything, it had to be the Lord because someone whispered in my ear to read Isaiah 54:9, and I have no idea what it says." All the time I was reaching for my Bible.

When I read those verses, we both wept and rejoiced because we knew we had our answer. The Lord was reminding me of His covenant with Noah in the ninth verse and plainly giving *me* His covenant of kindness, peace and mercy. By the thirteenth verse He included my daughter by saying, "All thy children shall be taught of the LORD; and great shall be the peace of thy children." Then it ended at the seventeenth verse by stating, "No weapon that is formed against thee shall prosper."

For this is as the waters of Noah unto me: for as I have sworn that the waters of Noah should no more go over the earth; so have I sworn that I would not be wroth with thee, nor rebuke thee. For the mountains shall depart, and the hills be removed; but my kindness shall not depart from thee, neither shall the covenant of my peace be removed, saith the LORD that hath mercy on thee. O thou afflicted, tossed with tempest, and not comforted, behold, I will lay thy stones with fair colours, and lay thy foundations with sapphires. And I will make thy windows of agates, and thy gates of carbuncles, and all thy borders of pleasant stones. And all thy children shall be taught of the LORD; and great shall be the peace of thy children. In righteousness shalt thou be established: thou shalt be far from oppression; for thou shalt not fear: and from terror; for it shall not come near thee. Behold, they shall surely gather together, but not by me: whosoever shall gather together against thee shall fall for thy sake. Behold, I have created the smith that bloweth the coals in the fire, and that bringeth forth an instrument for his work; and I have created the waster to destroy. No weapon that is formed against thee shall prosper; and every tongue that shall rise against thee in judgment thou shalt condemn. This is the heritage of the servants of the LORD, and their righteousness is of me, saith the LORD. (54:9-17)

Praise the Lord! God had heard our prayers and He wanted us to know that the answer was on its way. In no more than two days Candy called, crying. "Mama, I need the Lord," she sobbed, "I can't go on without Him." Her dad and I wept with her over the phone and told her to get her brothers and Sonja Goff, a close friend of hers who later became Pastor Doug Nolan's wife, together for a prayer meeting. And that's exactly what happened. When we got home, Candy had a wonderful salvation experience that continues to manifest itself to this day.

Her relationship with the Lord has matured to the extent that, as well as singing, she speaks often at women's conferences. Her engagement to Kent Christmas, a dynamic young minister, was more proof that all her future plans included the Lord.

I have found that raising girls takes much prayer and soul-searching and that you almost have to be a psychiatrist. They are complicated, complex and a lovely package of erupting emotions. But they are also loyal and tend to try harder to be the cohesive that keeps the family ties intact, or at least ours does. When her dad and I were at odds with each other, she was there for both of us. She helped in every way she could with her prayers and support. Candy continues to be a constant source of joy to me and to her dad and a consolation that far surpasses any discomfort that she has caused us. We could not imagine a more wonderful daughter.

And now she insisted on staying in the motel with me and spending the night so we could laugh and have fun and get ready for the big celebration, and celebration it was!

When Candy and I arrived at the church, we found it gaily decorated with big satin bows of lavender and purple, along with much greenery and brass. It was breathtaking!

Leah and Joel's sisters, along with the florist, had succeeded in making mine the most beautiful wedding I have ever attended. At 2 o'clock it started off with a medley of love songs sung by Joel's older sisters: Juanita, Verba, Bethel and Lois, wearing matching silk dresses of deep purple. Joel has eight remaining sisters and they all participated with the exception of Mary Evelyn, just older than Joel, who was unable to attend.

We both were deeply moved throughout the ceremony, but I think the most touching moments were when we pledged to each other our new covenants. Joel took me by the hand and quoted what he had written for me:

> LaBreeska, my love, I have truly found in you the woman King Solomon described as the virtuous woman whose value is far above that of rubies. I thought so at the beginning of our relationship—I know it now. Your husband and your children rise up to call you blessed.
>
> As in the past, I cannot promise you perfection, but I do take you by the hand once again to pledge you all my love and devotion. The Lord has always blessed my life, but never more than the day He gave me you.

I, in turn, had penned my covenant to him and responded with:

> Joel, my beloved, and husband that my soul loveth, when I was a young virgin you took me to your mother's house and I became the wife of your youth. We entered into a covenant of love. Since that time I have dandled your children upon my knees. I have opened my door to the stranger, and I have fed the poor. In our youth you were strength to me and I drew from that strength.
>
> But today I make a new covenant with you. From this day forward I shall be a tower of strength to you, as the Cedars of Lebanon. My love shall always cover you and undergird you and I shall give and not take away. I will always be beside you as we march through the remaining years of our lives, and together we shall go forth in victory conquering and to conquer. For you are my beloved and the husband that my soul loveth.

When I wrote those words I had no idea how prophetic they were or just how much strength I would need in the near future.

But for now a great victory had been won and it was time for rejoicing and making merry. When the ceremony came to a close we replaced the traditional recessional with a peppy Jewish congregational led by Candy.

Joel and I left the platform clapping our hands and singing,

Come let us sing, Let us rejoice,
Come let us sing, Let us rejoice,

Messiah is come and He brought life
And He put laughter into my soul![14]

Chapter 13

*Winds
of Change*

January 19, 1990

As I sat staring out the sliding glass doors of our den on that bleak, barren winter day, a chill of sadness crept into my heart. There in front of me sat our three adult children: Joey, Trent and Candy. Joel had called a family meeting to discuss the possibility of purchasing a new bus and upgrading our sound equipment for the upcoming year of touring which was to begin soon.

Then, without warning, Candy dropped a bombshell when she spoke up and said, "It doesn't matter to me, because I'm not going back on the road with the family this year." She went on to explain that her husband Kent was planning to quit his job and start evangelizing, and she believed that her place was by his side. Her words hung in the air like a thick fog. The rest of us sat and looked at each other in stunned silence. It had come so unexpectedly.

Then Joey broke the silence, saying, "I can't imagine us touring without Candy. She's such a big part of our sound, and SueAnn and I haven't started our family yet because I refuse to let her raise our children without me. So, if Candy isn't going to travel with us this year, I think I will stay home too and put more time into the bus business and plan a family."

Trent spoke up next. "Bethni and I have been putting off having children for the same reason, and it's harder every year to run our business from the road. I really need to be home as well."

In a dizzying fifteen minutes, our five-member family group had dissolved to just Joel and me. As we tried to grasp in our minds what had transpired and decide what course of action to take, I silently breathed a sigh of relief. I was burned out with life on the road and all the burdens that went with it. The fires of excitement from our minis-

try had long gone out for me. It had been years since I had felt fulfilled. It was as though our group had become a big machine of which
I was just a small part. The challenge was gone, as was the original joy
that I had once felt when I sang.

In the preceding days before this family meeting, I had·earnestly
brought this before the Lord in prayer. Down on my knees I offered
the year to Him, not even knowing how to pray about it. So many
lives would be affected by a decision on my part not to continue; now
it had been decided for me, just six weeks before we were to start.
There were no arguments and no harsh words, just shock and surprise.

For the past three years Kent had been very willing for Candy and
their baby girl Jasmine to travel with us, but now, if he were going to
evangelize, their place was definitely with him. Also, our daughters-
in-law had stayed behind in lonely houses week after week, year after
year, without protest. There were times that they traveled with us, as
they were always welcome, but touring gets old quickly if you aren't
called to it. This type of lifestyle was hard on them and their marriages, and I was well aware of that.

Where there is ministry, there is always sacrifice, and those darling
girls had done their share. It wasn't easy for them to make a life apart
from their husbands while we were away. Sleep didn't come easy
when they were at home alone. Taking this into consideration, we
were still sitting in our den grimly planning the demise of our life's
work, the thing that had held our family together as nothing else ever
would. The time had come to let our children go and to say good-bye
to life on the road with them as we had known it for the past
twenty-four years. That was a sad day, but all five of us would later
experience a deeper grief, much like the passing of another family
member, as our children walked away from the past and focused on a
new direction.

The next step was to contact our booking agency and get them to
cancel our dates for the year. These would have been the biggest

bookings of concerts and the best fees that The Hemphills would have ever received. We had been set to start on the Eastern province of Canada and work our way up to Nova Scotia.

Only Joel and I knew what it had cost to bring our group to this point of success: untold amounts of hard work and hundreds of thousands of hard miles on the road, sleeping in motel rooms and eating tasteless truck stop meals. We had spent year after year serving our apprenticeship by singing anywhere and everywhere in order to make a spot for The Hemphills in the gospel music field. Our accomplishments had not come easy, and it certainly wasn't going to be easy to toss them aside.

Ministry has always been a part of our lives. Joel and I were born into it. Now looking into the somber faces of our grown children as we sat there in the den, I was moved by all that they had so willingly given to *our* dream without a murmur. If there had ever been a complaint, it had never reached our ears. Each of them gave 100 percent while keeping their own lives on hold. It was understandable that they were now ready to pursue their own dreams and have a life of their own. No one could fault them for that—certainly not their dad and I.

There was no way of knowing then, but this day marked the beginning of a long journey of pain and trial by fire.

Almost everything around Joel and I that we thought to be stable and reliable began to shift. There was a storm brewing that had the potential to blow us into oblivion, and, like Job, we would "escape by the skin of our teeth" (see Job 19:20).

Saying Goodbye
Saturday, July 21, 1990

From somewhere in the distance I heard a horrible scream. Where was it coming from? I began reaching behind me for Joel, but he wasn't there. Those blood-curdling screams were making me weak, and I couldn't locate my husband.

It felt as if I were trying to wake up from a nightmare. Nothing seemed real. Then there were hands gently leading me from the coffin to a chair in the funeral parlor. My throat was dry and aching and my head heavy as I struggled to hold it up. I must have blacked out momentarily, because, when I came to myself, I was seated in an easy chair at the foot of Mother's coffin and came to realize those screams had been coming from somewhere down inside me.

Mother's death had come suddenly. She was not even bedfast for a whole day. The doctor had diagnosed her with lung cancer in May; now here in July, less than three months later, she was gone.

Just four days prior to this, around noon, the phone rang. Aunt Stella was on the other end of the line with concern in her voice. "Breeska, honey, it's your mother. Something's not right. You'd better get over here right away."

The twenty-minute drive seemed much longer. It was shocking to think that Mother would not live out the meager three months that Dr. Thompson had predicted to the family. The results of her test had come back positive for lung cancer. Mother was never told of the cancer nor of the fact that her days were so briefly numbered. She was a fearful person, so to speak outright the unspeakable and to declare that cancer would soon take her life was unthinkable.

In the weeks following the doctors' prognosis, Mother steadily grew weaker, and I felt she knew that her time was short. She seemed to struggle against it by talking of plans for the future and things she wanted to do for others. But Mother was wise enough to know that no one can win the race against time in life's final hours. How does one suddenly relinquish that God-given instinct for survival, that unquenchable thirst for life?

Even though we were aware that Mother would be leaving us, we never suspected it would be so soon.

I parked in Mother's driveway, and inside the house I found everyone congregated in the small living room, engaged in normal conversation. Bobby and his wife Frieda were down from Madisonville,

Kentucky. Aunt Stella, mother's only remaining sister, was there along with Mary, her daughter-in-law and her two teenaged children, who resided with Mother and Aunt Stella since the accidental death of Mary's husband, Jimmy.

Mother was also in the living room, lying on the half-bed that she and Stella had recently purchased for overnight guests. As I bent down to kiss Mother, I noticed a look in her eyes that reminded me of times in the past when she was feverish from pneumonia. Shortly after I arrived, she wanted us to help her to her bedroom, and we did. After we settled her comfortably in her bed, I walked to the kitchen for a glass of water.

Standing at the sink, Stella, Mary and I were discussing her condition and trying to decide whether or not to call an ambulance when we were jarred by a rumble of thunder just outside the window. The darkness outside and the noise of thunder caused me to hold my breath.

Knowing Mother's fear of storms, I rushed to her bedside and was shocked to find that she had already slipped away from us. It happened so quickly that I found it hard to grasp. I didn't even get to say good-bye.

Then I began to wonder if she had always known in her subconsciousness that a roll of thunder was going to herald her exit from this life into a world unknown. I have often heard that truth is sometimes stranger than fiction. The saying surely seemed to apply here. Yet the goodness of God continues to amaze me daily, for Mother's passing was without struggle or pain. She looked so peaceful lying there in her bed, as if she were just sleeping.

Knowing the ravages that cancer can bring, I realized it could have been so much different. I had asked the Lord to give her a peaceful passing when her time came, and He had granted my request. At that moment I was confident that Mother was safe in the arms of Jesus and that someday I would see her again.

Even though Mother had not been a Christian in my growing-up years, her influence upon my life was substantial. When I was a child, she was my best friend and confidante. I could talk to her about anything. Mother read my moods and helped me to know why I felt the way I did when the physical changes of adolescence were taking place in my body.

Being young and single after her divorce, Mother was familiar with the ways of the world and was constantly pointing out its many traps and pitfalls. She made me aware of empty promises in boy-girl relationships designed to steal virtue and self-respect, and she trusted me completely.

What Mother wanted for me more than anything was that I "hold my head high, my back straight, and look the world in the eye with confidence."

In the Bible when the Apostle Paul spoke of the faith in young Timothy that was first formed in his grandmother, then his mother, he could have been telling my story (2 Timothy 1:5). For although Mother did not respond to the faith she was taught by her mother until the last four years of her life, she always encouraged me in my Christian walk and moral lifestyle. That was a priceless gift. With her support and the influence of my two Spirit-filled grandmothers, Mama Goodman and Mama Rogers, I was never left without a reminder of God's love in my formative years.

The next step for me, being Mother's only child, was to make the three-and-a-half hour drive from Nashville to Jasper, Alabama to the funeral home to make the arrangements for her burial. Aunt Stella, Mary and I went ahead, leaving Joel, Candy, Joey, Trent and their families to come later. Joel and Candy were to meet me at the funeral home the following evening in time for the initial viewing.

To be so personally involved in the particulars of death was a first for me, and I had no way of knowing the impact it would have on my emotions. I realized that others had done this sort of thing and are doing it every day, and even though it was something I would rather have avoided, it had to be done. Going through Mother's things, I had chosen for her burial a lovely orchid dress that she had made and never worn. I also selected a broach and a ring that I had bought for her the year before as a gift from Hawaii.

Gathered at the funeral home on that hot July afternoon were Mother's remaining family—Howard and Vestal and their adult children and a host of Mother's aunts, uncles, cousins and friends—for the viewing that was set for 5 o'clock.

Just before we were allowed to go in to see Mother, Joel and Candy called from the motel to say they were in town and would be right in, but I assured them I was fine. I wanted them to take their time, as Joel had not been feeling well, and I wanted him to rest before he came. From the first of the year, I had noticed Joel's strength waning and I was concerned for him.

As we gathered in the foyer, Vestal looked at me and said, "Breek, darlin', do you want me to go in first and check your mother and make sure everything is all right?"

I declined Vestal's offer, wanting to be the first to see her, then turned and walked into the viewing room alone where Mother was lying in state. I began to check her clothes, hair and make-up in an automatic mode that turned to shock as I saw her lying there so cold and still. I began to fumble with her broach. It wasn't in the right place. I tried to adjust it but it wouldn't come unfastened.

At that moment the finality of death penetrated my soul, and I realized that I would never again hear the sound of her laughter. From my very first recollection, it was Mother's laughter that had set her apart from the world. It was so infectious. Mother had learned to laugh through her tears and disappointments. Her world had pretty much been a life of broken dreams. I was all that she could really call her own, and at times we had even been estranged. But from my earliest years, I knew it was she and I against the world. My mother loved me as much as she could love anyone, and we both knew that.

I redirected my attention to the broach. It had to be in the proper place, but I couldn't move it. At that moment I uttered those uncontrollable screams with such force that they left me limp.

The rest of the evening was a bit hazy, but I remember that Joel and Candy arrived later, as did my sweet, dependable daddy, Erskine Rogers, and my second mother, Lila. They and several of Dad's family members came at my request. Also present were our two sons and their wives and many of Joel's brothers and sisters. They were all supportive and held me when I was unable to hold myself and helped me through the difficult time of saying good-bye to Mother.

The next day under cloudless skies, there was a beautiful memorial service held at the little country church in Burnwell. This church had been founded by Mother's Uncle Hershel Nix when she was a child. It had always remained an anchor and place of refuge for her. Now the tall, stately pines nearby stood watch over the final portion of the service as the red soil received the earthly remains of my mother as she was laid to rest in the family cemetery by the side of her mom and dad, Mama and Papa Goodman.

For in death there is no remembrance of thee:
in the grave who shall give thee thanks?
I am weary with my groaning;
all the night make I my bed to swim;
I water my couch with my tears. (Psalm 6:5-6)

Chapter 14

*Our Time
of Crisis*

Tuesday, October 16, 1990, 11 a.m.

Scanning the two adjoining waiting rooms at Nashville Memorial Hospital where I sat, I noticed there were very few faces I did not know. Even our friends Doug and Laura Lee Oldham had come all the way from Lynchburg, Virginia.

The Kelleys were in from Birmingham, Alabama, as were Daddy, Lila and my sister Jane. Mom Hemphill, along with Joel's sisters and their husbands were up from Monroe, Louisiana. The Deasons, the Mayos and the Hicks families were present as well as a host of family and friends from Nashville, including Joel's nephew Tim McKeithen and his wife Dixie, and Pastor Doug Nolan.

I counted a total of forty-eight wonderful people that morning who had taken time from their busy schedules to offer their support to Joel and me in our time of crisis. A cancerous tumor about the size of a golf ball was located in Joel's lower colon and was about to be removed by Dr. Santi.

As the doctor was going over the procedures of the upcoming surgery just days before, he had asked Joel point-blank, "What kind of support system do you have?"

"What do you mean?" Joel asked.

"I'm talking about family, friends, church family," replied the doctor. "Who's going to help you get through this?"

"Well," said Joel, "I have a big family who is very supportive in every way, and, of course, my home church."

"That's good. You'll need them." Dr. Santi nodded, with a look of concern on his face. "Colon cancer is very serious and I have no idea how far spread this one is or if any other organs are infected. Your tumor is one of the lowest I have ever operated on. If this cancer were higher in the colon this conversation could be cut in half. But since the cancerous tumor is located low, it is considered rectal cancer. You have a fifty-fifty chance of a colostomy." Dr. Santi went on to say that he was going to use a new technique just recently developed that, hopefully, would allow him to staple the colon together during this particular surgery. If this procedure were a success, there would be no need for a colostomy.

Joel was hospitalized on Monday to begin preparation for surgery early the following morning. That was the time when this grand and wonderful group of friends and relatives started pouring in from all directions. We were held by the strength of their prayers, their faith and words of encouragement.

Even Dr. Santi sent a young minister friend of his by Joel's room that evening to pray with him and to read Scripture. It took both waiting rooms to accommodate us during the four-hour operation. No one, not even Dr. Santi, knew just what he would find once he got into the surgery. The news could be good or bad, but whatever it was, God had sent an army of loving and caring friends to help absorb the blow.

As for me, my faith was running high. I had taken the startling discovery of Joel's cancer with calm assurance. The Lord had come to our rescue in many a hopeless situation and I had no doubt that He would see us safely through this one.

Back in the waiting room at the hospital, all conversation was brought to a halt by the sight of Dr. Santi standing in the doorway. The clock on the wall read 3:30 p.m. Four anxious hours of waiting and reflecting had passed. Now came the report.

"Well, I put everything back normal," he stated, "and all other organs were clear. No more cancer and no colostomy." Dr. Santi went on to say that the cancer was localized and that he felt sure he'd removed it all. He found no signs of cancer anywhere else in Joel's body.

It was time for rejoicing! When the doctor left, the spirit of heaviness lifted, and with thankful hearts we crowded into the little prayer chapel to offer praise to our wonderful, prayer-answering God.

The days and weeks that followed the surgery were normal days of convalescence, and Joel's recovery was promising to be swift. In fact, three and a half weeks later, we answered a call to Bastrop, Louisiana for a church dedication.

The Bridge

We made the trip with no complications. We sang and Joel spoke and all went well. Then a couple of days after returning home, I woke up early one morning from a troubling dream. Easing from bed, so as not to wake Joel, I made my way downstairs to the kitchen.

While I was sitting on the sofa in the den sipping a hot cup of coffee, trying to understand why I would have such a troubling dream, Joel appeared in the doorway. Surprised to see him up so early and anxious to share my thoughts with him, I said, "Honey, let me tell you this dream I just had. I dreamt that you and I were traveling on the highway in our car, and you were behind the wheel. I was sitting beside you and looking ahead. Through the windshield I saw the steepest bridge I had ever seen, looming high in the sky, and it dawned on me that we were headed straight toward that bridge.

"The next thing I knew we were on this bridge and it was dark. There were no streetlights and no guardrails, not even a curb. The only thing to save us should our vehicle veer off the roadway was a solitary steel cable running along the sides of the bridge. I comforted myself by thinking, *A steel cable is the strongest kind of support. It will keep us from plunging off.*

"Then, as I looked down at the dark, swirling waters, I was seized with terror. We just inched along, and all we could see, as far as our headlight beam shone, was the bridge curved in several directions. As we came to the end of the bridge, we saw a man and a woman in what seemed to be a toll booth. They were laughing and talking when we pulled up, and I couldn't help wondering how they could seem so carefree and happy being connected with such a dangerous bridge.

"I leaned over and said, 'This bridge has nearly scared me to death.' And the woman answered, laughing all the time, 'I thought you looked scared when you drove up!'

"Then I woke up, still shaken by the whole episode."

When I finished telling my dream, Joel looked at me in disbelief. "You dreamed about a bridge. I too dreamed about a bridge," he said. "That's what I came down here to tell you."

Then he proceeded to relate his dream. "I was driving the bus, and we were all in it, our whole family. Then I found myself on this steep bridge that seemed to go straight up. It was so steep that I was actually afraid the bus would topple over backward, and I was thinking, *This bus is not made to climb like this,* but it did, though very slowly. I was really scared and started looking for the door to jump out, when I turned and saw little Jasmine asleep on the couch. That is the only thing that kept me from jumping. I knew I had to stay on board because of her. Then I woke up."

The Lord is so good. He was showing us both that He was about to take us across a great expanse. He was also giving assurance that we were going to make it across, no matter how treacherous it looked.

Unfortunately, that portion of the dream was forgotten in the midst of the fear and bewilderment that was to come in the months ahead.

Several days after our dreams about the bridge, Joel began having complications from his surgery. It started on a Saturday evening. We were both feeling good about how well Joel was healing, and we were still rejoicing over the fact that there had been no need for a colostomy and that there was no more cancer. It wouldn't be long before we could get on with our lives and continue our ministry. Some major adjustments would have to be made, since the children would not be traveling with us, but we had started without them in the beginning and we would do it again.

That night at bedtime after prayer, I noticed that Joel began to make numerous trips to the bathroom. There seemed to be no reason for alarm, and after I read a while, I turned out my light and fell asleep. But I was to be awakened throughout the night by Joel's recurring trips in and out of bed. His colon had become spastic and he must have made about fifty trips to the bathroom that night.

By early Sunday morning, he was in a very weakened state. All night long he had flushed important body nutrients down the toilet and, at one point, he had cried out in despair.

Just before daybreak, in order to try to get some rest, he found some diapers that had been sent home with him from the hospital and strapped one on. What began as a *temporary* relief became a five-week nightmare of continual use. The hospital had also sent Joel home with a prescription for Halcion, a potent sleep medicine, but he hadn't needed it until he started using the diapers. To quote Joel, "The only way a grown man can sleep through soiling a diaper all night long is to be knocked out." We then had to have the prescription filled so he could get some sleep through the ordeal.

Joel's condition did not change, and he became more and more stressed out. Our two doctors, one of them a gastro-interologist, could not diagnose the problem, nor could they come up with a solution.

His internal problems worsened. Every bite he ate was a potential time bomb. I allowed him to drink only distilled water and began steaming his vegetables, but most foods went straight through him. Any potential dietary hazard was eliminated from his menu. One morning a simple poached egg caused a fierce reaction; after that he couldn't even look at another egg.

Joel felt trapped in a body that no longer functioned properly and became extremely fearful. It didn't take long for his weight to melt away until he looked like an emaciated prisoner of war. He soon suffered from a full-blown sleep disorder and had horrible nightmares. During the night he would wake me up with his groaning and thrashing about, as he struggled to fight off his imaginary demons and monsters:

When I say, My bed shall comfort me, my couch shall ease my complaint; then thou scarest me with dreams, and terrifiest me through visions. (Job 7:13-14)

At this point we returned to our family physician for more sleep medicine. Joel had never taken much medicine in his life, and paranoia had already taken hold of him, so he requested a nonaddictive sleep medicine, as he didn't want to take any more Halcion. The doctor assured him that he had a nonaddictive type, but it had to build up in the blood stream gradually over a period of days.

The doctor did give Joel a prescription for something that *was* addictive for immediate relief until the other medicine would kick in. This frightened Joel more, and he started calling the doctor daily and seeing him as often as possible, yet nothing the doctor prescribed would allow Joel to sleep all night. In frustration the doctor finally told Joel he would have to will himself a good night's sleep, but, of course, this only made matters worse.

Then Joel's brother-in-law, Reverend Kelley, who is a light sleeper, advised Joel to do as he did, and softly play tapes of someone reading the Bible from a tape player beside his bed. Kelly believed that might soothe Joel and lull him to sleep.

It had the reverse effect. Joel didn't sleep at all that night. By that time bedtime became a time of dread and a nightmare within itself, all the more worsened because Joel had always been a sound sleeper. In times past Joel had fallen asleep in tree stands twenty feet high while hunting, and he had slept soundly while traveling down the highway in our bus, or while flying at 30,000 feet in an airplane.

Our physician realized that he could not help Joel and sent him to a psychiatrist. By then Joel was a bag of nerves. He talked in circles, repeating some of the same things over and over and wringing his hands while the psychiatrist evaluated him. Finally, the psychiatrist told Joel that he couldn't explain what was happening to him, but it was something that he was going to have to live with. It appeared to be something he had inherited in his genes.

Sitting there watching and listening to that conversation, it became apparent to me just how serious things had gotten, and I recoiled from the notion that we were now becoming involved with a psychiatrist on a continuing basis. It was easy to see that Joel's *physical* problem had evolved into an *emotional* problem. Being so completely out of control, Joel turned all his focus upon himself, searching for understanding, yet getting farther and farther away from it.

In a few weeks Joel was able to rid himself of the diapers. We both needed a change of scenery, so to take him on his first outing, I decided we'd go to the mall and just walk around.

This proved a disaster. The intercom that played music throughout the mall frightened him, and he convinced himself that songs being played were sending him hidden messages. And at every store we passed, he would look inside for the bathroom. In thirty minutes he used the bathroom five times. Frustrated, I finally gave up and took him home.

Good-bye to Rusty

In the middle of doing what we could to survive, we received the dreaded news of Rusty's death after a long battle with prostate cancer. Again I found myself seated in the pew of that same little church in Alabama. The thick aroma of fresh flowers combined with the stale odor of a country church hung in the air like a shroud and began to suffocate me with the smell of death.

A panic gripped my heart and suddenly I needed to get out of there. Joey sat beside me and held me in the grip of his arm while I stifled the strong urge to run away. Rusty was a rare individual and had been a vital part of my life. He was many things to many people: husband, father, gospel singer and songwriter. He had left an indelible mark in gospel music with the songs that he wrote and the way that he sang them, but he would always feel like a brother to me.

At fifty-six years of age, Rusty's untimely death brought a desolate sadness to my heart and made me think of King David's lamentation over his friend Jonathan, whom he loved like a brother: "The beauty of Israel is slain upon thy high places: how are the mighty fallen! . . . I am distressed for thee, my brother . . . very pleasant hast thou been unto me: thy love to me was wonderful" (2 Samuel 1:19, 26).

I'm glad I didn't know then that nine months later this same scene would be reenacted with his older brother Sam. There just didn't seem to be an end to our loss. My whole world was unstable. It was like trying to stand on a waterbed; the ground beneath me had turned to Jell-O. "My heart is sore pained within me: and the terrors of death are fallen upon me" (Psalm 55:4).

In reading my Bible I came across the words of Job, whose test of faith was so severe that ours paled in comparison, yet he stated in the midst of all his pain, "When he hath tried me, I shall come forth as gold" (Job 23:10).

I knew enough about the Scriptures to know that fiery trials were designed to burn the dross from our character, to eliminate impurities, leaving nothing but the purest metal. But when the heat is on and the suffering is so intense, it is hard to believe that you can survive, let alone be better for it. More than once I cried, "Lord, You're not only burning out the dross, You're getting the *good* too!"

So much of Job's writing resounded Joel's predicament. Job didn't know at that time that there was a contest going on between heaven and hell over him, but he felt the glare of God's spotlight when he said, "Will you never look away from me, or let me alone even for an instant? If I have sinned, what have I done to you, O watcher of men? Why have you made me your target?" (7:19-20, NIV). Actually it was more like an X-ray machine as poor Job was spread-eagled before it, so that all mankind after him might get a better glimpse of God the Father.

Job's example gave me hope. It was so good to know that someone, even in the distant past, had been to the precipice and had returned. Job ministered to me, as he has countless others down through the ages, through his suffering and vulnerability. The path to effective ministry always leads through that wilderness. There is *no* short cut.

Jesus our Savior was the prime example. How could deity such as He deal with mortal man unless He'd left His throne in glory and come down to earth as the lowly Christ, walking, living and suffering as a mere man? And to bring it right down to home, how were Joel and I to have the depth of ministry we had always desired if we bypassed this important place of trial by fire?

I found out during that time that my wanting to be Christlike did not include the part about being "a man of sorrows, and acquainted with grief" (Isaiah 53:3). What I had desired was spiritual gifts, wisdom and divine understanding. I hadn't taken into consideration the rough road that leads to that destination. But the Lord knew my heart and He knew Joel's, and we only wanted to be our best for God. That decision had been made long ago, and now there was no turning back.

Today I realize that our suffering has made me more tolerant of others' imperfections and has given me a measure of understanding of their actions. Fear is the opposite of faith and causes strange behavior. Previously I had been harsh in my judgment of the children of Israel for their crying, grumbling and complaining during their trek through the desert, where they even saw God roll back the Red Sea and perform miracle after miracle.

But what would I have done if I had been there? The picture becomes clearer when *we* are displaced and out of our *own* comfort zone. At a time such as this, it takes every ounce of faith that we can call forth to guard our hearts and our tongues that we might not do the same.

During Joel's and my trek through the desert, everything that we had believed, preached and sung about was laid on the line. Could I stand still and trust the Lord to see me through this? A scripture surfaced in my spirit that caused hope to arise once again: "Many are the afflictions of the righteous: but the LORD delivereth him out of them all" (Psalm 34:19).

Chapter 15

The Eclipse

Friday, March 15, 1991

As we stepped into the hollow corridors of the psychiatric ward of Nashville Memorial Hospital, the steel doors automatically locked behind us. Reluctantly Joel's brother David, Joel and I made our way down the hall to the nurses' station to sign Joel in. His sleeplessness had taken him to the limit and was causing bizarre results. He needed help. We all did.

The three of us were led into a dismal room that had been assigned to Joel. It was furnished with only a chair and twin beds. When we entered the room, I was repulsed at the sight of dirty laundry littering the floor and the strong smell of urine permeating the air.

It didn't take long to find where the odor was coming from when I sat down on one of the beds and got my clothes wet. Shaking with anger and fear, I darted out of the room looking for Joel's nurse, who at this point seemed to be my sole link to sanity. One look at me, I'm sure, was all she needed to see that I was in no condition to be put off when I demanded that Joel be placed in a clean, private room.

My request was granted almost immediately, as we were ushered into a nice clean room with a private bath. Flooded with relief and thankful for small favors, my emotions began to settle down enough to make some inquires.

"Why is this ward named Eclipse?" I heard myself asking a nurse.

No one seemed to know. David and I exchanged glances. He was standing over by the window, and I'm sure the question had already risen in his mind. We were both thinking about the prophecy back in 1986 that so forcefully came through David to his older brother when Joel and I were about to divorce:

"You are not as you shall be. As the moon before the sun, you shall have a total eclipse of the heart."

The prophecy at that time was a mystery to David, as well as to Joel, as to what the Lord was going to do or how and when He intended to do it. Now here we were in a mental hospital named Eclipse that had not even been in existence when the prophecy came forth.

Back to immediate matters, I had my hands full getting Joel settled in and trying to turn him over to strangers without feeling like I had abandoned him. It was a relief when the staff took him from me for evaluation and told me that I was no longer needed.

After saying good-bye to David, I drove home, emotionally drained and exhausted, with a sort of peace in my heart to have Joel in competent hands.

The first thing I did when I got home was to turn on the telephone answering machine and turn the volume up so I could hear who was calling and decide if I wanted to talk. I was certainly in no mood to answer questions, and I didn't want anyone to know that Joel was in a mental hospital. I thought it could jeopardize his ministry in the future. Who would ever want to hear someone preach who had mental problems? I felt that I had to keep it from everyone so Joel would not lose his credibility. Little did I know that later, after he was healed, he would tell it far and wide via television, radio, newspaper—wherever he had a chance—in order to give glory to the healing power of Jesus.

The day was surprisingly young in spite of all the happenings, and the sun still high as I climbed the stairs to our bedroom. It felt good to be alone, and I ran a hot bubble bath hoping to wash away some of the confusion I had just experienced.

While submerged in quiet tranquility and self-indulgence, my thoughts drifted back to 1986 and the awesome prophecy that Joel had received: "You have been strong in your own strength, wise in your own wisdom, and I'm going to take that away and cause you to sit at my feet as a baby and teach you My strength, My wisdom and My understanding."

I remember how Joel and I had received the prophecy with great joy. To think that the Lord would turn in our direction with such intensity was a humbling experience. Yet during all our married lives we had wanted to have greater results as ministers and soul winners. Now God was saying in essence that He was aware of our longing and that He was going to prepare us for a job that He had for us to do.

If we had examined those prophetic words more closely, we would have seen the tearing and the rending that was sure to come. But all we saw was the wonderful news that He was going to add to our ministry what was lacking, and we certainly had not dwelt on the word "eclipse." A solar eclipse occurs when the moon covers the sun from the earth with its shadow and for a space of time there is total darkness. There have been times in history that, during such an eclipse, chickens went to roost at midday because they thought it was night.

Well, it couldn't get much darker than being admitted into a mental hospital.

Still searching for some meaning for our predicament, I began to go over the events that had led up to this fateful day. Just two weeks back I had made the mistake of taking Joel to Monroe, Louisiana to his mother's house to convalesce. He had finally gotten past the need for diapers, but the bathroom was still the center of our small world.

We thought being with his mom and being in the house where he grew up would be good therapy. His three sisters, Gayle, Rita and Brenda, live near Mom Hemphill and are very loving and caring people. And I needed to be with them as badly as Joel did. Joel's home church is also on the same street as his mother's house, where he would also get to visit with friends from his childhood. Surely this would be the perfect setting for his recovery.

As we were about to leave home in Nashville, Joel did a foolish thing. He flushed all of his sleeping medicine down the toilet. Since he was going back to a very secure environment, he thought he wouldn't need his medicine to help him sleep. He also saw this as an

act of faith. When we got to his mom's, a few nights of sleeplessness
were expected until he got used to being without medicine.

Prescriptions, hospitals, surgery and psychiatric advice were all different languages for us and had not been much of a factor in our lives.
We were far too busy with our ministry working for the Lord to be
sick. We didn't have time for that. Of course, we didn't vocalize such
a foolish statement but that pretty well summed up our view on illness before it came our way. We sure had a lot to learn. Having no
previous experiences of this kind and no knowledge about sleep dis-
orders, we kept thinking that Joel would settle down and sleep, but
sleep never came.

Then after several days without sleep, Joel's mind began playing
tricks on him. He began to hallucinate, hearing strange noises, such as
motorcycles and dump trucks outside the bedroom window. Of
course they weren't there.

He even tried sleeping on the living room sofa, and his very concerned seventy-four-year-old mom made a pallet on the floor beside
him, hoping to coax him into relaxing enough to fall asleep. But nothing seemed to help, and the days started running into each other until
it finally soaked in on me just how serious things were. I immediately
packed our things so that we could get back to our home in Nashville
with our children and Joel's doctor.

By 3 that afternoon we had cleared Monroe and were headed for
Nashville as fast as we could go. We made the nine-hour drive home,
pulled into our garage around midnight and went straight to bed.
When I awoke the next morning, Joel had a feverish look about him.
His face was flushed, and he still had not slept a wink. Not only was
he not sleeping, but he also wasn't eating. He had hardly taken a bite
of food in days.

Frightened and upset, I tried to get him to drink a glass of milk and
at least take a Stress Tab, a vitamin that he had taken for years, but he
recoiled in fear.

Having no way of knowing what his overworked mind was telling him, I insisted that he at least take the vitamin tablet. I raised my voice, trembling with emotion, "Why won't you take the stupid vitamin?"

Paranoia had taken control of Joel's mind, and little did I know that he thought I was trying to poison him. In frustration I got on the phone and called David, who lives just a couple of miles from us. He was there in minutes as were Joey, Trent and Candy.

Still trying to understand where Joel was coming from, I continued to make an issue out of him not taking his vitamin. I had become almost as irrational as he, and the constant pressure I'd been under was now erupting. Something had to give. Finally, my poor husband took the vitamin reluctantly, convinced that he was committing suicide.

Then he left the den, walked out into the backyard where David followed him. Without our knowledge Joel had picked up a hunting knife and intended to open himself up and remove the "poison" he had just taken.

David had to wrestle the knife away from him. Of course after such a close call, the next move was the hospital. Joel went gladly and signed himself in, hoping they were going to pump his stomach out. We knew we needed professional help. At least the doctor would give Joel something to knock him out and he would get some sleep. The hospital was just a mile from the house, and it comforted me to know he was close.

Still alone with my thoughts, the bubble bath had refreshed me, and despite the bitter reality of our situation, I planned to take advantage of the time Joel spent in the hospital. For ten days someone else carried my burden while I gathered my wits. I did some shopping, spent time with Candy and just watched television.

Every evening at the hospital we were allotted some time with Joel, and the children and I stayed as long as visiting hours allowed. The staff would give Joel a pass and we'd go to the cafeteria for ice cream. He was a sad sight. They had Joel on strong medication, and I was glad because I knew he was getting the rest that he needed so desperately. But his reflexes were slowed down considerably. His hair was brushed straight back, a style he would have never created for himself, and even the sight of little Jasmine, his beloved granddaughter, made him nervous.

He told us that one of the doctors had brought two guitars in one day, and that the patients had a sing-along, and they knew his songs "He's Still Working on Me," "Consider the Lilies" and "Master of the Wind."

Lord, how can this be? I thought. *None of this makes sense. Have You forgotten us?*

When release day came, we were both ready for it. Being alone is fine during the day but when night falls, I sleep sounder with Joel beside me, no matter how sick he is.

Clinical Depression

Refreshed and ready to assume my responsibility, I gathered Joel's belongings and took him home. The first thing I did was draw him a hot bath and see that he styled his hair, shaved and put on the new clothes that I had bought for him. Then we went to a restaurant for a hot meal. It was good to have him back, but what I didn't know that day was that when he walked out of the hospital, full-scale clinical depression came with him.

Heavy medication was the only answer. Antidepressants and potent sleep medicine kept Joel sedated enough to live through it. His waking hours were spent engulfed in fear. He told me later that suicide rode his every thought. His emotions constantly ached like a bad toothache that never let up, and his only relief came when he was asleep. Every so often he would say to me, "Honey, if the Lord doesn't intervene, this is not going to have a happy ending."

My soul chooseth strangling, and death rather than my life. I loathe it. (Job 7:15-16)

I didn't know what he was talking about. When I saw Joel, I didn't just see what he had become—I saw all that he ever was, and suicide had never been a remote possibility with him. When he was well he was very outspoken on that subject and couldn't fathom someone doing such a foolish thing. He had stated that before he would consider suicide as a way out, he'd just change his identity and get lost in California or some other remote area and start a new life.

He had never known that emotional pain could be so severe that there is no escape, no matter where you go, and that dying could seem easier than living. But with emotional problems, you can't die, and your living is joyless, so you just exist and suffer it out.

Here is where many, seeking relief, take matters in their own hands and tragically end their lives. Joel knew, even in his pain and confusion, that death was not the answer; but the only thing that kept him from it was his strong Christian foundation and his knowledge of the Word of God. The enemy, whom the Bible describes as "the thief [who] comes only to steal and kill and destroy" (John 10:10, NIV) would then have done what he had set out to do.

When I say that Joel was in depression, I am saying that he faced every day with a feeling of foreboding and dread from the very moment he awoke. He was too paralyzed emotionally to do anything constructive. All he did from the time he shaved, showered and dressed, which took the greatest of effort on his part, was to come downstairs and collapse on the couch in the den.

I stood by helplessly and watched my strong, optimistic, hard-working husband regress and become fearful and withdrawn. He was like a little boy cowering with his arms up to shield himself from the next blow. He turned to me for comfort. I couldn't be out of his sight. Many days I'd sit and hold his head in my lap and talk soothingly to him as tears ran down his cheeks and remind him how much he was loved by all of us and especially the Lord.

None of it would sink in. Every positive word spoken to Joel at this time was like a candle in the wind: it didn't stand a chance. Even Joel's knowledge of the Bible became distorted and turned to accuse and condemn him. The Bible has been our guideline for living since we were both children. Both of us believe it to be the infallible Word of God. We have used it to measure ourselves by and to direct our actions and our goals. We believe the Bible holds the key to successful living. So naturally Joel began weighing his present situation by his knowledge of the Scriptures, and none of it made sense. He felt as if he must have done something terribly wrong to bring on all this suffering, but he couldn't figure out what it was.

Joel has been an avid reader and has always had a thirst for information. I have laughingly teased him through the years by accusing him of eating newspapers—several a day along with news magazines—yet that was never enough. The evening news on television or radio was always a must for him. Then suddenly all of that stopped.

He became overwhelmed by current events and could no longer handle the news which seemed to be filled with plane crashes, tragedy and human suffering. Not only was he suffering, but the whole world was hurting, and all he had was questions. What had he done? Where had he gone wrong?

His family spent hours, day after day, week after week, trying to reason with him. Candy and her family lived next door, and she spent countless hours talking to her dad, reading him Scriptures and praying with him, to no avail.

Joel's youngest sister, Brenda, was so patient and loving and spent hours on the phone with him. She even came up from Louisiana, as did his mom and other sisters, to pour out love and hope to him. But he could not assimilate a thing we were saying. The conclusion that had lodged in the depths of his soul was that he had miserably failed the Lord and blown his ministerial calling. This was something he could not live with. It had become a fixation in his mind that overshadowed everything else around him. He thought he was eternally lost, without hope, and all he could do was to lie on the couch in the den, stare at the ceiling, cry and break out in a cold sweat.

Many nights I would wake up to find Joel making his way down the hall to his prayer closet, then hear him struggling for his life by repenting over and over again. The pain that we both experienced is indescribable. At times I couldn't bear it anymore and I'd cover my ears so I couldn't hear him. Then I'd fall asleep just to wake up again to the sound of him easing from the bed to go back for another session of repentance.

When I lie down, I say, When shall I arise, and the night be gone?
and I am full of tossings to and fro unto the dawning of the day. . . .
I have sinned. . . . And take away mine inequity. (Job 7:4, 20-21)

Finally, I would step in and forbid him to go pray again. It would nearly tear my heart out. Here was my husband, a man of God, and I heard myself saying, "You cannot go back to that prayer closet again!"

Where are You, Lord? was the silent cry of my heart. *Can anything good come from all this insanity?*

Chapter 16

When Time Stood Still

Walking

Slowly making his way from the car to the pond, my husband resembled an old man stooped with time. He was snugly wrapped in a dark gray overcoat, wool scarf and a felt hat to ward off the March chill. Today marked our first attempt at walking for exercise. I had awakened early to a delightfully brilliant and crisp morning and was eager to get started with my new idea of how to coax Joel off the couch and back into the land of the living.

After he showered, shaved and dressed for the day, he then came downstairs for his daily breakfast of oatmeal and honey. Usually, after breakfast, he would head straight for the couch. I let him nap after the exertion of his morning routine, but by 11 o'clock he was awake and staring at the ceiling again.

This was the moment I had been waiting for, so I bundled him up and off we went. We drove to Cedar Hill Park, where there was a beehive of activity. There is a wide asphalt path, three-fourths of a mile long, that circles a duck pond. This path had been measured and marked for the convenience of walkers, which was what I intended for us to be.

It was a sad sight to watch Joel's feeble effort to circle the pond that first day. We started out walking together, but I soon seized the chance to get my adrenalin pumping again and made four rounds to his one. It felt good to be in the midst of all the hustle and bustle and to fill my lungs with the fresh morning air.

The sounds of Canadian geese honking, clearing the way for landings and takeoffs, were just another reminder that the park was teeming with life. These sounds made me feel alive. The mallards were simply gorgeous, glistening under the sun in effervescent hues of greens and blues, as cotton ball clouds floated lazily overhead.

Other walkers were friendly, smiling as they passed: some were in pairs chatting as fast as they walked. Others were in their own private musical worlds as they were plugged into their headphones, CD players and transistor radios. *Ah,* I thought, *this is the tonic we both need.*

After that first day of exercise and fresh air, Cedar Hill Park, only one mile from our house, became a regular part of therapy for us. Joel and I came to look forward to going there so much that we rarely missed a day of walking. It was so important to us that weather conditions made little difference. We had thick, warm jumpsuits that we had worn for fishing and hunting in extreme winter. We took umbrellas and wore slickers if it rained. During our exercise routine, I was determined that Joel was not going to forget who he was and what his life was about.

As we trudged along I would sometimes walk by his side and talk, filling his mind with positive thoughts of all the good things that God had poured down upon our lives. He would smile and agree, but within five minutes he seemed to forget all the good things we had shared and his demeanor was again one of depression.

On one such occasion I remember telling him that when men are enlisted in the army, the first part of their training strips them of their own identity. Their heads are shaved, their clothes are all identical and they go through grueling weeks of conditioning and responding to commands. They are no longer their own; they cannot do as they please when they please. They belong to Uncle Sam and they take orders from those in command.

These soldiers are told when and where to eat and sleep. It is a time of restructuring the soldiers' lives and the way they think. They are treated as though they have no wills of their own. But it is for the purpose of being built back up as good soldiers who are disciplined and who can obey orders within a moment's notice and carry them out. That day I reminded Joel that he was a soldier of the cross and this time was very important for us. I felt that the reason our ordeal was so severe was because the Lord was preparing to promote him to a higher command, and he must be able to carry out the will of the Father.

We both were learning the meaning of demoralization, since the bathroom now ruled our lives. Everything evolved around his trips to the commode. It reminded me of so many verses from the Old Testament referring to the dung heap. That seemed to be right where we were, but we continued to walk at the park daily, while Joel kept one eye on the port-a-john.

About a year after our jaunts around the pond, we graduated to walking along the road that wound two miles through the park. That was a happy day and we felt we had reached a major step up.

Playing Games

Walking was not the only method I used to try and motivate Joel. We also played games. We played every day. I got so sick of games that I thought I would go mad. Anyone that came by the house was immediately snagged to play with Joel.

Since Candy lived next door to us, Kent's son Josh, who was in his early teens, became a regular and burned away many summertime hours playing with Joel. Meanwhile, I was constantly trying to come up with ways to fill our days with some sort of activity. The pain of all that dull emptiness and wasted hours still smarts as I recall that period.

One hot summer afternoon, Joel was on the couch sleeping soundly and I was stir-crazy. I decided I'd just get in the car, drive out to the mall and walk around. As I was backing out of the driveway, little Jasmine, not quite four years old, crossed the front yard, so I stopped and rolled down the window.

"Where you going, MiMi?" called Jasmine.

"Honey, I'm going to the mall for a few minutes," I replied.

"Can I go?" she pleaded.

"No, baby, you don't like to go to the mall, so you stay here, I'll be back soon."

Then she clung to the door and sobbed in desperation, "But MiMi, I don't have anything to do." Her pleas, her face and her tears mirrored every pain I felt, and I knew I was taking her with me.

I said, "Go tell your mother you're going with me, and I'll wait for you."

She came back, hopped in the car and we went down the road for a couple of miles, only to get stuck in a traffic jam caused by highway repair. So I just turned the car around and we drove to Cedar Hill Park to say hello to the familiar ducks, which I had come to know so well. This was much better than a trip to the mall for Jasmine.

Today I now realize that I had to endure those quiet, silent days in order to learn from God. The Bible verse, "Be still, and know that I am God" (Psalm 46:10; see Exodus 14:13-14), became very real to me. Our lives had come to a dead stop. It seemed as though time stood still.

Going for Drives

Some afternoons I would take Joel for a drive, simply trying to kill time. We drove to many of the towns of Middle Tennessee and made several trips to Joelton and drove along the highway next to the Cumberland River. There we'd park a while, watching Ole Man River roll along, then turn around and make our snail-pace trip back home, trying to make it last as long as we could. Several times we drove to Ashland City, looking at the scenery, or to Dickson. But the trips began to torture me. They reminded me that I had no destination and no deadline, so I scratched those drives "to nowhere" from our miniature list of things to do.

On rare occasions Joel would try his hand at driving the car, and my spirits would rise. *Maybe he's coming out of it*, I would think. But it was not to be.

One morning he got behind the wheel and pulled the car out of the garage, but his judgement and his reflexes were distorted, and he scraped the front end of the car trying to clear the garage.

I said nothing.

Then he backed into the brick wall. I remained quiet, thinking things would improve, but they didn't. Next, we left our driveway for the main street, a busy four-lane road. Joel pulled in front of the on-coming traffic.

"Watch out!" I screamed as Joel swerved, just missing a car.

We heard brakes screeching and felt our blood pressures rising. When we finally gained our composure, Joel looked at me sternly and said, "Honey, you're going to have to quit hollering at me."

"If you think you're mad now, just wait until you wake up from this depression and find out that I've let you tear up this new car," I told him.

Joel has always been the handyman around our house. If something went wrong, he fixed it. But when he was in depression it seemed as though he forgot how to do anything. The weather stripping came off the door from the garage into the house, so I proceeded to put an-other one on. It was not a simple task for me. The metal strip, which held a flexible rubber blade that allows one to open and close the door while at the same time filling the gap between door and floor, had to be screwed to the bottom part of the door. I struggled and worked with it for an hour or so, while Joel just sat there watching me like a helpless old man.

When I finally got the door fixed, I was pleased with my labors and, looking up from the floor, I patted the door proudly, grinned and said, "That should do until my husband gets back."

Joel just grinned too, and I got up and went on to something else.

Sewing

Walking and playing games were just two of the routines we used to fill up our empty days. Another lifesaver for me was my sewing ma-chine, which I rediscovered. I used to love to sew when I was young and went from making doll clothes when I was small to making my own clothes as a teenager. By the time I married, the largest part of my wardrobe was of my own creation and design.

Sewing had been handed down to me from both my grandmothers and my mother. All three generations relished working with fabric. But my busy schedule over the past two decades had crowded out my love for sewing. Now I had the time.

Looking back I now know that the Lord was making us "lie down in green pastures" (Psalm 23:2), not just to rediscover the sewing machine but to find ourselves again.

The biggest part of our running around in the last years had been of our own doing and not for ministry. We'd worn ourselves out running back and forth to our farm in Monroe, Louisiana, a nine-hour trip each way. We would come home to Nashville from an exhausting performance tour, get off the bus and into a car or into Joel's truck and escape to the farm. Then when our concert schedule wound down in late October, Joel would have hunting trips lined up all across the United States, from Colorado and Texas to Kansas and Louisiana. I remember one year that Joel and I made seven trips to Mexico to fish at the bass camp.

All those miles were road miles too. We put our bodies through much wear and tear on the highway, and then we went out in the fishing boats with the Mexican guides, who took us over miles of choppy waters at breakneck speed.

I remember telling Joel one winter, when we were supposed to be resting because our singing year was up, "Honey, do you realize we have not spent three nights in the same place in months?" The short stays had become our lifestyle. Perhaps that is why the abrupt stop in our life was so hard on us.

I even remember how I wished that he'd break a leg on one of those hunts so we would have been forced to sit still. All that running here and there was killing me. Joel loved hunting wild game and went after deer, elk, alligator, turkey, pheasant, sheep and ducks. We have many trophies on the walls to prove his passion.

But the cause of this abrupt stop in our activity was not a broken leg, which can only take a few months to heal; this was something far more complex, and we had no idea how much longer it might continue. The sad thing is that we had no clues as to how to settle down and live a normal life. But we were learning.

I had never realized before how the Lord uses time to heal. Somehow magic and fantasy got all mixed with the truth of God's Word in my mind. I wanted Him to wave His magic wand and fix all of our brokenness, and I wanted that healing immediately. No one wants to wait on anything anymore. We live in a world of instant gratification and quick service on everything from breakfast to oil changes. I had become very impatient, but the Lord knew how to fix that. It did not matter to Him that I was a woman of the '90s with a microwave, fax machine and a remote control TV. He knew what was best for me, that I needed renewed strength and a renewed mind, and He had just the remedy for that—*be still and wait*.

In the New Testament, James says, "The trying of your faith worketh patience" (1:3) and to "let patience have her perfect work, that ye may be perfect and entire, wanting nothing" (1:4). Not only was I about to have my strength renewed, but I was also about to learn the definition of patience firsthand. The Lord set out to perfect Joel and me, but He did not make it happen overnight.

My poor little sewing machine. I attacked it with fervor and ran it day and night, as I worked out my frustration. I became lost in a world of eyelets, ruffles and ribbons, as I made scores of outfits for my two granddaughters. I sewed dresses, petticoats, pantaloons, bonnets and tams, going through miles and miles of lovely materials.

All the while, Joel lay tucked beneath a blanket on the couch and watched as I planned, cut and created as I never had before . . . and we waited.

My Surgery
January 14, 1992

"Mrs. Hemphill, you need a complete hysterectomy."

Those were the words I was hearing from my doctor, who had been my gynecologist for the past eighteen years. He continued, "The tumors I found last year are growing rapidly, and one is as big as my fist."

His words filled me with dread, but I knew that this could not be put off any longer and a date was set for my operation. Once again both our families were called, and they came without hesitation. And once again I found myself back at Nashville Memorial Hospital for major surgery, but this time it was for me.

Joel was still wrestling with his demons of depression. His sisters took turns caring for him at home while I was hospitalized. Mom Hemphill came prepared to stay with us for a week or so until I was back on my feet.

Everyone was surprised at how quickly I bounced back, and I was pleased with myself for having braved another storm without my husband to lean on. Before surgery I had become quite resolved to the way things were with him and had doggedly pressed forward with our daily routine with the hope of finding the light at the end of the tunnel.

After surgery something happened to me that I wasn't expecting. A strong case of hopelessness took over and plunged me headlong into a low emotional valley. Oscillating mood swings are commonly connected with this type of surgery, but when it happened, I was caught off guard. I felt as close to rock bottom as I had ever been in my life. It was as though being weak physically had opened up a highway into my spirit, giving the enemy full access to torment my mind. A little imp seemed to be perched upon my shoulder whispering doom and gloom into my ear, and I was too weak to fight back. Something had gone out of me during surgery that left me vulnerable to Satan's attacks.

As rough and unsettling as things had been up until now, I had coped pretty well, believing that the Lord would not let more come upon us than we could bear. But now my faith was being tested severely. For over a year I had been Joel's connection with the real world; consequently, he looked to me for everything, even such normal tasks as taking him to the barber to get a haircut.

As long as I was near him, Joel was at ease, but he could not bear to have me out of his sight. We laugh about it now and say we were velcroed together; but while it was happening, it was no laughing matter. We both had sunk into a deep, dark hole with no light to show us the way out.

Many nights at prayer time, all I could do was cry or sit before the Lord in stunned disbelief. Other times, especially if Joel were having what we called a "bathroom night," I would lie in my prayer closet and beg the Lord to come to our rescue. Many nights I prayed myself hoarse. Almost every night, when we started for our separate prayer closets, Joel would clutch me in desperation and with pleading eyes beg me to pray for him. There was no place for me to hide, nowhere to run to escape my burden.

The gamut my emotions swung, like a pendulum, dashed hope against hope until my internal feelings were raw. Through all my Christian walk and in all I had learned about the Lord, I could not put this crazy jigsaw puzzle of our lives into place. Nothing seemed to connect. From childhood I had relied on the Lord, and He had rescued me many times in desperate situations. The Lord had always been there for me, and now it seemed as if He were nowhere to be found. The silence of unanswered prayer was deafening. My faith was tested to the core and I felt alone.

Joel had always been a tower of strength to me, but his strength had melted away like hot wax. Now he leaned on me and I was doing my all to lean on Jesus. The Lord was wanting me to learn that He was my source, not Joel. If I were going to get out of this unscathed, it would be by His hand and through His tender mercies. "Blessed is he, whosoever shall not be offended in me" (Matthew 11:6).

But Lord, I countered, *I'm hurting and You could fix it if You would.*

I had no idea that Joel was struggling with suicide, but I kept assuring him that the Lord knew where we were and would come to our rescue, while silently my soul kept crying out in desperation, *Where are You, Lord?*

Yet unbeknownst to me, He was there all the time. It was similar to the tale of the little Indian boy that I read when I was a child. According to the story, the day he turned twelve years old, his father took him deep into the forest and left him to spend the night alone. If he could stay in the same spot where his father left him all night, midst the frightening sounds of howling wolves, screaming panthers, screech owls, rustling leaves and other unknowns of the nocturnal world, he would be made a brave of the tribe.

What the little boy didn't know was that his father, after walking away, slipped back and stayed the night with him, hidden behind a big tree just a few feet away. He was there in case there was real danger. The same was true of my Heavenly Father, even though I was in fear and trembling as I'm sure the little Indian was.

I stand amazed at how well the Lord does things. His understanding is as far above ours as the heavens are above the earth. He loves us too much to leave us the way we are. He teaches us His strength through adversity. To prove Himself to us, He sometimes has to strip away all the earthly foundations that we stand on. He is the only true Rock.

Once we turn our will over to Him, He gently draws us into His presence and holds us tenderly as we weep in His loving arms. "My grace is sufficient for thee: for my strength is made perfect in weakness" (2 Corinthians 12:9).

My understanding at the time was very finite, yet I still trusted the Lord. I knew He was ordering our footsteps, but my shades of doubt caused fear, and my personal endeavor of maturing without Joel as a support was painful.

The Fallen Tree

Our situation was not unlike what happens when a giant tree is felled in the forest. Once the tall timber falls, the little saplings that once stood in its shadow have full access to the sun and rain and plenty of space to grow. "Hew down the tree, and cut off his branches, shake off his leaves, and scatter his fruit. . . . Nevertheless leave the stump of his roots in the earth" (Daniel 4:14-15).

Joel was the tree. I was the sapling. Now that Joel had been cast down with his illnesses, I had been granted all the space I needed to mature. My decision concerning our affairs became the only decision, for better or worse. My old excuse that Joel could do it better no longer covered my inaction.

Like it or not, I had been placed in the driver's seat with the wheel in my hands. Before his illness Joel had been a perfectionist, demanding perfection from himself as well as those who worked with him, including me and the children. So, rather than take a chance of making a mistake, most of the time we left the decision-making up to him. Joel had been a driven man, working day and night. Even when he played he worked. When hunting season came Joel found as much satisfaction erecting the camp house or building the tree stands as doing the actual hunting. I sometimes felt that the sport was just an excuse for him to do more work.

In all fairness, Joel had often encouraged me to expand my horizons, to be more independent. But the fact that we had married when I was seventeen and had our first child when I was eighteen brought me in closer to home. By the time I was twenty-one, I not only was the mother of three small children but the mother of a church family as well. Somehow during those early years of mothering and ministering, my personal identity seemed to have gotten lost in the shuffle. Now the Lord was calling me forth to be all that I could be.

He knew my capabilities. He knew that at some point my inner strength, fueled by His power, could do these things. Still, God gave me plenty of room to make mistakes and time to find myself.

Initially I fought the change. It isn't easy to break old habits and thought paths that one has followed for years. I cried and I fretted, but the Lord was with me and I continued to grow.

The Piano

Soon after my surgery, an old urge returned. I felt an overwhelming desire to try my hand at the piano again. I could chord a bit, but never was accomplished enough to sit down at our beautiful white Kawai grand and play a tune. We'd had the piano several years, and I doubt that I had tried to play it more than a half dozen times. Because my musical knowledge was very limited, just a few chords here and there, I was extremely embarrassed for anyone to hear me. Since the piano was located in the living room, I had no way of closing myself off to find out what I did know.

I fought my urge to go to the piano for several days. No one was in the house but Joel, but I still thought it would aggravate him if I went to the wrong key change or made a mistake. It's amazing how long it takes for our minds to comprehend change. But Joel was in another world, paralyzed by unreal fears, and he could have cared less what I did on the piano.

So I slowly familiarized myself with the keyboard again, very timidly at first. I found a home-study lesson book and pounded away for hours a day, improving my skills and learning how to accompany myself as I sang.

Before long, the piano became a great source of joy to Joel and me, filling the house with music. We had stacks of songbooks from the past, wonderful old songs from the church that we had loved and cherished from childhood. These are what I practiced on.

The piano soon made me abandon my sewing machine, and I found an incredible source of joy in making music. This would later be a major key in unlocking the way to Joel's and my restoration.

Chapter 17

Hang in There, Baby!

Mental Hospital No. 2
March 18, 1992

"Would LaBreeska Hemphill please come to the phone." I was being paged while buying groceries at Sam's.

"Mom, this is Candy. Trent just called me from the doctor's office. He says Dad is definitely on too much medication, and he wants to put him in the hospital and try to wean him off as much medication as he can and replace it with something lighter."

"That's fine with me," I replied, feeling as if my load had just gotten lighter.

So now it was back to another psychiatric ward, and all I could feel at that point was a sense of relief. The doctor that Joel had been seeing was a dedicated young psychiatrist who kept trying to find a medical cure for Joel's depression. When Joel pressed him for help, the doctor would then try a different prescription until Joel was taking seven antidepressants at one time: Prozac, Xanax, Lithium, Zoloft, Wellbutrin, Haloperidol and Halcion.

After Joey and Trent came to realize how much medicine their dad was consuming, they began searching for another psychiatrist and found Dr. Joseph Fishbein, a much older and more experienced doctor.

That morning Trent had taken his dad for his first visit, and after consultation, the concerned doctor called him a "walking drugstore." Dr. Fishbein wondered how Joel was standing on his feet and described him as "looking like a zombie," with "blunted facial expression."

In other words, the lights were on but no one was at home. Joel was immediately admitted into the Parthenon Pavilion, a modern facility

located in downtown Nashville. This kind old doctor was a
God-send, but although he altered Joel's prescriptions significantly,
Joel's depression didn't alter a bit.

One of the most meaningful contributions Dr. Fishbein made to
our peace of mind was the search for a medical remedy for Joel's
loose bowels. With much trial and error we landed on the simple solution of Metamucil, an over-the-counter medication that we thought
to be just a laxative. However, it caused Joel to have a formed stool
and brought a semblance of normalcy to our lives by cutting his trips
to the bathroom in half.

All through Joel's illness, we received a steady stream of encouraging cards, letters and calls from a multitude of concerned and caring
friends. These were reminders to "hang in there," and that we were
not forgotten. Their concern was a great comfort to us.

Joel's sisters wrote almost every week with an outpouring of love,
as did other members of the family. Churches and Sunday school
classes from various denominations, who had been touched by our
music, sent get-well cards to remind us that they were "still praying."
There were also times when ministers and pastors would call and give
Joel scriptures or pray for him over the phone.

Pastor David Mayo called many Sunday mornings before service
from Monroe, Louisiana to find out how we were and to assure us
that his church was still praying and expecting a miracle. Brother
George Guy, a very dear and longtime minister friend from Louisiana, never gave up, and even called a three-day fast that same year just
for Joel. He included many of the churches where he'd held meetings,
then he and Pastor Merle Ewing flew to Nashville to anoint Joel and
pray for him.

Even with all of this, our dilemma was unchanged, and I had come
to the end of my "bungee cord." There seemed to be no more bouncing back for me. Forced by circumstances from my secure world into
one of stark reality, I was left dangling somewhere in between. I had
been under the false assumption that, as a Christian, I was somehow

insulated from heartache and pain. But the raw truth is, as Job so aptly put it, "Man that is born of a woman is of few days, and full of trouble" (Job 14:1). Now I was finding out, just as Job had, that pain and suffering are a part of life and are essential in the Christian walk, just as dying is a part of living. We all come into this world with a death warrant on our heads, and the sooner we prepare for that journey into the vast unknown, the better we are prepared to live life to the fullest. I had prepared for eternity but not for suffering. Well, prepared or not, I was in the middle of it, hanging by a thread.

In June I was summoned to perform jury duty, but because of Joel's continued depression, Dr. Fishbein wrote the following letter to request that I be excused, and I was.

> To Whom It May Concern:
> Mrs. Hemphill has been summoned to appear for jury duty in your court. Her husband Joel W. Hemphill is under my medical care for a severe psychiatric problem requiring major psychiatric medication and attention. Mrs. Hemphill is the sole party in charge of his care, and she can only be away from him for a short period of time without it having catastrophic effect on his therapy. It is my opinion that her attendance to his psychiatric needs is paramount and she should be excused from jury duty.
> Yours truly,
> Joseph H. Fishbein, M.D.

As kind and attentive as family and friends were, I knew that at some point they would have to get on with their lives and leave us alone. Even our children were so busy with making a living and raising a family that it would not be fair to burden them with our daily struggles.

All this had really been hard on them. They all had their own special rapport with their dad and depended on his input and counsel in many areas of their lives. Through the years it has given me a lot of satisfaction to see Joel and his boys get their heads together, talking and planning. Buses were a mainstay of conversation most of the time, as Joel gave them pointers on leasing and taught them many facets of the business. They have since taken that knowledge and added their own expertise and brought the bus leasing business to a height that Joel never dreamed of.

Candy too was strongly affected by her father's illness. She had been the apple of his eye from the moment he first saw her in the hospital nursery. We were so proud of her when she came into her own in the field of Christian music, displaying her talent for singing and writing gospel songs. It has been a joy to watch her mature and develop with her dad's tutoring her on her writing and her stage performance.

Before her father got sick, she had leaned on him heavily, needing his endorsement. Now seeing her dad, who in her eyes was the epitome of strength, become fragile and weak left Candy confused. She carried him heavy on her heart with a lot of prayer and words of encouragement, and she often read scriptures to him. It was like a role reversal. She was strong and supportive, just like her brothers, but this could not go on indefinitely.

Not having their father's strength and guidance to rely upon left a void that no one else could fill. Like it or not, our children stood at the helm of their own ships and they were having to find their own way. Without a doubt, our world had fallen apart.

Still Searching for Answers in Job

The big question is: Do we *blame* God or do we recognize His sovereignty, and say as Job said, "Naked came I out of my mother's womb, and naked shall I return thither: the LORD gave, and the LORD hath taken away; blessed be the name of the LORD" (1:21)?

Job and his wife had learned a valuable lesson, and now I found myself enrolled in the same school, taking the same course. Job's and his wife's pain, in comparison, was far greater than ours. But I was convinced that ours was meant to bring about the same results. Maybe that is why I kept reviewing their situation. I was looking for answers.

There is not a lot of mention about Job's wife in the Bible. The contest seemed entirely between righteous Job and the forces of evil. But when his wife saw him sitting there on the ashes of all she held dear, including the loss of her ten beautiful children, the sight of him must have been more than she could bear.

There sat Job in a heap of rubble, covered from the crown of his head to the soles of his feet with putrid, runny sores, scratching himself with a piece of broken pottery (Job 2:8). Sometimes the most unlikely things trigger an outburst of our pent-up emotions. I cannot help but believe that it wasn't just the sight of Job but the piece of pottery that stirred her emotions. Perhaps it signified all that had been and pinpointed where they were at this very instant—shattered and hopeless with nothing left.

Job's wife lost it. She must have felt that God had turned against them and wondered why Job was still hanging on—and to what? With all of her children gone, how could there be anything left to live for? She knew more than anyone that Job was a righteous man and had lived an honest and sinless life, but she was hurting. She wanted out and begged him to do something, anything to get them out of God's spotlight. The words of Job's wife have always made me cringe and clearly show that her pain had crowded out all sense of reasoning when she told him to "curse God, and die" (2:9).

I cannot imagine anyone coming to that place. But having learned a little more about the heart of God, His infinite wisdom and mercy, I have hopes that her insanity was covered by His grace. Perhaps she was not responsible.

I have heard many sermons on Job, his test of faith and all that he lost. But we must remember that when the fire was turned up to the intensity that it was, his wife was still there, reeling from each blow. Those ten children that died were her babies too. Her loss was of such a magnitude that it staggers the mind.

I also believe that her "giving up" was the acid test of Job's integrity toward God. She was all that he had left on the face of the earth. How could he make it without her? Yet, knowing that she might leave and that he would be totally alone without help and without pity, there was no hesitation. Righteous Job still chose God!

Finding the Way Out

My husband had also made this choice, and while reading the little books of Bible promises, he found what he thought to be the ticket out of the living hell that he was mired in. He clung to this verse tenaciously. "He that cometh to God must believe that he is, and that he is a rewarder of them that diligently seek him" (Hebrews 11:6).

Joel had found the solution, and it was simple.

Did he believe in God? Of course he did. Then he must also believe that God would reward our diligent effort to find Him in the midst of all our pain and confusion. This spark of hope found lodging in the depths of Joel's spirit and began to flame up into faith.

The hardest part for me was not knowing how much longer it would last and how much farther I could carry on. At what point would I snap under the stress? I had no doubt that Joel was going to come out of this storm a stronger man. The spiritual encounter that we had experienced in 1986 left me knowing that the Lord had a plan for his life. Until now I'd felt that I was included in that plan, but I was ready to confess that I was at the end of my endurance and facing the possibility that I might not make it. There was nothing left inside me to draw from.

Little did I know that this was the place where the Lord wanted me—not my power nor might, but on His Spirit. "Fear thou not; for I am with thee: be not dismayed; for I am thy God: I will strengthen thee; yea, I will help thee; yea, I will uphold thee with the right hand of my righteousness" (Isaiah 41:10).

"But *when*, Lord?"

Dr. Fishbein's report taken from his journal of Joel's 1992 office visits sheds light on the pain of his unstable emotional condition, but it tells nothing of *mine.*

Dr. Joseph H. Fishbein, MD
Psychiatrist for Joel W. Hemphill
Patient in Parthenon Pavilion Psychiatric Hospital:

March 18, 1992-March 25, 1992

Office visits:
  March 30, 1992: First office visit
  April 3, 1992: Depressed, can't travel, no control of bowel movements
  April 10, 1992: Improving, planning a trip to Louisiana
  May 13, 1992: Returned from Louisiana, still depressed
  May 27, 1992: Agoraphobic, avoiding people and crowds
  June 20, 1992: Family reunion, sing along, more initiative
  July 24, 1992: Each day an ordeal
  August 7, 1992: Went to Monroe, fearful of losing grip on reality, paranoid thoughts
  August 21, 1992: Dramatic improvement, sense of humor returning
  August 24, 1992: Recurrent depression

The ground beneath my feet continued to feel like shifting sand, but with prayer and praise I held on to the Lord, and He was my solid rock. "I will love thee, O LORD, my strength. The LORD is my rock, and my fortress, and my deliverer; my God, my strength, in whom I will trust" (Psalm 18:1-2).

I was learning that His grace is sufficient, and that He was all I needed.

Hast thou not known? hast thou not heard, that the everlasting God, the LORD, the Creator of the ends of the earth, fainteth not, neither is weary? there is no searching of his understanding. He giveth power to the faint; and to them that have no might he increaseth strength. (Isaiah 40:28-29)

Chapter 18

Mexico

October 21, 1992

As we cleared the runway, our plane ascended into the heavens, penetrating the dense clouds that hovered over Nashville. I shut my eyes, letting my head fall back on the seat, and took a deep breath. I had made it.

I was actually on the plane and we were airborne. Up until the last moment, I'd halfway expected something to interfere with my plans and keep me from making this trip. Sure enough, after painfully tearing myself away from Joel, with just enough time left to get to the airport, my young and inexperienced secretary at that time dropped me off at the wrong level.

I realized it when I couldn't find a place to check my bags, and glanced up just in time to see the taillights of our car fading out of sight. With that, I ran up the stairs, luggage in tow, to the ticket counter and then to the departure gate. I was a nervous wreck by the time I boarded the plane, out of breath and fully convinced that Murphy's Law was working overtime. It was a relief when I finally collapsed into my seat.

But now all was well and I was soaring through the air on silver wings, and as the plane continued to climb, so did my spirits. Then like a flash we broke through the thick maze of clouds and there, to my surprise, was the sun in all its dazzling splendor. What a welcome sight. The sunlight burst across the sky, filling every visible mile as far as the eye could see, and came splashing through my window, dousing me with the warmth of its radiant beauty.

The panorama of the stratosphere was absolutely breathtaking and made me feel as though I had a hug from the Lord. As we glided through those celestial regions, the drone of the airplane engines numbed my painful memories and my thoughts turned reflective.

We had been dealing with Joel's illness and all the baggage that had accompanied it for almost two years now. I had hung in there, giving him my undivided attention and doing all that I could do to make him well. Still there was no change, and I was running on empty.

Joey and Trent had noticed that my twenty-four-hour-a-day vigilance had taken its toll, and they had a growing concern for my health as well their father's. They feared that I might become permanently affected by the burden of Joel's constant care. The emotional drain had been exhausting: it was like walking an endless tightrope.

Today though, my heart was full of gratitude toward our two precious sons. Not even a week ago Trent had said, "Mom, you've got to get away. You've been under the load too long, and we don't want to lose you too."

Joey spoke up. "Trent and I are going to pay for you to go on a trip. Just decide where you'd like to go, what would give you some joy, and we'll pay the plane fare." He continued, "Now Mom, this has to be planned immediately. Don't wait and don't tell Dad until we've made all the arrangements or you won't go."

Even though this was completely unexpected, my mind started traveling as they spoke. I immediately thought of the fishing camp in Mexico and Rita and James Mayo. Oh, to be there once again with Rita, my sister-in-law and dear friend.

In my mind's eye I could envision the cascading hot pink bougainvillea at the entrance to the camp. And I could see the lovely hibiscus in varying shades of red, orange and lavender greeting me with an explosion of color. The flowers were always an uplifting sight after the long and tiring trip down on their bus.

The camp lies sprawling along the bank of a freshwater lake teeming with bass. The tropical environment is a great place to escape Middle Tennessee's winter months. The sun is warm and inviting and the breeze always seems to be blowing from the lake. And I love hearing the musical inflections of the Spanish language that come from Romana, the head cook, as she issues orders to her assistants. Those pleasant sounds are accompanied by tantalizing aromas that waft out of the kitchen all day long.

Pure tranquility is what it is.

And there are the many friendships. Missionaries Jerry and Pat Wiley live there, as do camp managers Raphael and Maria.

My heart smiled as my mind drifted to that wonderful spot where Joel and I had spent so many cherished days. The possibility of being there again filled me with hope.

Quickly I decided to go to Mexico with Rita and James if they were going any time soon and had room for me. Rushing home from my sons' bus shop just a couple blocks from the house, I found Joel still asleep on the sofa. I went into the office to make the phone call. To my great joy the Mayos were headed for Mexico in a few days, and Joel's sister, Anna Gayle, volunteered to drive to Nashville and stay with him in my absence.

I was to fly to Houston, where Rita would meet me, and we would spend the day shopping. From there we would fly to the border where a vehicle would take us the remaining 200 miles into Mexico to the fishing lodge. This was excitement to my long-dulled senses. I was actually making plans again. Everything was happening fast. I knew that Joel was not going to take this well—and he didn't.

He and Anna Gayle, just two years apart in age, had always been close, but at this point in his life he thought no one else could take my place. However, the boys were adamant about my getting away, and I desperately needed the break. Now here I was on the plane.

All the right connections were made. Rita met me at the airport in Houston. It was like a dose of good medicine to see her again. We hugged and laughed and cried at the same time. It was a gorgeous day and a feeling of lightheartedness was like salve on my threadbare emotions. All my troubles for the moment were several hundred miles behind, and for a few short days I was out of my prison.

Shopping with Rita is a trip in itself. She always has the poor and needy of Mexico in mind. It isn't unusual to go into a shoe store with her, simply to look around and leave with *ninety* pairs of shoes. More than a few times we've gone into a store, any store, and if there is a sale table with candy, backpacks, tennis shoes or anything that she can take to the children in Mexico, she'll come out with all of it. Soon we'll have several sales clerks helping us to the car, packing the trunk and stuffing the backseat to the ceiling with treasures for the under-privileged.

On one occasion, when she was in Nashville for a visit, I took her to the big monthly flea market at the state fairgrounds. One of the first vendors we approached was selling socks. Rita bought all that he had—hundreds of pairs. Our shopping in Houston that day was equally and deliciously bizarre. Because of their business, Rita and James have access to the wholesale markets, so we made the rounds. When the day was over, we had so much loot that we hardly had a place to sit in Rita's big Suburban.

Angel of Mercy

Rita is a missionary at heart. Her family's fishing camp in Mexico was an opportunity that she seized to make a difference in that impover-ished land. For many years she has tediously gathered and "exported" tons of clothes, Bibles and food supplies across the border in the bays of the busses that carry sport fishermen and hunters to "El Campo."

Once she gets to camp, she then travels hundreds of miles in old pickup trucks and four-wheel drive vehicles, searching out isolated villages. She has entered countless dirt-floored houses with walls made of sticks and plastered with cow manure. Most of those shanties have holes in the floor where fires burn in the wintertime as the fami-lies' only source of heat.

Many of the children are covered with sores and head lice, suffer-ing from malnutrition and in need of medical attention. When any of our family goes to Mexico with Rita, we know that we will be going with her on these missions of mercy, passing out clothes, food and tracts. This trip was no exception.

It wasn't long after reaching the fishing camp and catching up on a little rest that Rita and I took off for parts unknown. She was happy to have me back in Mexico and talked nonstop, filling me in on all the latest happenings. She was so full and eager as she shared the latest miracles of God's grace as He had led her from one family to another to minister to them. She shared the good news that there were now nine native pastors and eighteen small churches scattered throughout the villages of that region. She told me of the plans of Jerry and Pat Wiley to build an orphanage and Bible school on the thirty-five acres which they had recently purchased in a village not far from the fishing lodge.

Rita recounted in detail the many cases that she had uncovered in out-of-the-way villages, poor families who hadn't had a decent meal in days; or others in need of specific items, such as an elderly person needing a potty chair or wheelchair that she would just happen to have with her that day.

She was the most excited about building a block house with indoor plumbing for a blind woman and her family. She had taken money that others had contributed, along with her own offerings, and was having a house constructed on a concrete slab. She laughed and told me how the whole village came and stood in line to look at the shower. They had never seen one.

Our first stop that day was to check on two elderly sisters, one blind and the other bedfast. She was lying on a piece of plastic curtain on a filthy bed in her own fecal matter. We found the blind sister behind the house trying to wash out some clothes by hand in a big washtub.

They were thrilled to hear Rita's voice. She hugged them and told them she'd brought "java" and food and seemed not to notice the filth and overpowering stench. When Rita had first found these poor women, the rats had had command of the house. The pair were help-less to do anything about it—but Rita wasn't.

After we'd visited a while, leaving the things we'd brought for them, we took off for another village further in the hills. It's a good thing we had a four-wheel-drive vehicle that day, because we found ourselves in a monsoon-like downpour; and we slipped and slid our way across near-impenetrable terrain to reach the village. I held my breath as Rita fearlessly accelerated through deep mud holes.

When we drove as far as possible, trying to reach a particular hut, we got out and walked the remainder of the way. Mud that was ankle deep finally pulled my sandals off. This was a far cry from the asphalt path Joel and I used to circle in Cedar Hill Park back home. Here it was easy for an American to count her blessings.

Some young village girls came out with a bucket of fresh water to wash our feet. Water is a priceless commodity for these people. Here it is hauled in on a truck once or twice a week. When we finally reached the hut, there, on a small cot attached to the stick wall of a one-room shanty, sat a lady not as old as myself. She rocked back and forth. She had been stricken with an illness that had left her paralyzed from the waist down. A small, naked boy about the age of two was running around in the mud. It was obvious to my eyes that he suffered from malnutrition.

Nearby in the yard sat the grandfather in an old makeshift chair. The mud was nearly as deep inside the hut as it was outside—still ankle-deep. This poor Christian woman was imprisoned in her own home. She could not help herself or the infant grandchild that her daughter had left at her door. All she could do was rock and pray. I've never seen a more hopeless sight. Rita, full of compassion and ever an angel of mercy, had found this woman and attempted to relieve her misery by bringing food and clothing. I left that place with a pain inside my heart.

The last stop that day was another construction site. Rita had been blessed to build four block houses for some of the most needy cases. This one was at the top of the list. It would soon be home for a large family of mentally challenged children, including one child with a cleft palate. They lived in the poorest of conditions.

Back at the fishing camp that night, my exhaustion made sleep come easy. But the following day I couldn't shake the many scenes of despair that I had witnessed. So many people were in straits of helplessness and hopelessness, with an almost unlivable environment and yet, with practically no creature comforts, they survived and were glad to be alive.

Much to Be Thankful For!

I realized that God had arranged this entire trip for me to put things in the proper perspective. After my excursion with Rita into a third-world lifestyle, my problems back home took on a new light. By the time I had boarded the plane and was homeward bound, I saw things much more clearly.

My home, which in some ways had become my prison, was plush and comfortable, loaded with luxuries that we Americans so take for granted. Now I had something to compare my trials to, and in view of all that I had just witnessed, my load suddenly became lighter.

As we got closer to Nashville, I became anxious to see my husband. It is a good feeling to know you are needed and loved, and that I was. But that was not all the emotion I was feeling. A warm rush of heartfelt gratitude welled up inside me. I began to count my blessings anew. How thankful I was that Joel was still alive and how glad I was to have someone to come home to that loved me more than anything in the world.

That made me feel good and I actually found myself smiling.

Chapter 19

*A Time
to Heal*

November 8, 1992

It was Sunday morning. On our way to church I was feeling old. My body had developed aches and pains that weren't there before all our troubles began. Even with our daily routine of walking, we both had gained about twenty pounds over our normal weight. A great part of that was due to one of the final comforts we had held on to: going out for meals. We looked forward to going to the Piccadilly for lunch and to Morrison's for supper. For variety we would occasionally go to the food court at the mall in the evening, but wherever we went, it had to be agreeable to Joel's delicate emotional condition.

It's hard to get me back to any of these places now because we wore them out then, and in turn they wore us out. I saw the same food day in and day out for the better part of two years. But if that was what Joel needed, so be it. I really was thankful that he was able to go anywhere.

One invaluable asset was that we both loved church on Sunday morning. Evening services were too much for Joel, but we looked forward to Sunday school and morning worship every first day of the week. Early into this ordeal we had felt a need to be close to our children, and so we left our own home church in order to attend where Trent and Bethni were members, Word of Life Fellowship. Trent is the pianist there, and he and Bethni had helped start this new, swiftly growing Full Gospel Church, founded by Pastors Doug and Sonja Nolan. It was a place of blessed assurance. We were immediately wrapped in a cocoon of love by a body of people who knew how to pray and how to minister to hurting souls.

When the service was over we always looked forward to eating Sunday dinner with our children, rendezvousing with Joey and Candy and their families when we could make the connections after their churches let out.

God Speaks to Joel

A few days before what was to be a monumental morning, I was surprised to find Joel searching for his Bible. He still wasn't reading it, just the little promise books, and he was still depressed out of his mind. But that day he came from the bathroom and said that Hebrews 6:10 had strongly impacted his mind and he felt that the Lord wanted him to read it, but he had no idea what it said.

Eager to find out, we looked it up, and were blessed when we read the verse: "For God is not unrighteous to forget your work and labour of love, which ye have shewed toward his name, in that ye have ministered to the saints, and do minister."

Joel and I marveled at this sacred thought. We hadn't considered the fact that our music and our songs were continuing to air on the radio, and were still ministering in countless homes across the nation—*still ministering*. Even while we were at a dead stop and feeling useless, our work continued, through our past labors.

We were still working for the Lord! What a comfort. God had not forgotten. We had, but He hadn't. There was my poor darling in the bathroom, dealing with his torturous ailment, an accepted way of life by now, and the Lord looking down had given a word of encouragement.

During this same time frame David called Joel from out of town. He was checking into a motel, but before he'd gotten his room, he felt an urgency to call from the lobby and assure Joel that "everything was still covered by the blood of Jesus." Candy also came by with more assuring scriptures. Suddenly there began to be a lot of "spiritual activity," and by that we should have known that God was about to do a marvelous thing.

That is how things stood as we entered church that eventful Sunday morning, November 8, 1992. When we walked in, the congregation was singing, and as always it soothed my aching soul. There sat Trent at the piano. The warm feeling of being surrounded by our church family as they sang and worshiped was a comfort to both of us.

The tears flowed in abundance. I couldn't help it. I cried all the way through praise and worship. It had become the norm for me, along with the feeling that I would never smile again. I also knew that before the service was over Joel would embarrass me, as he had so many times, by going down front to petition Pastor Nolan and the elders of the church to pray for him.

We were like spiritual sponges trying to soak up every prayer we could get. This was not an easy place for me to be, as we had always been the ones doing the ministering, and now we were on the receiving end. This particular Sunday morning seemed no different than the rest, but what I didn't know was that our Heavenly Father had said, "Enough."

Joel did walk down front for prayer that day, but it was at the request of Pastor Nolan. As the worship service was coming to a close, Brother Nolan stepped to the podium and halted the music. Then he looked directly at us and motioned Joel forward. He said, "Brother Hemphill, would you please come and let us pray for you? The Lord just spoke to me that He's going to heal you today."

With that invitation, Joel left his seat and walked down the aisle for prayer. Brother Nolan and the elders gathered around and prayed for Joel, and he was *instantly healed*. That was the last day of depression he ever had! The fear, the dread, the gnawing ache inside him were all lifted away during prayer that morning, never to return again.

My Skepticism

When Joel told me the next morning that it was gone, I wanted to believe him, but my faith had been exhausted, and I couldn't grasp what had happened.

I was like Rhoda, the maiden in the early church in Jerusalem who went to the door and heard Peter's voice, for whom the church had been praying for his release from prison. "And when she knew Peter's voice, she opened not the gate for gladness, but ran" (Acts 12:14).

It was practically impossible for me, after all the muck and mire that we had been bogged in for so long, to clap my hands in joy and say, "Yes, I believe you are healed!" At one time I had been that kind of person, so trusting, so believing, so innocently naive. But now I had come to view life with skepticism. This had caused me to accept Joel's healing experience with much more caution. I wasn't going to let myself in for more disappointment. Time would tell if he was really healed—and it did.

The healing was instant, but restoration was gradual. I made a short entry in my diary just a week later, stating: "Joel is laughing, telling funny stories and doing great."

When we went back to see Dr. Fishbein for his regular two-week visit, the doctor was amazed. He asked, "What happened to you?"

Joel replied, "I was prayed for at church and the Lord healed me."

The doctor wrote in his journal: "Prayers lifted his depression." He moved Joel's next visit to six weeks, and on that occasion, January 20, 1993, the physician discontinued Joel's medications.

I was thrilled over the change in Joel but was far from totally accepting his healing. I was afraid that anything might throw him back into the pit of despair the Lord had just delivered him from.

The sad thing about emotional pain is that no one can see it. Those of us who have had to deal with a loved one suffering from it could comprehend a broken limb much easier. Through all our struggles, Joel had become so different from the man I thought I knew, and he had no earthly idea how to get back into the flow of life. Now, since depression was gone, Joel ventured to his brother's house one day to ask his advice on what he should do to get back to being productive. David counseled him by saying, "You are a songwriter. Go home and try to write songs. No matter how childish they may sound, or even if they don't rhyme, just go ahead and write."

When Joel began trying to write, sure enough, it was very simple and lacked the finesse that had always made Joel's songs appealing to the public. Of course, Joel's body still retained much of the strong medication that he had been taking. It can take years for some of these drugs to work their way out of the body.

In spite of this, Joel still came up with two or three ideas and made a pretty good attempt at structuring a song. One title was "I'd Like to Say It Again." The song had potential and its words said, "I've told the story of Jesus many times before but I'd like the chance to say it again."

In my daily piano practice I took the song and started playing around with a melody, a liberty that I had never taken with one of his songs before. Then I began to polish the song as Joel would have done in earlier days, and before long we had a pretty good song. It delighted us both to get around the piano and sing a brand new Hemphill song again, something that hadn't happened in a long time.

In order to break the habit of lying on the couch every morning, after his healing Joel would shower, shave and dress, then come to the piano with me. We sang every gospel song we could think of for hours. We filled our spirits and our minds with those great uplifting songs of faith. It worked wonders. Gradually we began to rebuild our lives on that firm foundation that was strong and solid, and still miraculously in place, the rock which is Jesus Christ.

Again, I couldn't help reflecting on the vision and the prophecy that came to David in 1986 for Joel: "Tear the house down, leave the foundation, and I will build a greater house for my glory, nail upon nail, plank upon plank, and brick upon brick."

The old house was gone. The Lord Himself had declared it, but the next house was one that He was going to erect. A promise concerning the Lord's house in Jerusalem seemed to fit us also. "The glory of this latter house shall be greater than of the former, saith the LORD of hosts: and in this place will I give peace" (Haggai 2:9).

The song "I'd Like to Say It Again" was a real breakthrough for us. It came before Joel's songwriting and ministry talents were fully restored, but it was a cry from within expressing his desire to continue to carry the Word. And it set a precedent for our new ministry, which brought me more into the songwriting process.

A great day for rejoicing came when The Cathedrals, one of the top Southern gospel quartets of our time, decided to record our new song. It was a new day, and we were about to embark on a fresh ministry. The Lord had done away with the old and was now erecting the new and establishing me as a full-fledged partner. Once again God remembered LaBreeska Hemphill.

Amazingly, our Heavenly Father is not like we are. He has no problem with His memory. That is why it is such a miracle that our misbehaving or wrongdoings are blotted out by the precious blood of His Son. When He applies the blood of Jesus to those guilt-ridden areas of our past, they are no more. It's as if they never were. Thus, we are thoroughly washed clean and stand guiltless before Him.

The marvel of it all is that every good deed we do and have done is ever-present before Him. Things that we have long forgotten stand before Him as a memorial, giving testimony in our behalf. The times that we chose to do right in the face of adversity when it cost us friends, family, possessions—whatever—the Lord has promised to repay it all a hundredfold in this life—not to mention life everlasting.

The boundaries of our lives began to expand as we continued our ascent from that deep, dark pit, but my faith was still lacking. Like a soldier who had been on the front lines in the heat of battle, I was combat fatigued. The change in Joel seemed too good to be true. I still had my guard up and was proceeding with extreme caution.

The Fast: April 1993

One morning in early April, Joel came downstairs and announced that he felt the need to go on a three-day fast. He said that he was having difficulty with unwanted thoughts and had discussed it with our pastor. Brother Nolan told Joel that it had happened to him before, and that he had fasted a few days and resolved the problem.

When Joel explained all this to me, I didn't know what to think. I could visualize his becoming weak and plunging headlong back into depression. I had been halfway expecting something like this to happen, and now here it was. I was inconsolable and cried so hard I fell to the floor. My knees just buckled beneath me as I begged Joel not to put us back through that again. Thank the good Lord, he relented. Later during the day, I called his family in Louisiana and told them I needed them. So two carloads of his sisters, Lois, Bethel, Juanita and Verba, along with Rita, Gayle and Brenda drove 500 miles to be with us for a day of moral support and encouragement.

Then on the twelfth of April, Joel hesitantly told me again that he felt he must go on a three-day fast. I took it more calmly this time and consented. Actually, I was feeling the need to put food back in its right perspective and decided to join him.

For the next three days we both drank water while giving up all food. I was surprised at how easy it went. I also gave up my daily walking trips at the park since I didn't have the strength. But Joel was *gaining* strength.

On the third day we went to Christ Church in Brentwood, Tennessee to attend a convention. People had gathered from many states. In attendance were the Kelleys from Birmingham, Aunt Vestal and Uncle Howard Goodman, and many other minister friends whom we had known from the past.

Everyone commented on how good Joel looked and how strong he seemed to be. Yet when we got home that night, I warned him that if he continued with the fast any further, it would definitely be against my will. The next morning when I went downstairs to the coffeepot, I found that I had no appetite for it or for food. I decided not to mention it to Joel. If he wanted to go on with the fast I would acquiesce.

Sure enough, when he came downstairs, Joel really wasn't ready to quit fasting, so we agreed to continue on. To my amazement, he sailed through it, walking daily and getting stronger with each step. I was forced to eat a bit in the evening to keep from getting sick, so I drank a glass of skim milk with two pieces of dry toast, but the rest of the time I stuck to water.

One day about midway through the fast, Joel came by the piano where I sat playing and gave me a kiss. I noticed for the first time since his illness that his breath didn't have that unbearable odor any longer. It surprised me.

I said, "Honey, your breath has sweetened up." He was surprised too. We had been forced to keep breath mints on hand at all times to combat bad breath, something that had never been a problem before he got sick. The problem may have been caused by the combination of medicine and inner turmoil, but we rejoiced that day to find that it was gone. We knew too well what Job meant when he said, "My breath is corrupt" (Job 17:1), and, "My breath is strange to my wife" (19:17). We knew, because we'd lived it.

Joel was feeling so good during his fast that he started walking twice a day, morning and evening, and rejoicing and praising God all the way.

Looking back, I believe that this fast was divinely inspired to help flush the remaining medicine from Joel's system. I really believe that Joel's obedience helped complete his restoration, and when it was over, his reflexes were back to normal and his thinking was clear. Not only had Joel recovered his mental stability, but he was becoming tanned and healthy looking from walking in the sun. Also, we both lost the excess weight that we had gained throughout the ordeal.

Dr. Fishbein had taken Joel off all his medicine on January 20 and told him there was no more need for it since he had recovered. Joel's next scheduled visit, April 22, came on the tenth day of our twelve-day fast. When Joel went in to see the doctor, the physician couldn't believe the changes in him. He said, "Man, you're doing great. You look athletic and tanned!" When we started to leave, Dr.

Fishbein said, "No need to come back. Just call me if you ever need me."

Joel has not been back since. He walked out of the doctor's office a new man. He had been to hell and back. The fast, only two days from completion, had been an assault against the enemy in pursuit of stolen goods. Jesus our Savior warned us that "the thief comes to steal, kill and destroy, but that He [Jesus] came that we might have abundant life" (John 10:10, my paraphrase).

Joel was taking back what the thief had stolen from him. From that day forward I was convinced of Joel's complete healing and never again feared his returning depression.

Chapter 20

The Unstopped Well

Thursday night, May 13, 1993

One of the first things that we added to our agenda after Joel's healing was attending night services at church, and it felt good. Not far from our house a small Full Gospel assembly started a revival, and we gladly took advantage of it.

The first night we went, the pastor recognized us when we entered and invited us to sing a special. It had been years since we'd sung in public and certainly not with my playing the piano, but Joel jumped at the chance and accepted. We sang a song that we had been singing in our daily hymn times at home, and I played the piano.

Brother Henry Willis, a wonderful man of God, was the evangelist, and after he preached, he began praying for various people. He laid hands on Joel and prayed for him and gave him some words of encouragement. This specific night was very important because Joel's well of ministry needed to flow again.

The following day, Joel drove to our sons' bus shop and ran into a long-time friend, country singer Marty Stuart. One of the first things Marty asked was, "Are you writing again?" When Joel said he wasn't, Marty became concerned. That same day Marty placed a call to evangelist Jerry Sullivan, a mutual friend of his and ours from Alabama. Marty urged Brother Jerry to call a special prayer at church so that Joel's songwriting gift would be stirred and in operation once again. It is amazing how the Holy Spirit seemed to be nudging so many people in this area of Joel's restoration.

The very next day, Joel and I drove to Birmingham and stayed overnight in a motel. The following morning we went to Sunday school at Brother Kelley's church. They had prayed faithfully for us throughout our test. Juanita Kelley had made sure of that. For that reason we were eager for them to see just how healed Joel was. We had a wonderful time that morning. Everyone greeted us with such love, and we even sang several special songs. They had a guest speaker, Brother Greg Ellison, whom we had never met before. He called Joel forward and prayed over him and told him that he would write songs that day.

After church we went to lunch with the Kelleys, then began the three-hour trip back to Nashville. Joel was behind the wheel, and I was on the passenger side dozing. He was enjoying driving again. It was a gorgeous, sunny spring day.

In a few minutes Joel nudged me awake and said, "Honey, listen to this," and he began to quote the words of a new song. I straightened up, all excited, and began to write it down. We had crossed the Warrior River, and he was inspired with the thought for the song "A Mighty Warrior for the Lord."

I don't think Joel had ever written three songs in one day, but he was so overjoyed to realize that his gift of songwriting was in bloom again that he began writing about everything. Intoxicated with all the beauty of the day, he penned "My Father Made It All." Before we got home he wrote one more song. All of them were strong lyrics.

Joel had only penned the words, not the melody. Then, the following morning, we went to the piano and were working on the melodies when the telephone rang. It was Michael Sykes, Rusty's son-in-law, who is married to my cousin Tonya.

Michael asked, "What's happening?"

"Well, Joel and I are putting melodies to his new songs. He wrote three yesterday," I told him.

Michael was speechless. When he found his voice, he said, "I've got chills on me as big as goose eggs. I was going to call Joel this one last time and try to encourage him to get back to writing. Then I just wasn't going to bother him again."

That evening Michael came over, and we made a rough demo of the songs. From there more words began to flow from Joel's pen, and there was a great deal of excitement in the house on the hill on Dickerson Road.

Before long we had enough songs for a new album, which Michael produced for us and George Hairr engineered. Michael took us under his wing and ever so gently honed and polished our duet vocals and came up with our "Partners" album. Thirty years earlier Rusty Goodman had done the same thing for us, and both did it with tender love and care.

Satanic Attack

What happened next was a series of misfortunes that befell our family. These odd occurrences took place in such a short span that they seemed to be more than coincidence. The majority of these "accidents" involved our grandchildren.

We had waited a long time for our children to give us grandchildren, and now it was happening. Candy and Kent had presented us with Jasmine, our first grandchild, an energetic and feisty blond-haired, blue-eyed doll whom we just adore.

Then three months before Joel's healing, Sue Ann and Joey had blessed us with Taylor, a beautiful little girl with a porcelain-like complexion and hair that lay in naturally curly ringlets. Next Bethni and Trent had little Madeleine Grace, who was now just two-and-a-half months old. She was another beauty with olive complexion and penetrating eyes just like her father's, so brown they almost looked black. Joel and I were enjoying our new role as grandparents, and the babies had opened new little windows of love in our hearts.

Then the troubles began.

It was on that same Monday that Michael came over to hear the songs that Joel had written on Sunday. At around 8 o'clock that evening we decided to walk next door to Candy's to check on her. She was early into her second pregnancy and doing great, but we wanted to spend some time with her and Jasmine before retiring to bed since Kent was away ministering in South Africa.

We didn't stay long, said our good nights, and had started back across her lawn, when we heard Candy scream, "Mother!"

Rushing back inside we found her crying and pale. She was hemorrhaging and was sure she had lost the baby. When we called the doctor, he said there was nothing he could do at this time, for her to go straight to bed and he would see her the next morning. We prayed with her and stayed until all was calm. Then she assured us that she was OK and insisted that we go home. When we left, we told her that we would leave our phone on in case she needed us. Otherwise we switch it off at night, leaving the answering machine to record all messages. After we prepare for bed, we go to our separate prayer closets and do not like to be interrupted when we are praying or sleeping. But that night the phone was left on.

Near midnight the ringing telephone broke the silence, and jumping out of bed, I rushed to answer it. Knowing it must be Candy, I picked up and said, "What's wrong?"

It gave me a start to hear Trent's voice on the other end of the line. He sounded drained. "Mom, you and Dad had better get down here to the hospital right away. We've had a problem with Madeleine, but I think she's OK now."

I hung up the phone, and Joel and I hurriedly jumped into some clothes and rushed to the hospital. When we got there, we found Trent in a blue hospital scrub uniform, as he had arrived in only his underwear.

He began to relay how he had found Madeleine cold and stiff in her crib at about 11 that night when he picked her up to take her upstairs.

"Mom, she was as dead as she'll ever be," Trent began. "When I took her into my arms she wasn't breathing. She just had a death fix on her face. She had been lying on her stomach and her arms were frozen in place. Mama, I just started screaming at the top of my voice, 'No! Jesus, no! Jesus, please give me back my baby!' "

Trent was in his undershorts when the near tragedy began. Spying his pants lying across a chair, he tossed Madeleine on the sofa, hoping to jar her and get a response. When she showed no sign of life, he forgot about his pants, grabbed her up and ran for the car.

Meanwhile, Bethni came running down the stairs crying, "Is she dead? Is she dead?"

"Mom, she was!" Trent told me. "I ran out the door and held her up toward the sky, praying loudly, 'Lord, I'll serve You—I'll do anything—please give me back my baby!' Then we ran to the car. Bethni drove and I held Madeleine, screaming 'Jesus!' and praying all the way. Just before we arrived at the emergency room, she whimpered and then fell back into lifelessness. We just kept doing all we could do, and by the time we got inside, she was screaming to the top of her lungs. The nurses tried to quiet her down, but I told them, 'Let her cry! That's the sweetest sound I have ever heard.'

"Then they gave me this uniform to put on," he added with a grin. The doctor sent Bethni and Trent home with a monitor for Madeleine to wear as she slept. It went off about three times during the next several months. This indicated that she was prone to sudden infant death syndrome (SIDS), but there was much rejoicing that God had come through for us on this.

We went home from the hospital reminded that Jesus had said, "I am the resurrection, and the life: he that believeth in me, though he were dead, yet shall he live" (John 11:25). When Trent called out to Jesus, he was calling on the name of resurrection and, praise the Lord, it worked.

Before dawn that morning there was a loud crash outside, almost like an explosion. When I went to see what had happened, I found where lightning had hit a tree just a few feet from our house and had burned a wide streak all the way to the ground, knocking a big chunk of concrete from the sidewalk.

When I saw it I thought about the prophet Elijah hiding in a cave fearing for his life.

And a great and strong wind rent the mountains, and brake in pieces the rocks before the LORD; but the LORD was not in the wind: and after the wind an earthquake; but the LORD was not in the earthquake: and after the earthquake a fire; but the LORD was not in the fire. (1 Kings 19:11-12)

I believe strongly that the Lord was not in the lightning that struck on that gray morning. That same Tuesday morning at 9 o'clock, Joel had a dental appointment not far from the house. He was only gone a short time when I received a call from him saying he had a wreck. A woman rammed into him as he cut through the parking lot, broadsiding our car, but thankfully they both escaped without injury. Determined to turn a mishap into a blessing, they shared Jesus and held hands and prayed in the parking lot until the police arrived.

We found out before the day was over that Candy was still carrying a baby. It was thought that she may have lost a twin. However, we rejoiced again, knowing that she was still "with child" and another grandbaby was still on the way.

On Wednesday we received yet another call, this time from Rachael, Joel's niece. She was beside herself. Jasmine and Candy had come to her house, and her husband Scott's big chocolate Labrador dog, not used to small children, got nervous when Jasmine tried to pet him and bit her in the face.

Rachael told me, "They have gone to the emergency room. We don't know how bad it is, but we do know it just missed her eye." A short time later, Candy called with good news that Jasmine had come out with only a minor injury, which did not leave a scar.

We were appalled at how much havoc had broken loose, but at the same time, happy to know that we were protected. Years ago I heard a little homemade song that went, "The devil's mad and I am glad, glory hallelujah, he lost my soul he thought he had, glory hallelujah!"

To know that it mattered whether we wrote songs or not was very encouraging. Each mishap could have meant disaster, but the Lord turned it all around. Thank God for the blood of Jesus, the healing, cleansing, protecting flow from Calvary. All we have to do is claim it for ourselves, as Joel stated so well in the words of his song "I Claim the Blood."

I have a source
Of strength when I am weak
That takes me through
When life is pressing me
I have a source   •
Of power from above
I'm covered over
By a shield of love

I do not know
How others make it through
Who never go
To Calv'ry as I do
For there the healing
Cleansing stream still flows
With peace that only
His redeemed can know

I claim the blood
Jesus shed on Calvary
Those precious blood stains
Were made there just for me
For all my sin
My sickness and my pain
When I need healing
I claim those precious blood stains.[15]

Chapter 21

Happy!
Happy! Happy!

Joel appeared in the doorway of the kitchen. It was late in the evening and he had been gone most of the day. He and a couple of guys were working on one of our rental houses, trying to make it livable again, after a family who had been raising Pomeranian dogs inside had moved out.

So much of our property had deteriorated into poor condition during Joel's absence. We both understood that it was only by the grace of God that nothing was lost while he was incapacitated, but almost everything was in need of repair. I was concerned that Joel might be overwhelmed by the amount of work he faced, but to my amazement it had the opposite effect on him. He was like a kid smacking his lips over the dawning of each new day, eager to work and play. He was just glad to be alive.

However, the grind of everyday toils has a way of knocking the sheen off the beauty of our surroundings, and I was in no hurry for Joel to wake up to that realization. His fresh approach to life after his healing was infectious and uplifting, and I wanted to protect that, but I wasn't sure I could.

With all this disturbing my thoughts, I was startled when I turned from the kitchen sink to find him standing there. He was a mess, sweaty and grimy. He had been under one of the houses searching for a water leak. My heart sank. That's when I expected the "old Joel" to surface and start griping about it all—the house, the renters, the mess. But before I had time to say a word, he clapped his hands and said, "Happy! Happy! Happy!" with a twinkle in his eyes that not even the dirt smudges could dim.

Such an unexpected outburst of joy made me laugh out loud, as I rushed over and gave him a big hug, dirt and all, and said, "Glad! Glad! Glad!"

At that moment I knew that things would never be the same. God had given Joel a new lease on life. He said with a big grin, "Honey, this is a good day. I've seen some bad ones, and this is not one of them."

That was a phrase I was to hear often in the days ahead, and I loved it! Where Joel had an unexplainable feeling of foreboding and doom while in depression, he was and still is experiencing little explosions of joy going off day after day, and he knows why. He credits it to his thankfulness to the Lord for rescuing him. Joel has learned to walk in praise. He says if we walk in praise, we'll walk in joy.

It reminds me of the valuable lesson that King David learned through his dark days when he said, "Praise the LORD, O my soul. While I live will I praise the LORD: I will sing praises unto my God while I have any being. . . . Happy is he that hath the God of Jacob for his help, whose hope is in the LORD his God" (Psalm 146:1-2, 5).

To better illustrate this, early one morning I had put the coffee on and then discovered that we were out of creamer, a necessity for us. When I told Joel, he hopped in the car and ran to Kroger's. In a few minutes he came back with a big smile recounting what had happened while he was gone.

He said, "Honey, it's such a beautiful morning I couldn't help praising God. I parked the car in the lot and looked around to make sure no one was there." Joel hesitated for a moment with mischief in his eyes, then went on, "You know, I don't want people to think I'm crazy, even if I have been in two mental hospitals. I didn't see anyone, so I just clapped my hands and said out loud, 'Thank You, Jesus! Father, I love You and praise You for this good day.' Then I turned and saw to my surprise, a man sitting in one of the parked cars just a few feet away, with his window down. I figured I ought to give him some kind of explanation so I said, 'Sir, you'd feel this way too if you'd been where I've been.' "

"The man said to me, 'Where've you been?'

"I told him, 'In depression.'

"The man misunderstood and said, 'In Nebraska?'

"I said, 'No, depression. I had cancer and depression and God healed me and I'm not depressed anymore!'

"The old gentleman kinda mumbled and said, 'Well, I guess a day like this does make a person feel good.' "

Joel and I had a hearty laugh. His stay in a mental hospital was such a far cry from where we are today that it isn't a factor in our lives, except that Joel loves to tell it to the glory of God.

Our story is similar to those souls in the Bible who were healed of various problems: the blind man, for instance, who said to the amazed onlookers, "I was blind but now I see!" (John 9:25, NIV). Joel is quick to give testimony to the healing power of God.

Sometimes I tease him and tell him he's like Rip Van Winkle, the fictitious character who woke up from a twenty-year nap and discovered a brand-new world. But more than that, Joel came out of his "sleep" with a brand-new heart, one full of love and compassion. Before his illness he was a workaholic and a perfectionist, and I sometimes felt as though I had to earn his love, but today, his love for me is as close to unconditional as I'll ever find this side of heaven, and it's wonderful. He still enjoys work, but he now loves to play, and it's a good thing.

We have six grandkids, so Joel has plenty of playmates. They ride horses, go boating, four-wheeling and fishing, and he has even taken Jasmine, our oldest, to the deer camp to hunt. Taylor and Madeleine love to ride the donkeys. Nicky, only five, follows PaPaw everywhere. He loves to talk about the donkeys and horses, but fishing is his passion and he has even been found sleeping with his fishing rod. Sarah Kate and little William love to come to PaPaw's and MiMi's house to play with Midnight the cat.

I thank Jesus every day for sparing my marriage and my husband. Things could have been so very different had we not called out to

God when our world was falling apart. I thank the Lord that His eye is upon His children, that His ear is open to our cry and His heart is touched with the feeling of our infirmities. We do worship an awesome God, a loving Father and a very present help in time of trouble. Life is fragile and comes with very few guarantees, and as the marquee in front of one church so aptly put it, "must be handled with prayer."

God is sovereign and does according to His good pleasure. We, His offspring, are blessed beyond measure because He is merciful and righteous, and only allows adversity to come our way to cause us to seek Him. If He came immediately every time we cried out, we would be spoiled children. But when He causes us to wait, He is honing us to perfection and building our character. He also knows that as soon as we receive what we desire from Him, we oftentimes go on our own way, without so much as a thank-you. How soon we forget where our blessings come from when things are going good.

Back in the Ministry

Nine months after Joel's healing, we were called upon to pastor a small rural church thirty miles south of Nashville, and Joel took that assignment with enthusiasm. He knew that this was exactly what we both needed: to be immersed in ministry. When we took the pastorate of a church in Peytonsville in August of 1993, we immediately found ourselves participating in all the functions that cause the world to go around. There were weddings, funerals, hospital visitations, baptismal services, baby dedications, plus many enjoyable social functions.

And Joel was digging in the Word. I'm sure this little church needed us, but they didn't need us nearly as much as we needed them. For thirteen months we enjoyed a rich interchange of spiritual fellowship with the members of that little church. It was a cherished time that we will never forget.

Then Paul and Sheila Heil, producers of "Gospel Greats," a popular syndicated radio show, wanted to interview Joel about his deliverance from depression. The "Gospel Greats" program presents the latest recordings and provides updates on the lives of gospel music artists on more than 150 stations across the country. The interview was extensive, and after it aired, things started to happen. The word was out that Joel was healed and The Hemphills were back.

The next call came from Bill Gaither, founder and producer of the popular "Homecoming" videos. He invited us to appear on his and Gloria's next taping. These gospel music videos had already caught the attention of gospel fans all over the world and were being seen nationwide on many cable networks, including The Nashville Network. TNN is a powerful country music channel owned and operated by Gaylord Productions, which also owns the Grand Ole Opry. Through these videos Gaylord finally found the vehicle through which they could include gospel music in their programming on a regular basis.

We gladly accepted the invitation and made the trip to Alexandria, Indiana to be a part of one of the most exciting events to ever come along in our field of music. At the taping we found ourselves surrounded by over 100 of our peers and long-time friends. What a gathering it was! And what a video—about ninety minutes of solid gospel tunes sung by some of the greatest voices in the field. Joel was called to sing "He's Still Working on Me," and there was hardly a dry eye in the room. The words to that song had never been more meaningful than at that moment.

He's still workin' on me
To make me what I ought to be
It took Him just a week to make the moon and stars
The Sun and the Earth and Jupiter and Mars
How loving and patient He must be
He's still workin' on me

There really ought to be
A sign upon my heart
Don't judge me yet
There's an unfinished part
But I'll be perfect just according to His plan
Fashioned by the Master's loving hand

In the mirror of His Word
Reflections that I see
Make me wonder why
He never gave up on me
But He loves me as I am and helps me when I pray
Remember He's the Potter, I'm the clay.[16]

The "Homecoming" event prompted more phone calls and offers. Promoters across the land wanted to book us on their concert dates and more television appearances beckoned. We found ourselves on *Music City Tonight*, a secular television show hosted by Lori Ann Crook and Charlie Chase. We had no idea that they would want Joel and me to talk about his being healed of depression, but they did. Lori Ann was intensely interested as she asked both of us probing questions. I think I spied a glimmer of a tear in her eye as we told our story.

Then Joel and I did a television show called *Prime Time Country* with host Tom Wopat, one of the former stars of *The Dukes of Hazard*. After we sang our joyful gospel songs, we presented him with some choice alligator skins to have made into boots. We had presented country-rock singer Charlie Daniels with a pair of gator skins just months before when he was taping a video of one of Joel's gospel songs, cowritten with Frank O'Brien, titled "Two Out of Three." The gift made such a hit with Charlie that we thought we'd do the same for Tom.

In the meantime we were doing religious television appearances on the Trinity Broadcasting Network. We were also called on to relate our experiences of depression and Joel's healing on Pat Robertson's well-known *700 Club* in Virginia Beach, Virginia.

Before long we were caught up in a whirlwind of activities and loving every moment of it. We had been down and out of commission for a long time. Now we wanted to do it all. Joel was writing some of his best songs, and they were being recorded by a variety of singers. Needless to say, we could not do all this traveling and pastor a church, so we regretfully said good-bye to the sweet little congregation in Peytonsville. Then we purchased a beautiful bus, hired David Hall, a gifted young Christian man, to sing with us and play the keyboard, and we were off and running.

During our absence a lot of changes had taken place on the gospel music scene. These were changes that we found to be good ones. The audience had a greater acceptance of solos and duets, and modern technology had made it simple for the artists to sing with tracks while accompanied by whatever instrumentation they desired to add.

What this translated into was fewer people on the bus and fewer expenses, but it still allowed us to retain a full sound. Because of these evolutions in the business, Joel and I have more freedom to focus on ministry and the delivery of our songs. We have always wanted our audiences to understand every word of each song. To us this is most important, because if it were not for the message of gospel songs, then our music could not be distinguished from any other genre. The good news message of hope, victory and joy must come through very clearly.

This is not to diminish what we did with our family and the fine performers who traveled with us previously and played in our band. Those were exciting, happy times, and because that was the norm back then, our audiences came expecting a stage full of people. But this truly is a new day.

The new trends came gradually, but being out of circulation as we were, the changes were easy for us to spot. A whole crop of new talent was making waves and occupying the top positions on the radio charts, a most important position for artists of any type of music. If you wish to fill the seats of an auditorium, you must be heard on the radio. To be heard on the radio you must have a good song. Among many of the popular groups, lead singers have gone on their own and are performing solo with great success. As Joel points out, "You can always tell the health of a species by the number of young it produces."

Gospel music is alive and well, and the fans are accepting Joel and me as easily now as they did when we performed with our family.

Chapter 22

Time to Celebrate!

The brass knocker resounded with a bold clank-clank-clank from the front door of our home. Someone was coming at the wrong time.

Today was the day Joel and I were to celebrate our fortieth wedding anniversary, and we were rushing around trying not to be late for the festivities.

Rita and James, in town on business, had come earlier and were going with us to meet our children for an evening of food and fellowship. The kids had chosen a restaurant and Candy had called to tell her dad to be sure to wear a dinner jacket. That was a hint that it must be a pretty classy place, even though she didn't clue us in as to where that might be. The children had taken us to nice places before on special occasions, but tonight had been kept top secret.

The knocks came again, louder this time.

By now Rita was close enough to the foyer to answer the door and called up excitedly to Joel and me as we were coming down the stairs, "It's a chauffeur. There's a limousine here for you!"

Well, this was a first.

Rita started apologizing to us, saying, "We feel awful, barging in on you at this time. We'll just drive our car and follow you."

But Joel and I insisted they ride with us. This was a real treat, and we have the philosophy that everything is better shared. So the four of us hopped into the limo and were off, giddy as children going to an ice cream party. Everyone likes a good surprise, even those of us who have been married forty years. While trying to plan this night, Candy told her father and me the week before, "I've checked your schedule with Kim [our secretary], and you'll be in Texas Wednesday and get back into Nashville sometime Thursday morning. Then you leave again Friday for a concert in Chattanooga and on to Tulsa for another five days. Thursday is the only night you'll be at home. Do you think you'll feel up to doing anything for your anniversary? Joey and SueAnn, Trent and Bethni, Kent and I and all the grandchildren would sure like to get together with you and go out to eat or something."

"Of course we will," Joel and I responded.

We always jump at the chance to be with our family. Most of the time, when we are in town long enough we have supper at our house; I make a great duck gumbo, or sometimes I fix Italian spaghetti and meatballs or just a big pan of roast beef topped with carrots and potatoes. It doesn't matter, just as long as we get together. When the weather is cool, we always have a big crackling fire in the living room fireplace. These good times usually end up around the piano, with all of us singing gospel songs as the grandchildren skip around the room clapping their hands. But tonight was our night to be treated in grand style.

As we drove along, our driver made a few turns and wound up on Briley Parkway. It occurred to me again that I had no idea where he was taking us. So I sat back and enjoyed the ride. As I did, a panorama of past events began to flood my mind.

Forty years is a long time was the thought that struck me with force. Yet it didn't seem that long ago that Joel and I had stood under the big oak tree on the courthouse lawn in Greenville, Mississippi, bravely pledging our troth to each other. I in my little yellow homemade taffeta dress and Joel in his light blue suit, we promised to love and cherish one another, till death do us part. At that moment we were confident that nothing could arise in the future that our love could not withstand.

What an awesome decision we had taken upon ourselves to make at such a young age! At seventeen we may have been young, but we felt sure that we had found in each other the right ingredients for a happy future. For Joel and me to have found each other in this big world was a miracle within itself and nothing less. Our faith in each other and in the Lord is what gave us the courage to take that forever plunge.

I smiled inwardly as I remembered those happy, carefree days that we spent fishing with Rusty, and how Joel and I enjoyed each other's company from the start. *We still like doing things together and still have the ability to make one another laugh,* I mused. The characteristic that I most love about Joel is his unselfishness. He is selfless almost to a fault and is acutely aware of the feelings of those around him. To be a firsthand recipient of this wonderful trait has challenged me over the years to be equally thoughtful and kind.

Momentarily I was brought back to the present when Joel loudly called out to our chauffeur as we zoomed past OpryLand, "Are you sure you know where we're going?"

The driver glanced back at us with a broad grin and responded, "I have no idea. You mean you don't know?" He turned back around and kept driving.

It is so like Candy to come up with a fun plan, I decided, remembering how sweet and helpful she had been on our thirtieth anniversary when we had renewed our vows. My heart still thrilled over the beauty and excitement of that anniversary ten years before.

Our limousine finally came to a stop in the circle drive in front of Two Rivers Mansion, a beautiful old Italiante estate built in 1859. "They must have secured a room for our family to dine in," I said aloud as the car door swung open. Then, before we could get out, we were met by a professional photographer. Those kids had thought of everything!

My heart swelled with gratitude as I realized how blessed we were to have children who cared enough to go to all this trouble and expense. They had been with us through some rough times, and it was easy to see that they were glad to have those times behind. They were happy that we were healed and restored and back in ministry once again. I was certainly enjoying all the hullabaloo, but as mothers do, I was also worried about what they must have spent on such extravagance.

Then when we entered the mansion, Joel and I were thunderstruck! There to greet us were more than 100 of our dearest friends and family from everywhere, even Daddy and Lila. Many had driven a long distance and some had flown. Those three wonderful children of ours had coordinated a grand bash and had kept it completely secret from us.

They had also rented the entire mansion. Trent had the idea of hiring a small orchestra that played beautiful music throughout the evening, including many of Joel's compositions. Each of our kids had written some amusing reminiscences of childhood that kept us chuckling with laughter, as they stood and read them, one by one.

Marty Stuart, Woody Wright and Joel's brother David also had funny tales to tell. Jasmine, Taylor and Madeleine were dressed like little angels and sang their favorite song, "He's Still Working on Me."

And eight-year-old Jasmine wrote a poem for us and read it:

MiMi and PaPaw, you're the best,
Although I see you work very hard,
MiMi, your love never fades nor your spirit,
And PaPaw, your compassion will never lose its touch,
Nor your spirit. You have always made it through,
And stuck together. You're the best!

Joey read congratulatory letters from Tennessee Governor Don Sunquist, Senator Fred Thompson, Vice President Al Gore and President Bill Clinton. The meal was a scrumptious, catered buffet, and they even had a gorgeous pink wedding cake covered with confectionery roses. It was such a lovely party and must have taken months of planning and laborious legwork.

What a night!
What a family!
What a God!!

The Grand Ole Opry

Along with that unforgettable anniversary celebration, a kaleidoscope of exciting events continued to unfold for Joel and me. Of course the call to make a guest appearance on the Saturday night Grand Ole Opry was at the top of the list.

The Opry was certainly not a door that we could have opened for ourselves. Just being on that program made us know that God was with us and was paving the way for us. Once again we identified with Job. When God restored him, He blessed him with twice as much as he had lost (see Job 42:10). The Bible states, "The LORD blessed the latter end of Job more than his beginning" (42:12). And it looked as though the Lord was doing the same for us!

After our performance on that legendary stage of the Grand Ole Opry, Joel and I went home that night still savoring the sweet taste of victory. In retrospect, I thought of the winding path that had led to such an eventful occasion and became acutely aware that it really doesn't take long to live a life. But thank the Lord ours isn't over yet.

While preparing for bed, the excitement of the evening was soon tucked away like a lovely garment and stored in our treasure chest of memories. My heart was still smiling as we thanked the Lord in prayer for His abundant mercy, grateful that we are able to enjoy each day to the fullest as we look toward the future with great expectations.

There's a song that I have recorded and sung that sums up the way I feel about my past, present and future. The song was written for me by country singer Marty Stuart and Joel on the floor of my den, in front of the fireplace.

Before Marty began writing this song, he quizzed me, "LaBreeska, tell me in your own words what heaven means to you." As I talked he began to write "Someday When I Go Home":

Life has been good for me on this earth
With loved ones and friends I have known
Some joy and some pain
Some sunshine and rain
In my weakness I've tried to be strong
But I've had a glimpse of my Father's house
Felt the warmth of the love He has shown

Where all of my dreams at His feet are fulfilled
Someday when I go home

There are times that I feel I could stay here forever
Pursuing my hopes and my plans
But often enough to make heaven seem sweeter
He lets them slip right thru my hands
One day I'll abide in His presence forever
Where no tears and disappointments are known
And for this pilgrim, it's the end of my journey
Someday when I go home.

Home where my Father waits
Home, home beyond heaven's gates
Forever with Jesus is where I belong
Someday when I go home.[17]

Epilogue

by Joel Hemphill

The prophetic utterances that came to me from God in 1986 through my brother David included, in addition to what was said regarding our situation, four specific messages to others.

To gospel singers

God said that many of the singers had said in their hearts, "We get paid and the people get blessed, so it doesn't matter how we live." God said, "It's not so." He said if we make our living by singing and testifying to His name, we are as the Levites, and we must offer an acceptable sacrifice of our lives to Him. He said that His anger had come up in His face because His body had been wounded by His people, by seeing that some of the singers sang one thing and lived another. He said if we do this we are as moneychangers in the temple or as foolish children who take up a pretty serpent to our bosom to play with it, and we would be bitten by it.

To preachers

God said that many preachers had tried to package Him, or merchandise Him as the healer, or the solver of financial problems, or as the quick and easy way to success and prosperity, and God said, "It's not so." He said, "I do heal and I do meet financial needs but I am the Lord God of the Mighty Host, the Great King soon coming back in majesty as the Bridegroom to receive a bride who has made herself ready," and He wanted to be presented in that manner.

To the large Christian family

God said that many are careless and foolish, and their hearts are not turned toward Him, but they are turned toward the world and playing near the darkness. God said, "Return to Me and seek My face and I will stretch forth My healing hand and heal your wounds, for if you do not return to Me, I will soon stretch forth My hand in wrath."

A general warning

God said, "I am soon going to shake the nations with a demonstration of the power of my wrath." He said, "Many will think that it is the end but it is not; it is just to show My power to the nations." God said that He did not want His Church stirred by the shaking, but He wants us stirred by the Word now, so that we will be able to reap the harvest of souls that the shaking will bring. (We later found scriptural references to this shaking in Ezekiel 38:20; Haggai 2:6-7; and Hebrews 12:26-27.)

Endnotes

1. Available: www.coloradohealthnet.org/depression/depression_
facts.htm; www.usnews.com/usnews/issue/990201/1proz.htm; cnnfn.
cnn.com/2000/08/09/companies/lilly/; www.nimh.nih.gov/publicat/
depresfact.htm; mentalhealth.about.com/health/mentalhealth/library/
mh/dep/bldepress.htm; Shankar Vedantam, "Would You Take Prozac
for PMS?" *The Washington Post*, n.d., n.p.

2. Joel Hemphill, "Partners in Emotion" (Copyright 1995, Trumpet
Call Music/BMI).

3. "Looking for a City" (Copyright 1943, renewed 1971, Hartford
Music Co.). Used by permission; license ID#78662.

4. The correct spelling of LaBreeska was lost over the years. My
mother came up with her own spelling and punctuation.

5. " 'Tis So Sweet to Trust in Jesus" (public domain).

6. "He's All I Need," writer unknown.

7. Joel Hemphill, "The Way Is Made" (Copyright 1967, Trumpet
Call Music/BMI).

8. LaBreeska Hemphill, "Life Evermore" (Copyright 1966, Journey
Music/BMI).

9. Albert E. Brumley, "I'll Meet You in the Morning" (Copyright
1964, Hartford Music Co.). Used by permission; license ID#78663.

10. Ruth Munsey, "An Unfinished Task" (Copyright 1969, Hemphill
Music Co.).

11. Joel Hemphill, "He Filled a Longing" (Copyright 1967, Trumpet
Call/BMI).

12. Joel Hemphill, "God Likes People" (Copyright 1985, Hemphill
Music Co./BMI).

13. 1986 message from God to Joel.

14. "Come Let Us Sing," writer unknown.

15. Joel Hemphill, "I Claim the Blood" (Copyright 1984, Hemphill
Music Co./BMI).

16. Joel Hemphill, "He's Still Working on Me" (Copyright 1985, Hemphill Music Co./Family & Friends/BMI).

17. Marty Stewart and Joel Hemphill, "Someday When I Go Home" (Copyright 1997, Trumpet Call Music/BMI).

For more inspirational material from Joel and LaBreeska Hemphill:

Books
CDs *(Music and Preaching)*
DVDs
Songbooks

P. O. Box 656
Joelton, Tennessee 37080
Phone: 615/299-0848
Fax: 615/299-0849
Email: jhemphill@wildblue.net
www.thehemphills.com
www.trumpetcallbooks.com

"Partners In Emotion"
By LaBreeska Hemphill
Trumpet Call Books

"My Daddy Played The Guitar"
By LaBreeska Hemphill
Trumpet Call Books

"To God Be The Glory"
(Examining The Bible View of God)
By Joel W. Hemphill
Trumpet Call Books

Books available from the above address or wherever fine books are sold.